DOMESTIC CULTURES

ISSUES in CULTURAL and MEDIA STUDIES

Series editor: Stuart Allan

Published titles

News Culture, 2nd edition
Stuart Allan

Modernity and Postmodern Culture
Jim McGuigan

Television, Globalization and Cultural Identities
Chris Barker

Ethnic Minorities and the Media
Edited by Simon Cottle

Cinema and Cultural Modernity
Gill Branston

Compassion, Morality and the Media
Keith Tester

Masculinities and Culture
John Beynon

Cultures of Popular Music
Andy Bennett

Media, Risk and Science
Stuart Allan

Violence and the Media
Cynthia Carter and C. Kay Weaver

Moral Panics and the Media
Chas Critcher

Cities and Urban Cultures
Deborah Stevenson

Cultural Citizenship
Nick Stevenson

Culture on Display
Bella Dicks

Critical Readings: Media and Gender
Edited by Cynthia Carter and Linda Steiner

Critical Readings: Media and Audiences
Edited by Virginia Nightingale and Karen Ross

Media and Audiences
Karen Ross and Virginia Nightingale

Critical Readings: Sport, Culture and the Media
Edited by David Rowe

Sport, Culture and the Media, 2nd edition
David Rowe

Rethinking Cultural Policy
Jim McGuigan

DOMESTIC CULTURES

Joanne Hollows

Open University Press

Open University Press
McGraw-Hill Education
McGraw-Hill House
Shoppenhangers Road
Maidenhead
Berkshire
England
SL6 2QL

email: enquiries@openup.co.uk
world wide web: www.openup.co.uk

and Two Penn Plaza, New York, NY 10121–2289, USA

First published 2008

A catalogue record of this book is available from the British Library

ISBN-13: 978 0335 22253 7 (pb)   978 0335 22254 4 (hb)
ISBN-10: 0335 22253 6 (pb)   0335 22254 4 (hb)

Library of Congress Cataloging-in-Publication Data
CIP data applied for

Typeset by RefineCatch Limited, Bungay, Suffolk
Printed in the UK by Bell and Bain Ltd, Glasgow

The **McGraw·Hill** Companies

For Chris Lee
who offered me a home when I needed one.

CONTENTS

FOREWORD

In Raymond Williams's 1958 essay 'Culture is Ordinary', he suggested that it is the very *ordinariness* of culture that is deserving of careful consideration. It was necessary to distinguish the contours of the ordinary processes of culture as 'a whole way of life', he believed, to facilitate an analysis of its lived negotiation in the times, spaces and places of the everyday. At stake, it followed, was the pressing need to better understand the means by which society is 'made and remade in every individual mind,' that is, the ways in which the very materiality of culture is intimately imbricated in the varied realities of our ostensibly mundane, even banal experiences. In considering how people engage with televised news or drama in the privacy of their households, for example, this perspective encourages us to examine the ordinary activity of 'watching TV' in relation to the (unspoken) rules by which the very normality of everyday life is defined, and as such rendered meaningful. The integration of television viewing into our daily routines is clearly informed by this sense of normality in the home, with important implications for how we relate to the world around us; and yet, to the extent that it is regarded as simply a casual, habitual part of domestic life, it is likely to escape the attention of our more traditional modes of enquiry.

In exploring this question of how society is 'made and remade' through ordinary cultural practices in the domestic realm, the contribution of feminist researchers has been invaluable. The idea of home, they have pointed out, is central to many people's experience of everyday life, and as such requires us to move beyond familiar academic boundaries in order to properly attend to its significance. Joanne Hollows's *Domestic Cultures*, using an interdisciplinary approach, proceeds to show us why an understanding of the home is of crucial importance for cultural and media studies thinking and research. In contrast with cultural critics who have represented the home as a stable place, she demonstrates how the meaning of domestic culture is produced, maintained, reworked and challenged both within and across different historical formations. While the distinction between public and private spheres has shaped modern conceptions of domestic cultures, she argues, this distinction has not been as clear-cut as is often assumed. Not only do activities associated with the public sphere – such as paid and unpaid work – frequently take place in the home, but 'homely' values are often mobilized within the public sphere. Examples are everywhere, ranging from politicians' appeals to domestic 'common sense' at election time to the comfy sofas of a Starbucks café. While certain critics have claimed that the home is little more than a repressive space, one which works to reproduce unequal power relations, *Domestic Cultures* offers a more complexly dynamic understanding of the place of the domestic in everyday life.

The *Issues in Cultural and Media Studies* series aims to facilitate a diverse range of critical investigations into pressing questions considered to be central to current thinking and research. In light of the remarkable speed at which the conceptual agendas of cultural and media studies are changing, the series is committed to contributing to what is an ongoing process of re-evaluation and critique. Each of the books is intended to provide a lively, innovative and comprehensive introduction to a specific topical issue from a fresh perspective. The reader is offered a thorough grounding in the most salient debates indicative of the book's subject, as well as important insights into how new modes of enquiry may be established for future explorations. Taken as a whole, then, the series is designed to cover the core components of cultural and media studies courses in an imaginatively distinctive and engaging manner.

Stuart Allan

ACKNOWLEDGEMENTS

I would like to thank various people who have sent me copies of articles that have informed this book or put up with me discussing ideas with them: these include Neal Curtis, Lydia Martens, Alan Metcalfe, Shaun Moores, Rachel Moseley, Gary Needham, Caroline J. Smith, Nick Stevenson, Ben Taylor, Lisa Taylor, John Tomlinson, Dave Woods and probably other people that I have neglectfully forgotten to mention. The anonymous readers provided reports that were extremely generous and helpful in their advice (some of which I have taken on and others aspects of which were beyond me on this occasion). Nottingham Trent University offered the research leave that enabled me to get the book started and I would like to thank my colleagues in the MCS team for taking the strain while I was on leave.

Special thanks go to Steve 'will I be receiving a cut of the royalties?' Jones and David Bell. Steve not only generously shared sources and ideas but also co-devised and co-taught the course on 'Home' and Cultural Identity that provided the impetus for this book. The students on this module also deserve acknowledgement, both for their willingness to be so enthusiastic about a topic which they initially approached with caution and for the ideas that they generated in their research projects on different aspects of domestic life. David kindly blitzed me with articles that he had discovered, photocopied pieces from his rather better resourced university's library, gave me generous and useful feedback on the chapters, and kept me relatively sane with emails.

I am very grateful to Stuart Allan and Chris Cudmore who, in their respective editorial roles, were very supportive and *extremely* patient.

Thank you, as ever, to Mark for all his help on the book and in domestic life, and for living with my verging on maniacal ideas about the importance of windows, kitchens and relatively small TVs in making a home.

INTRODUCTION

1

Meet the au pairs

As this book neared completion, I watched a TV documentary called *Meet the Au Pairs* that followed three British households through the process of hiring – and living with – an au pair.[1] While the households involved were all families, their living arrangements varied: one household was comprised of a heterosexual couple and their three boys; the second contained a single-parent mother and her daughter; and the third household consisted of two boys who lived with their father but maintained a close relationship with their mother who lived locally. In each household, the parents worked or studied full time. The au pairs who joined the families came from Turkey, Brazil and the USA.

While having an au pair is hardly typical, the documentary raised a range of wider issues about domestic cultures. First, it showed how even among people living as families, domestic living arrangements are far from standardized, fixed and simply routinized. Indeed, these families' narratives demonstrated how domestic culture required complex co-ordination and scheduling to ensure that houses are cleaned and children are fed and to ensure that people could actually experience living together as a family (DeVault 1991; Douglas 1991). Second, the documentary demonstrated how domestic cultures are not bounded and fixed but are always interconnected with life outside the home: the decision to employ an au pair was triggered by questions about how adults could manage the relationship between home and work. Furthermore, the domestic spaces in this documentary were also workplaces in which parents were employers and the au pairs were employees – indeed, for the au pairs there was no separation between domestic space and the workplace. Finally, this TV show high-lighted how our place of residence does not necessarily equate with a sense of 'home': two of the au pairs were painfully aware that home was elsewhere. For the Brazilian au pair, home was a place where her family employed servants to do the domestic labour that she performed in the UK while attempting to improve her English. For the Turkish au pair, home was a place by the sea: if the domestic culture in which she found herself felt alien, she only felt at home in the UK in a public space – sitting on Bognor beach, looking out to sea.

While cultural theorists have often represented domestic spaces as fixed, bounded and static – as sites of tradition and reproduction where people go about mundane tasks – this example demonstrates how domestic cultures are instead the site for complex negotiations about how to live (Felski 2000). Furthermore, although routine domestic tasks such as setting the alarm clock and brushing our teeth are easy to take for granted, just because these activities appear repetitive and everyday does not mean that they are without cultural significance. As Ben Highmore (2004: 307) argues, routines are not simply imposed on us and they are not just endlessly reproduced: instead 'we establish our own daily routines to give our lives rhythm and predictability'. Indeed, the extent to which these routines feel 'natural' contributes to the extent to which we feel 'at home' in a particular domestic culture. For example, au pairs rarely feel 'part of the family' in their workplace because 'they just do not understand the house, its rhythms, norms, and expectations, whether they should respond to the calls of children when they are off-duty, which meals are for them, whether it is appropriate to watch the television with the family or discuss their relationships with them' (Búriková 2006: 103).

The documentary about au pairs highlights how we need to be wary of making generalizations about domestic culture. Many critics have assumed that we know all about domestic life and have merrily asserted the characteristics that unify domestic cultures. One of the key themes underpinning this book is that we need to look at domestic cultures in their specificity. Domestic cultures take various forms both across – and within – different times and places. In studying domestic cultures we need to look at the specific ways in which they have been practised and imagined and to think about how domestic cultures produce ways of organizing, managing and doing everyday life. We also need to examine how people construct and give meaning to their lives through domestic practices, and how these meanings are also constructed for us as well as by us. Through domestic cultures, people attempt to negotiate particular temporal rhythms and spatial relations. And although, like the au pairs, we may not reside in a place we call home, domestic cultures are frequently organized around an attempt to reproduce, create or sustain a connectedness to a sense of home.

Public and private spheres

The distinction between the **public sphere** and the private sphere structures the way in which the modern world is organized and lived. The public sphere is seen as the realm of industry, economics and politics, and the private sphere is seen as the realm of the family, personal life and the domestic. These spheres have also frequently been understood as gendered: masculinity is associated with the public and femininity with the private. This distinction between public and private has been a key means of imagining the modern world and, therefore, it is not surprising that this distinction has been a central assumption in much social and cultural theory. The distinction between public and private has also been a key means of organizing both space and time. The public sphere is not only associated with spaces such as the factory, the office and the street, it has also been associated with the fast-paced rhythms of the industrial work-place and global trade. Likewise, the private sphere is not only associated with the domestic home but it has also frequently been associated with a slower, more organic sense of time.

Throughout this book I demonstrate how ideas about public and private have been used in particular ways at particular times and with particular effects. However, at the same time, I also show how the conceptualization of public and private as distinct and bounded spheres is deeply problematic. From the outset, it is important to note that 'Home is not separated from public, political worlds but is constituted through them: the domestic is created through the extra-domestic and vice versa' (Blunt and Dowling 2006: 27). Furthermore, while domestic cultures have frequently been represented as a retreat from the public sphere, they are also sites of interconnection where ideas, things, images, resources and people come together in particular combinations. In creating and living domestic cultures, people are always involved in negotiating relationships to the public sphere. They are also responding to – but also helping to create – wider cultural formations and transformations at local, national and global levels. As Nigel Rapport and Andrew Dawson argue, the world is 'no longer . . . divided up into units, territorial segments . . . each of which shares a distinctive, exclusive culture'. Instead, 'traditionally fixed, spatially and temporally bounded cultural worlds from which to depart and return no longer exist' (cited in Morley 2000: 10). Through domestic culture we negotiate and make sense of our relationships to a variety of places, spaces and scales.

Not only are aspects of 'the outside world' tangled up within the places we live but aspects of domestic culture are themselves mobile. The meanings, values, practices and traditions that are associated with domestic cultures can themselves have a currency within the public sphere.[2] Aspects of domestic culture are transported beyond the domestic home to a range of public spaces (for example, the home-like wooden floors and comfy leather sofas found in Starbucks), and are mobilized in public debates (for example, in political parties appeals to domestic 'commonsense' when they discuss national economic policies). These themes are developed in Chapter 7.

However, just because domestic cultures are porous and mobile does not mean that we should ignore their specificity. Since the eighteenth century in the UK, domestic spaces have been identified with very particular values and responsibilities and it is necessary to identify how these ideas of home have been reproduced, negotiated, resisted and transformed. Studying domestic cultures enables us to understand how social, cultural, political and economic processes at a larger scale are bound up with –

and *lived* through – in everyday life. Yet at the same time, we can also learn about how domestic activities have contributed to these large-scale transformations, how the impact and orientation of domestic practices have 'reached out beyond the home to the city, the country and the globe' (Marston 2000: 238). It is so as to maintain the focus on domestic cultures in their specificity that I have limited the scope of this book by focusing on domestic cultures in the West, and concentrating on those in the UK and USA. For people wishing to gain a more global understanding of domestic cultures, work by Cieraad (1999), Birdwell-Pheasant and Lawrence-Zúñiga (1999) and Blunt and Dowling (2006) provides a useful starting point.

While I frequently use the terms 'domestic' and 'home' interchangeably in this book, the concept of home is not tied to the domestic but can also convey a sense of belonging tied to non-domestic spaces (a pub or football ground or even an office). Furthermore, the idea of home can operate at regional, national and transnational scales (Morley 2000; Blunt and Dowling 2006). As I go on to discuss in Chapter 6, the media can transport us beyond our place of residence, enabling domestic space to be connected to a national or transnational sense of home. Likewise, as the au pairs discovered, we can be part of a domestic culture in which we do not necessarily feel *at home*. These themes are discussed in more detail in the following chapters.

Domestic cultures and cultural studies

This book started life as a second-year undergraduate module called ' "Home" and Cultural Identity' that I team-taught with Steve Jones at Nottingham Trent University for a number of years. When we introduced the module, we were interested in how studying home offered students an opportunity to develop their understanding of lived cultures. The module encourages students to 'do' cultural studies, enabling them to reflect critically on the apparent obviousness of everyday life by doing research projects into various aspects of 'home'. During the period in which we have taught this course, we found that we weren't alone in developing an interest in home. In recent years, numerous studies and collections have interrogated the meaning of the domestic home and analysed the complex structures, processes and practices that underpin seemingly mundane aspects of domestic life (see, for example, Jackson and Moores 1995; Cieraad 1999; Chapman and Hockey 1999b; Miller 2001c; Pink 2004). These debates have taken place across a range of disciplines – for example, anthropology, geography, design history, history, sociology and media studies – although the spirit of enquiry has often been interdisciplinary. A new journal – *Home Cultures* – has been established to provide a 'home' for the interdisciplinary study of domestic cultures (Buchli et al. 2004: 2).

Putting 'home' into the curriculum offered a way of introducing our students to a tradition within cultural studies that concentrates on lived cultural practices and the rich textures of everyday life, a tradition that can be traced back to the work of critics such as Richard Hoggart and Raymond Williams. Although Hoggart constructed a pessimistic narrative in which he argued that domestic cultures were increasingly divorced from a living cultural tradition and became mass-produced and conservative (see Chapter 3), Williams's essay 'Culture is Ordinary' offers a way into thinking about the cultural significance of home. Rather than understanding the significance of 'plumbing, baby Austins, aspirin, contraceptives, canned food' as signs of how ordinary domestic cultures became centred around a mass-produced commercial culture imposed from above, Williams (1997: 11) suggests that these commodities provide resources through which people reworked the meaning of everyday life and produced distinctive cultural responses to a changing experience of modernity.

While this tradition offered a way into thinking about the meaning domestic cultures, recent academic work on home has largely been outside of cultural studies (although see, for example, Jackson and Moores 1995; Morley 2000; Highmore 2004; Johnson and Lloyd 2004; Moran 2004 and 2005b). There has been far more interest in domestic cultures within media studies where a range of research has explored how media technologies and texts are used to produce the meaning and experience of domestic life (see Chapter 6). However, while this research offers a useful framework for understanding the cultural processes that might underpin other aspects of domestic life, cultural studies has frequently remained preoccupied with the spectacular and transgressive dimensions of cultural life and ignored seemingly mundane cultural practices such as preparing meals and mowing the lawn.

By representing some forms of cultural experience and some types of cultural practice as more significant than others, cultural studies has frequently reproduced the idea that certain aspects of everyday life and certain social groups aren't worthy of our interest. Indeed, some of the everyday practices that were included in Williams's conception of culture have become marginalized because they are seen as somehow intrinsically conservative and fundamentally boring. As Ben Highmore (2002: 10) notes, designating cultural practices as boring is usually as a means of 'denigrating the everyday life of other social groups' (see Chapter 3). This book hopes to contribute to a developing strand in cultural studies which aims to identify how those aspects of life that have been dismissed as 'banal and boring' may also offer ways of understanding 'a significant area for an unacknowledged cultural politics' (Moran 2005b: 11).

However, the marginalization of home within cultural studies needs to be understood in terms of the assumptions that have underpinned wider theories of modernity and the ways in which these theories are gendered. In Marshall Berman's (1983) now classic account of modernity he argues that the processes associated with modernization – **capitalist industrialization**, developments in science and technology, **rationalization, urbanization**, the development of the mass media and so on – brought about a radically new experience of the world in which people's relationships to time, space and each other are transformed. Berman argues that these changes, in which 'all that is solid melts into air', provoked a sense of both excitement and anxiety. Yet Berman –

like many critics and artists before and after him – represents the experience of modernity as a distinctly masculine experience. As critics such as Rita Felski (2000) and Judy Giles (2004) have pointed out, theories of modernity focus on the dynamic experience of a modernity that is lived on the streets of the city, in factories and in forums of political debate. This emphasizes a masculine experience of modernity that tells us little about how women, who frequently were excluded from these spaces, made sense of the social changes around them. Furthermore, it tells us little about how people made sense of the experience of modernity in their domestic lives. Giles (2004: 4) argues that we also need to focus on domestic modernity and analyse how 'modernity was lived, expressed and imagined in the private worlds of women as well as the ways in which public discourses about domesticity shaped those experiences and imaginings'.

Focusing on domestic cultures can tell us about another side of modernity, a domestic modernity that is excluded from most accounts. However, thinking about domestic modernity requires more than simply adding the domestic to the inventory of quintessentially modern sites and experiences. This is because the home has frequently been seen as somehow 'outside' modernity and as a 'a refuge from the modern, a repository of traditional values, a haven from the excitement and dangers of living in the modern world' (Giles 2004: 4). Therefore, many Victorian commentators stressed the value of home because it connected people to traditional values (ignoring how their very ideas about domestic culture were a modern invention). The assumption that the domestic lay 'outside' of modernity was also reproduced by theorists of modernity, although many of these theorists adopted a more critical stance and argued that the traditional values nurtured in the home produced conformity, conservatism and constraint. As Meaghan Morris notes, 'There is a very powerful cultural link . . . dear to a masculine tradition inscribing "home" as the site both of frustrating containment (home as dull) and of truth to be rediscovered (home as real). The stifling home is the place from which the voyage begins and, to which, in the end, it returns' (cited in Morley 2000: 68). Indeed, as Felski (2000: 86) argues, 'The vocabulary of modernity is a vocabulary of anti-home. It celebrates mobility, movement, exile, boundary crossing. It speaks enthusiastically about movement out into the world, but is silent about the return home . . . Home . . . is the space of familiarity, dullness, stasis.' As I go on to demonstrate throughout this book, the idea that the domestic can simply be understood as a site of tradition and conservatism continues to be mobilized across a range of debates from the late eighteenth century to the present day.

Indeed, this assumption that home is a space of containment and conservatism was also reproduced in some of the key early work within cultural studies. The fascination with masculine subcultures who occupied public spaces (see, for example, Hebdige 1979 and Willis 1977) not only celebrated young men's escape from the confinement of home but also rarely recognized that even punks go home. As Angela McRobbie (1981: 116) observes, identities are shaped by what goes on 'around the breakfast table and in the bedroom' as well as by the public sphere. Because cultural studies has been informed by the very theories of modernity that celebrate transgression and mobility, it is perhaps not surprising that there has been very little interest in home. Furthermore, the celebration of mobility and dismissal of the domestic in some cultural theory is also profoundly gendered. As Beverley Skeggs (2004: 51–2) observes, 'mobility is itself gendered on a variety of scales . . . male subjectivity is discursively linked to narratives, of travel, adventure and discovery whereas female subjectivity is mapped as a fixed place on the itinerary of the male journey.'

As Giles (2004) and Felski (2000) suggest, it is difficult to simply incorporate domestic cultures within theories of modernity because these theories do not simply *ignore home* but are also frequently constructed *against home*. Likewise, because of the close associations between home and femininity, these theories of modernity do not simply ignore women's experience of modernity but also are defined against the home as a feminized space. To think about domestic modernity and the complex contribution of domestic cultures to modern life means that it is necessary for us to 'question the assumption that being modern requires an irrevocable sundering from home, and simultaneously explicate the modern dimensions of everyday experiences of home' (Felski 2000: 89). While theorists of modernity frequently assumed that the meaning of home was easily understood and knowable because it was familiar and unchanging, in this book I bring together work from across a range of disciplines to explore how domestic cultures have a history and are a key site through which the meaning of modern life is constructed, negotiated and lived.

Domestic cultures as family cultures?

It would be easy to assume that domestic cultures are in fact family cultures. One of the most common meanings associated with the idea of home is family. Likewise, frequently the concept of private life is associated with family life. Policies about work–life balance (see Chapter 7) presume that the 'life' we have outside work is primarily organized around the family. And even academic studies of domestic life frequently assume that domestic cultures are organized around the family. Indeed, it is entirely conceivable that a book on domestic cultures might be primarily about the family. However, while the idea of family is undoubtedly central to the ways in which domestic cultures have been understood, this book does not assume that domestic cultures are always oriented around the family because this not only excludes the experiences of those people who live outside of 'conventional' family structures but it also limits the range of questions we can ask about the cultural significance of the domestic.

Nonetheless, it is important to question how and why domestic cultures are so often seen as familial cultures. The idea that domestic life and family are synonymous is far from natural or traditional but was the product of a series of cultural, social and economic transformations that took place from the late eighteenth century onwards in the USA and the UK (see Chapter 2). During this period, the emergent industrial middle class invested home with specific meanings: distinguished by its difference to the public sphere of work, domestic culture was imagined as a moral and familial culture. The nineteenth-century middle-class family was structured around the idea of a male breadwinner who provided economic support for his wife and children, and a female home-maker who was responsible for producing and maintaining domestic culture and the socialization of children. As I go on to explain in Chapter 2, this ideal model of family life was not necessarily reproduced in practice, even by the middle classes. Nonetheless, the association between the home and the family would have a profound impact on the way in which later domestic cultures were imagined, organized and lived.

While there have been key transformations in – and struggles over – the meaning and nature of family life since this period, the association between the domestic and the family has been naturalized so it appears as normal. As Barrett and McIntosh (1982: 31) argue, 'Just as the family has been socially constructed, so society has been familialized'. In the post-war period, it was frequently assumed that domestic life was focused around – or *should* be focused around – the **nuclear family** unit, comprised of a male breadwinner, female housewife and two to three children. Despite significant transformations in how people live, domestic life is still frequently organized as if everyone lives within nuclear families. Food is often sold in 'family-sized' packages while the idea of 'the family home' with three to four bedrooms remains central to the housing market. Likewise, despite significant social change, the idea that people live in heterosexual couples in which there is a male 'breadwinner' and a female 'home-maker' still structures many aspects of everyday life. For example, the school day and school year still operate as if there is a member of the family who is not in full-time employment while the content of daytime TV programmes is frequently constructed around the assumption that this person is female. Therefore, the assumption that domestic cultures are familial cultures structures everyday life and must be negotiated by those whose domestic life is not experienced within the nuclear family.

While film and TV representations of domestic life have become open to more expansive and diverse notions of home and family (Chambers 2000; Tincknell 2005), the idea that domestic life should be organized within and around the nuclear family continues to structure many political debates and social policies. At the time of writing, David Cameron – the leader of the right-wing Conservative party in the UK – announced plans to introduce tax benefits to married couples as a means of reinforcing the importance of marriage and a 'stable' family life as the foundation of a 'moral' and 'stable' society. As he put it:

> Here's an easy question: what institution looks after the sick, cares for children and the elderly, supports working people and the unemployed, and provides people with their most fulfilling relationships and their most cherished memories? The answer is not the welfare state; it's the family. That is the institution Britain

depends on for its wellbeing. And what is the institution that, in so many cases, holds families together? Most of all, it is marriage.

(Cameron 2007)

Although, in order to avoid charges of discrimination, he would quickly revise this policy in order to promise the same tax benefits to gay and lesbian couples who had entered into a civil partnership, Cameron's statement reinforces the relationship between a stable society, a strong nation and the family. A familialized domestic culture is seen as playing a key role in maintaining moral order but is also seen as fundamental in providing emotional, economic, medical and social support for its members. While many of the functions that Cameron ascribes to the family *could* be provided within the public sphere (or within non-familial domestic arrangements), he appeals to the commonsense idea that these functions are best catered for within a familial domestic culture.

These images of 'normal' domestic life are also reinforced by pathologizing people who live outside of 'normal' families. For example, Deborah Chambers (2000: 201) highlights how Britain's 'socialist' Labour government led by Tony Blair demonized those people who were outside the nuclear family in the late 1990s. Blair presented the decline in the number of people living within nuclear family structures as a threat to social stability, claimed that ' "problem families" bring up problem children' who were partly responsible for rising crime, and singled out single-parent families as a particular form of 'problem family'. In the process, Blair reproduced the idea that specific forms of familial, domestic culture are essential to the moral stability of the nation – people living outside the nuclear family are associated with the threat of moral disorder.

Such interventions contribute to the naturalization of domestic culture as a particular form of familial culture that is central to a stable social life. These images work to suggest that people who do not live within nuclear families are *unnatural* and to imply that these people's domestic lives cause a problem for society as a whole. These representations of 'problem' homes are frequently inflected by 'race' and class. For example, in the USA, there is a recurring tendency to represent the relatively high numbers of African-Americans living in poverty as a result of 'deviant' family structures. The well-publicized Moynihan Report of the mid-1960s indulged in 'blaming the victim', claiming that it was black family structures – rather than structural economic equalities and racism – that kept many black families locked in poverty. This opinion was revived by Moynihan (1986) in the mid-1980s when he claimed that 'a breakdown in family values has allowed Black men to renounce their traditional breadwinner role, leaving Black women to bear the economic responsibility for children', resulting in high levels of poverty among African-Americans (Baca Zinn 1989: 859). These views, which received a significant amount of media coverage, not only diverted attention from the real causes of black poverty but also pathologized the black family and, in the process, reaffirmed the value of nuclear family structures associated with the white middle class. In this way, the severe problems of poverty were seen to result from 'deviant' domestic cultures.

Furthermore, familial ideologies are used to legitimate actions against those who are represented as a 'threat' to hegemonic ideas about family life (although the significance and meaning given to the family is transformed in different historical and national contexts). For example Jackie Stacey argues that, in the 1980s, the right-wing British government represented gays and lesbians as 'outsiders' who were a threat to family life (and, therefore, to the nation as a whole). These ideas were used to legitimate an attempt to introduce new legislation that discriminated against gays and lesbians (resulting in the attempt to pass a new bill, **Section 28**, which specifically prohibited the promotion of homosexual relationships because they were seen as 'pretend' family relationships). Stacey (1991: 287) argues that media representations in the period told 'a familiar story of the innocent family, site of health happiness and normality, which was under threat from the evil, deviant outsiders, lesbians and gay men, who signified the more general decline in moral standards'. Therefore, although some critics have argued for expanding the idea of family to include households that live outside of the heterosexual nuclear family, familial ideologies tend to reinforce the idea of nuclear family households as the only legitimate basis for domestic culture.

Therefore, the familialization of domestic culture works to exclude certain cultural identities. As a result, for gay men and lesbians, the family home is frequently represented as a site in which it is impossible to be 'at home' and to 'be yourself' and, as a result, narratives of leaving home are often central to gay and lesbian identity (Johnston and Valentine 1995). Nonetheless, the idea of home is frequently invoked by gay men and lesbians to identify 'a desired site of familiarity, comfort and belonging' (Fortier 2001: 410). While this sense of 'home' may be found in bars and clubs rather than domestic space, Andrew Gorman-Murray's (2006b: 153) research into gay and lesbian couples' homemaking practices identifies that places of residence were also important as 'private spaces' in which his interviewees could 'be themselves'. He argues that domestic spaces operated as 'sanctuaries from wider social sanctions against same-sex relationships'. While this sense of privacy and control can be threatened by 'the prying eyes of parents, relatives and neighbours' (Johnston and Valentine 1995: 106), domestic space can take on a heightened importance precisely because there may be the ability to control access (Gorman-Murray 2006b). Therefore, while the domestic has frequently been associated with the nuclear family – and hence as hostile to people who live outside these family forms – domestic cultures are not inherently heterosexual. Indeed, as Gorman-Murray (2006c: 54) argues, they can operate as a sanctuary 'from **heteronormativity**'.[3]

While understanding how the idea of family is given meaning, inhabited, structured, struggled over and experienced is a valuable field of academic endeavour, focusing on the family alone is not sufficient if we want to understand the complexity of domestic cultures. Critics such as David Morgan (1999) have used the idea of 'family practices' in an attempt to conceptualize the complex range of activities and processes that are oriented around *the idea* of family (not all of which take place in domestic space – for example, paid work may be oriented towards the idea of family and is a practice that helps to produce and sustain the family). Rather than assume what 'the family' means, Silva and Smart (1999: 5) argue that the concept of family practices enables us to study the range of ways in which people ' "do" family life' rather than 'passively residing within a pre-given structure'. Tony Chapman (2004) has suggested that we can gain a more expansive notion of domestic life, one that is not simply tied to family, by employing the concept of 'domestic practices'. This concept is useful because it doesn't presume that domestic cultures are necessarily family cultures but instead enables us to consider the range of practices that go into creating and sustaining the idea of the domestic. While I rarely explicitly employ Chapman's idea of domestic practices in what follows, I share an interest in thinking about the sheer range of practices that are oriented towards and around the idea of home. Likewise, drawing on Silva and Smart, I am also interested in the range of ways in which people *practise* domestic cultures rather than assume from the outset that we can know exactly what domestic culture actually means.

For this reason, I have resisted the temptation to offer a definition of domestic culture that attempts to pin down its essential meaning. Instead, I consider how domestic cultures have become attached to particular values, meanings, structures, living arrangements and practices and how these have been reproduced, resisted and transformed both across, and within, different historical formations. *Domestic Cultures* brings together a range of different voices that have spoken for, about and through 'the domestic' (and the related concept of domesticity), voices which also are produced by – and help to produce – the wider social and cultural context out of which they arise (Hebdige 1988; Gray 2003).

Using this book

The approaches I use in order to make sense of domestic cultures in this book are informed by work in cultural studies. However, given that relatively little has been written about domestic cultures within the field of cultural studies, the spirit of this book – like cultural studies itself – is interdisciplinary. This interdisciplinary approach has been essential in order to begin to grasp the complexity of domestic cultures and in order to map some of the key ideas about how domestic life has been represented, organized and experienced. While readers with an investment in approaches to the study of home within a particular discipline may feel that I haven't done justice to the key ideas and work within their field, I hope that the strength of this book lies in the way it brings together theories and research from across disciplines.

While there is certainly scope for a book that focuses on the ways in which the meaning of domestic cultures are constructed through representation, I have instead opted for an approach that examines how the meaning of domestic culture is con-structed across institutions, industries, texts and practices. Drawing on Paul du Gay et al.'s (1997) conception of 'a circuit of culture' (see also Johnson 1986), I examine the complex relationships between the ways in which the meaning of domestic culture is produced through representation (for example, in domestic advice literature and on lifestyle television); production (from the construction industry to domestic labour); regulation (from housing policy to initiatives on work–life balance); consumption (for example, the arrangement of family photographs and the ways in which we use furniture); and cultural identity (for example, gendered or generational identities). By thinking about how these different processes interrelate, we can begin to examine the complex, diverse and sometimes unpredictable ways in which domestic cultures are produced, managed and lived.

Chapter 2, 'Histories of domestic culture: gender and domestic modernity', explores how a new conception of the meaning, value and functions of domestic cultures emerged from the late eighteenth century onwards as part of wider processes of modernization. I examine how the public sphere of work, politics, industry and commerce was imagined as distinct and separate from the private sphere of the home that was seen as the site of family and morality. Furthermore, these spheres were also gendered with the public sphere imagined as masculine and the private sphere as feminine. However, I also demonstrate that public and domestic life were never truly separate. The chapter offers an understanding of the history of domestic cultures by identifying some of the key changes in both domestic cultures and domestic femininities across the nineteenth century and through to the interwar period of the 1920s and 1930s. In the process, I consider how domestic cultures were also shaped by class, ethnicity and 'race'.

In Chapter 3, 'Home-centredness: suburbia, privatization and class', I explore how domestic cultures have been seen as a political problem. Mapping a series of debates from the 1920s through to the present day, this chapter identifies how a series of critics have claimed that being home-centred causes people to becomes privatized and to withdraw from public life and any sense of social and political responsibility. These critics frequently claim that suburban domesticity produces a trivial, conservative and conformist culture that, in turn, helps to sustain a wider conservative political system. I demonstrate how these arguments are problematic and argue that it is necessary to explore how an investment in suburban domestic culture instead needs to be taken seriously and does not automatically result in political conservatism.

Chapter 4, 'Home-*work*: feminisms, domesticity and domestic labour', also examines how domestic culture has been seen as a problem, considering how feminist critics have portrayed the home as a problem for women. In this chapter I explore how domestic cultures are work cultures and focus on the amount of unpaid labour that is required to sustain domestic life. Many feminists have criticized how labour is organized within domestic culture and argued that domestic cultures are sustained by – and also help to sustain – an unequal division of labour in which unpaid domestic work continues to be primarily seen as feminine labour. Using the example of cooking, I demonstrate how domestic work is also a key home-*making* practice which not only physically sustains household members but is also a form of emotional labour that helps to create the meaning of home. I finish this chapter by thinking critically about feminist perspectives on domesticity, arguing that there is scope to develop a more complex understanding about the contribution of domestic culture to social and political life.

In Chapter 5, 'Home-*making*: domestic consumption and material culture', I examine how the meaning and experience of domestic cultures are constructed through consumption practices. While lifestyle media encourage us to see the home as a site in which we can play with our identity, this chapter suggests that consumption practices are frequently mundane and oriented towards actively maintaining the very idea of home. Not only do people use things – from photographs to kitchen cupboards – to construct the meaning of domestic culture but material culture can also shape the ways in which we relate to the places we live. I argue that housing also needs to be thought of as a form of material culture: housing can be appropriated and invested with meaning by its residents but it can also constrain the forms of domestic cultures that can be created and place limits on our ability to experience our residence as a home.

Chapter 6, 'The media in domestic cultures', also focuses on consumption practices, demonstrating how people use media technologies to negotiate the meaning of domestic cultures. In this chapter I explore how media technologies undergo processes of domestication in order to render them at home in domestic space. I also examine how media forms are used to create relationships between the domestic space and forms of belonging at national and transnational levels. In the process I demonstrate how the media are used to 'stretch' domestic space and contribute to the blurring of boundaries between public and private.

The final chapter, 'Dislocating public and private', expands on these themes and considers a range of debates that demonstrate how the meanings associated with public and private spheres have become mobile, and how the distinction between public and private is not only porous but also sometimes unhelpful. I explore how the values associated with domestic culture have been mobilized in a wide range of ways within the public sphere. I also examine how the distinction between home and work – which was central to ideas about separate spheres – is not clear-cut: as the workplace becomes increasingly domesticated, domestic culture is also shaped by the values and rhythms of the workplace. Finally, I identify how the blurring of spheres does not erode the significance of domestic culture but instead can result in an attempt to protect the values and experiences associated with domesticity. Throughout the chapter – indeed, throughout this book – I demonstrate how distinctions between domestic and non-domestic spaces can never be assumed but are continually in process.

Further reading

Blunt, A. and Dowling, R. (2006) *Home*. London: Routledge.
Felski, R. (2000) *Doing Time: Feminist Theory and Postmodern Culture*. New York: New York University Press.

Morley, D. (2000) *Home Territories: Media, Mobility and Identity*. London: Routledge.

Silva, E. and Smart, C. (eds) *The New Family?*. London: Sage.

Notes

1 This was shown as part of Channel 4's documentary series *Cutting Edge* and was first broadcast on 21 May 2007.

2 However, the ability to capitalize on aspects of domestic culture as a form of currency may be circumscribed: see, for example, Reay (2004) and Silva (2007).

3 Gorman-Murray (2006c: 54) argues that gay men's investments in home must be ultimately described as 'unhomely' because they involve inviting into domestic space ' "external" non-normative discourses, bodies and activities in order to *queer* domestic space and engender non-heteronormative socialization and identity-affirmation'. However, his reading rests on the assumption that the domestic home has a singular and fixed meaning: rather than thinking about how gay men make domestic space unhomely, it might be more productive to think about how they are involved in attempts to resignify home. Furthermore, Gorman-Murray's approach identifies the primary meaning of home in terms of sexuality: such an approach might miss the similarities between gay and straight home-making practices by focusing only on the differences (a problem which is implicitly addressed in Gorman-Murray 2006b).

2

HISTORIES OF DOMESTIC CULTURE:
GENDER AND DOMESTIC MODERNITY

Introduction

In order to understand contemporary domestic cultures, it is necessary to take a historical approach to understand the meaning of home. Such an approach highlights how the meaning of domestic culture is subject to change and reveals how domestic cultures are shaped by – and, crucially, also shape – specific historical contexts. Put simply, contemporary domestic cultures are significantly different from nineteenth-century domestic cultures. At the same time, some meanings of home also have considerable longevity: for example, some of the qualities that people associate with home today – such as comfort, security, warmth, family – were also identified with the meaning of home in the nineteenth century. However, these are not 'timeless' and 'natural' aspects of home but were distinctively 'modern' ideas that became dominant in the Victorian era (1837–1901). In order to understand domestic cultures, we need to be aware of both continuities and discontinuities in the meaning of home in different historical formations.

This chapter offers an overview of the distinctively 'modern' domestic cultures that emerged from the late eighteenth century onwards in the UK and the USA. I focus on how the public sphere and the private sphere were imagined as distinctive and separate spheres of modern life and how they were associated with specific meanings, values, identities and functions. In particular, I examine how domestic cultures – and new ideas about domesticity – came to be seen as feminine and identified with women. As the chapter progresses, I explore how the meaning of domestic cultures in the Victorian period was produced across a range of sites and practices. Particular ideas about domestic cultures – and women's role within them – were represented through the places where housing was situated, how homes were produced, designed and furnished and in the advice given to women about home-making. However, I also identify how these ideas could be negotiated, resisted and reworked through women's home-making practices. Furthermore, I demonstrate how domestic cultures were not simply gendered but were also differentiated by class, 'race' and ethnicity.

Throughout this chapter I highlight how nineteenth-century domestic cultures are characterized by an apparent contradiction: they are 'modern' inventions but frequently identified with 'traditional' values (Bennett 2002; Giles 2004). For example, during the nineteenth century, home came to be seen as a haven from the pressures of the modern world, a site of tradition and moral values that provided a bulwark against the apparent immorality and chaos produced by modernity. This chapter demonstrates how the seemingly paradoxical representation of home as *both* modern and traditional is central in understanding the complexity of domestic cultures. As I argued in the last chapter, while domestic cultures are frequently represented as 'outside' of modernity, they also play a key role in producing modernity. In the latter part of this chapter, I go on to explore how this antinomy between the modern and traditional was negotiated in domestic cultures in the interwar period of the 1920s and 1930s.

Before proceeding, it is necessary to understand how the concept of separate spheres has been central for many critics who have sought to explain the differences between 'pre-industrial' and 'modern' domestic cultures. Pre-industrial households are usually characterized as a site of production (work) and reproduction (family life). While home is now frequently seen as synonymous with family, many critics argue that pre-industrial households made little distinction between family and other people who lived there (workers, lodgers, servants, and so on). In these households Tamara Hareven (2002: 34) argues that 'the family's public and private activities were inseparable': relations within the household were based on '*sociability* rather than *privacy*' and there was little distinction between public and private spaces within the home. While men and women were frequently involved in different forms of labour and while women were seen as inferior to men, the pre-industrial home is frequently seen as a place in which men, women and children all contributed to production.

Many critics argue that this form of pre-industrial domestic culture was torn apart by processes of modernization that segregated home and work into separate private and public spheres, each with their own specific functions, values and meanings. There is considerable debate about *when, how* and *where* this shift took place (although these transformations are often identified with the late eighteenth century in the UK and France and the early nineteenth century in the USA). However, many critics would agree that 'following the removal of the workplace from the home as a result of industrialization and urbanization, the household was recast as the family's private retreat' (Hareven 2002: 35). As a result, it is claimed that domestic life took on increasingly specialized functions – it was no longer seen as a place for work and the production of goods but as a site for child-rearing and the consumption of goods. However, while such arguments offer a useful way of understanding large-scale social changes, it is crucial to remember that these changes occurred in uneven ways over a long period of time.

The distinction between public and private life was reinforced through their association with opposing meanings and values. For example, the public sphere was associated with 'chaos, pollution, moral and sexual dissolution and the erosion of the traditional order' in 'counterpoint to the idea of a virtuous and harmonious domestic existence' (Nava 1997: 60). Home came to signify security, comfort, intimacy and a moral life and was imagined as a haven from an unsettling, dangerous, impersonal and immoral public sphere. Indeed, by the mid-nineteenth century in both the UK and the USA, home had come to be seen as a special place; a place to be 'yourself' and put down roots; a place of innocence, warmth, intimacy and hospitality; a site devoted to marriage and the family, to religion and morality, to leisure rather than labour; a stage to display status through the exercise of 'good taste' through appropriate consumption; and a place of national importance (Ryan 1981; Matthews 1987; Sparke 1995; Hepworth 1999; Tosh 1999; Davidoff and Hall 2002). While the public sphere was frequently represented as an 'unnatural' place, the home was represented as having a 'natural' association with timeless and traditional values, despite the fact that nineteenth-century domestic culture was distinctively new and modern. A further crucial distinction separated these spheres: the public sphere was identified with masculinity and the public sphere with femininity. This distinction is the focus of the next section.

Separate spheres?

For many critics the organization of economic, social and cultural life into two distinctive spheres brought about a profound shift in gender relations. As production and business moved out of the household into the public sphere, it is frequently argued, it also became defined as a masculine activity. In the process, women became responsible for maintaining domestic and family life and became economically dependent on men. This section explores these debates in more detail, examining how femininity became identified with domesticity. However, I also highlight how we need to be wary of generalizing about gender and domestic cultures: class and 'race' cut across the experience of women during this period and distinctions between 'public' and 'private' were never as clear-cut as is sometimes implied.

For many critics the simultaneous separation and gendering of public and private spheres was a decisive moment in women's history, producing deeply embedded inequalities between men and women. For example, in one of the most oft-cited pieces on the subject, Barbara Welter (1966) argued that new ideologies of domesticity – what she terms 'a cult of true womanhood' – emerged in the nineteenth century: these not only identified women with the home but also effectively kept them confined there, producing profound constraints on women's freedom. From the 1820s to the 1860s, she suggests, this ideology was promoted by US women's magazines that defined femininity in terms of 'piety, purity, submissiveness and domesticity' (Welter 1966: 152). Evangelical religions, which exerted considerable influence during the period, also reinforced the importance of women's domestic role, suggesting that their domestic responsibilities offered women the opportunity to exercise moral authority. While Welter's argument is useful in highlighting how femininity was identified with domesticity during the period, she assumes that these ideologies were unquestioningly accepted by the readers of women's magazines and evangelical literature, suggesting that we can 'read off' lived experience from an analysis of texts.

A further problem with Welter's work is that she suggests that ideas about gendered spheres applied to all women. However, other critics in the USA have argued that these 'modern' ideas about domestic culture – and women's place within it – were distinctively urban, white and middle class (Cott 1977; Ryan 1981).[1] For example, in her study of the formation of the middle class in Oneida County, New York, Mary Ryan (1981) argues that new ideas about domesticity did not simply work to position women in the home but also played a crucial role in producing and legitimating a distinctive form of domestic culture that was central to the identity of an emergent urban middle class.

Ryan's study highlights how domestic cultures did not simply produce ideas about gendered identities and relations but also played a key role in processes of class formation. While many theories of modernity assume that class identities and class cultures were principally a product of the public sphere, this ignores how domestic cultures also contributed to the formation of both gendered and class identities. The middle class that emerged from the late eighteenth century onwards produced a distinctive form of domestic culture based around feminine domesticity and a morality of 'domestic moderation' that helped to distinguish them from both the new urban working class and the aristocracy (Davidoff and Hall 2002: 21).

Leonora Davidoff and Catherine Hall's *Family Fortunes* – a study of gender, domesticity and the provincial middle classes in the UK between 1780 and 1850 – provides a useful way of examining how nineteenth-century ideas about domestic culture were shaped by – and helped to shape – the emerging middle class. They argue that evangelical religions influenced these new middle-class cultural identities and provided a justification for gendered spheres. These religions promoted the idea that the home was 'the basis for a proper and moral order in the amoral world of the market' (Davidoff and Hall 2002: 74).

Women's role was to produce and represent the moral virtues ascribed to domestic culture, a role they were seen as 'naturally' suited for because women were seen to be 'naturally' more nurturing and hence more Christian, gentle and passive. These were qualities that made women seem unsuited to the competitive and amoral public sphere (Davidoff and Hall 2002: 115). Therefore, it was believed that middle-class women were best suited to operate as guardians of morality: although men had to operate in the public sphere, they could maintain a Christian heart and mind because 'they could be rescued by women's moral vigilance at home' (Davidoff and Hall 2002: 74). These religious ideas also helped to legitimize a **sexual division of labour** based on men as breadwinners and women as economically dependent home-makers: masculinity was defined in terms of a 'man's ability to support and order his family' while 'a woman's femininity was best expressed in her dependence' (Davidoff and Hall 2002: 114). Although these ideas gained a more secular flavour in the 1830s and 1840s, domestic advice literature continued to promote the importance of home as 'a bedrock of morality in an unstable and dangerous world' (Davidoff and Hall 2002: xiv). In this way, while women's responsibility for domestic culture was founded on the dubious premise that they were 'naturally' suited for this role, women were not necessarily seen as inferior to men but different to them: 'they were equally important in their distinctive domestic sphere' (J. Williams 2000: 23).

For the emergent middle class, domestic life was also important because it was the site of family life. Marriage became increasingly centred around ideas of romantic love and operated as 'the economic and social building block for the middle class; it was the basis of a new family unit' (Davidoff and Hall 2002: 322). Middle-class femininity was not only identified with the role of wife but also, more crucially, with the role of mother (a role women were also seen to be 'naturally' suited to). As mothers, women played a crucial role in creating and reproducing middle-class culture because they were responsible for the socialization of their children. The importance of family life to the middle classes was also reinforced in the new status they gave to childhood as a period free from adult responsibilities and characterized by 'innocence'.

However, while home was seen as the natural place for women and children, men also had a key role in these domestic cultures. Because the masculine role of breadwinner required men to engage in the competitive world of the market, they were also the family members most likely to experience the home as 'haven' from the public sphere (Tosh 1996). Fatherhood was taken seriously and this can be seen in new ideas about 'family time' that emerged, a period after men returned from work that enabled all members of the household to enjoy the collective experience of family life (Tosh 1999: 84). This suggests that the importance of home was not only maintained through the spatial separation of private life from the perceived dangers of public life but also maintained through temporal rituals that enabled a collective experience of home and family togetherness. Although occupation and wealth have frequently been used as indicators of class position, Davidoff and Hall clearly identify just how central domestic cultures were in producing middle-class cultures.

However, Davidoff and Hall primarily focus on *representations* of domestic cultures, examining how ideas about class and gender were mediated. Many other researchers have also analysed texts such as domestic advice literature, women's magazines and religious materials to understand how the meanings of domestic culture were constructed and negotiated in the nineteenth century. While such an approach can offer invaluable insights into how ideas about domesticity were mediated, we cannot simply assume that these ideas were unquestioningly accepted by middle-class women and reproduced in their practices (Vickery 1993). There is considerable evidence to suggest that middle-class women were not simply confined within the home. Indeed, Amanda Vickery (1993: 400) argues that 'the stress on the proper female sphere in Victorian discourses signalled a growing concern that more women were seen to be active *outside* the home rather than proof that they were so confined'. Although nineteenth-century urban spaces were represented as immoral, dangerous and no place for 'respectable' women, large numbers of middle-class Victorian women did venture into this space to carry out philanthropic work. Furthermore, in the second half of the nineteenth century, a number of 'respectable' public spaces – department stores, tea-rooms, galleries, libraries, and so on – attracted large numbers of female visitors (see, for example, Hollis 1979; Chaney 1983; Wilson 1985; Walkowitz 1992; Laermans 1993; Nava 1997; Rappaport 2000). Middle-class femininity may have been identified with domesticity but this did not necessarily mean that these women were trapped within the home.

The idea that there were strictly delineated gendered spheres has also been problematized in other ways. Not only did men take an active role in domestic life, but many middle-class women were involved in their husband's businesses: as Davidoff and Hall (2002: 330) argue, 'public was not really public and private was not really private'. An ideology of separate spheres may have identified women's role as consumers with their responsibility for the private sphere, but this role not only took them out into public spaces such as department stores but also gave them opportunities to exert political pressure in public life. For example, British women were encouraged to use their power as consumers to protest against slavery by boycotting slave-grown sugar (Davidoff and Hall 2002: 442) while American women were encouraged to boycott British goods as an expression of their national identity (Matthews 1987). As Joan Williams (1991: 79) argues, middle-class women 'seized the opportunities domesticity offered to bring virtue out into the public sphere'. This problematizes the idea that women were simply made 'a hostage in the home' (Welter 1966: 151): while ideologies of domesticity may have worked to naturalize women's position in the home, the same ideologies also offered ways of criticizing the forms of competitive self-interest that underpinned capitalist modernity (Cott 1977).

As we have already seen, the meanings of middle-class domestic culture – and middle-class domestic femininity – were defined through their distance from the world of work. However, this obfuscates the extent to which the middle-class home was also a place of labour. While middle-class women were unlikely to perform their own domestic labour, their homes were often a workplace for the working-class women who they employed as servants. Indeed, the very idea of the middle-class home as a haven from the world of work was frequently only sustained by domestic servants whose labour kept 'dirt, chaos and disorder . . . at bay' (Giles 2004: 71): as Carole Dyhouse (1989: 107) notes, 'servants with their separate entrances and staircases protected their employers from the dirt and drudgery' that might threaten to 'contaminate' their middle-class status (see also Walker 2002). Therefore, like many middle-class men, middle-class women were employers of working-class labour (Glucksmann 1990: 254).

As I go on to explore in the next chapter, working-class women's position *as workers* problematizes any simple notion that the ideology of separate spheres effectively contained women within the home and made them economically dependent on men (although women's pay was frequently significantly less than men's pay). In the USA in particular, the differences between women's experience of domestic modernity was also sharply differentiated by ethnicity and 'race'. Under slavery in the South, black women were effectively excluded from the ability to participate in domesticity and 'normal' family life because they were seen as part of slave-owners' families. In the North in the nineteenth century – and in the South after **Abolition** – many immigrant and African-American women were locked into work as domestic labour (J. Williams 2000: 162–5). Indeed, Aida Hurtado argues that the distinction between public and private is largely irrelevant to 'Women of Colour [who] have not had the benefit of the economic conditions that underlie the public/private distinction' (cited in Morley 1992: 223). These ideas are explored in more detail in the next section.

In this section, we have seen how an opposition between the feminine private sphere and masculine public sphere was central to the experience of modernity. The home became associated with a range of distinctive values and gained a range of specialized functions, many of which continue to influence how contemporary domestic cultures are lived and organized. However, while the *idea* of clearly delineated and gendered spheres was central to the ways in which modern society was organized, in practice the boundaries between spheres were rather more fluid. While 'viewed as a "haven from a heartless world", the organization of the home was in fact profoundly determined by the forces arising out of the external world it was meant to be a retreat from' (Bennett 2002: 7). Furthermore, although imagined as a retreat from the public sphere – and a realm of relative freedom – the home also became subject to surveillance and regulation by an increasing array of public policies and institutions that sought to 'improve' the nation's 'private' life. Indeed, working-class domestic cultures have frequently been under scrutiny and subject to intervention because of their perceived 'deviance' from middle-class models of domestic culture (Donzelot 1979; Skeggs 1997). Yet at the same time, as we have seen, domestic cultures were not simply determined by external factors nor did they simply reflect the needs of the wider social and economic system: the values of nineteenth-century domestic culture also had an impact on the public sphere.

Nineteenth-century home-making

Many accounts of separate spheres stress how, from the end of the eighteenth century onwards, the home moved from being a site of production to a site of consumption. In the process, its frequently argued that women were transformed from active producers to passive consumers. In this section I look in more detail at consumption in the nineteenth century and suggest that domestic consumption is not only productive because it is a form of domestic labour but also because it is an active process of home-*making*. While nineteenth-century women's roles as consumers are frequently associated with conformity and the reproduction of patriarchal gender ideologies, this section demonstrates how women played a key role in *producing* domestic cultures. Furthermore, working-class women used their home-making practices to negotiate and resist bourgeois definitions of home, producing homes that articulated other classed, 'raced' and ethnic identities.

During the nineteenth century, middle-class women were offered advice on their new role as consumers who were responsible for creating 'good' homes and were encouraged to see the exercise of 'good taste' as a key element of domestic femininity (Sparke 1995). Advice on how to *make homes* was necessary in a world in which an expanding array of consumer goods were available and where the meaning of everyday life was transformed by the social and cultural changes associated with modernity. Anthony Giddens (1991) argues that one way in which these changes were managed – and made sense of – was through the rise of 'expert systems' that offered newly developed forms of 'professional expertise' and acted as **embedding mechanisms**, which helped people come to terms with living with modernity. Nineteenth-century domestic advice can be understood as an example of these new forms of 'expert' guidance, offering 'guides to living' in changed conditions (as can more contemporary forms of expert guidance such as the lifestyle TV programmes discussed in Chapter 5).

The boom in domestic advice literature in both the UK and the USA can be understood in this context. Initially, this advice was strongly influenced by religious discourses demonstrating how Christian values could inform domestic culture and aesthetics: for example, in *The Frugal Housewife* (often recognized as the first American domestic advice manual), Lydia Maria Child demonstrated that 'good' middle-class homes should reject 'indolence, frivolity and waste' (Leavitt 2002: 10; see also Matthews 1987; Blumin 1989; Davidoff and Hall 2002). More generally, domestic advisors encouraged their readers to understand everyday objects in terms of character traits in order 'to demonstrate that the home could embody values' (Leavitt 2002: 37). While this literature (like lifestyle TV today) frequently only dealt with *fantasies* of how homes might be, domestic experts instigated 'a national dialogue' about domestic culture and 'gave white middle-class women a common vocabulary and place to begin their own journeys with home (and moral) improvement' (Leavitt 2002: 39).[2]

If domestic advice literature offered one set of guides to imagining the meaning of domestic culture, then planning and architecture also reinforced the meaning of separate spheres. As I go on to discuss in more detail in Chapter 3, the development of suburban housing on the fringes of cities, produced a spatial separation between work and home. Many of the stylistic features of nineteenth-century suburban developments symbolized a distance from modern urban life and an identification with a rural and 'natural' pre-modern world. An attachment to 'nature' was signified through the conservatories and gardens of suburban houses and the use of potted plants and floral motifs in suburban interiors (Ryan 1981; Sparke 1995; Hepworth 1999; Davidoff and Hall 2002).

Divisions between spaces within the Victorian middle-class home also reinforced ideas about separate spheres. For example, within the middle-class home, there was often a clear demarcation between spaces of work (for example, the kitchen was associated with servants), private life (for example, bedrooms) and public interactions (for example, the **parlour**). As a public space within the home, the parlour operated as a space for display: furnishings and ornaments were used to display familial identity and status to the outside world. The use of domestic space represented 'dominant middle-class beliefs about "proper" social relationships and the different roles and capacities of men and women' (Walker 2002: 824).

The objects that the middle class used to furnish their homes also reinforced the distinction between public and private in Victorian Britain. Domestic **material culture** signified the idea of home as haven from an industrialized public sphere. As John Ruskin put it, the home 'is the place of peace; the shelter, not only from injury, but from terror, doubt and division' (cited in Cohen 1980: 753). This image of home was produced through the use of traditional and old objects and in the use of 'soft textures and surfaces, and soft blends of colours, by gentle curved forms and patterns . . ., by visual references to the natural world rather than the man-made world of technology' (Sparke 1995: 27). Heavily upholstered furniture and an excessive use of textiles (especially as window coverings) worked to 'increase the sense of privacy and soften the environment, both visually and to the touch' (Sparke 1995: 39). However, although these styles were based on a rejection of the values associated with the public sphere, they were nonetheless dependent on it. New fashionable domestic goods were produced through the very industrial technologies – alongside a globalizing capitalist market – that the domestic interior sought to disavow.

Nonetheless, by the mid-late nineteenth century, there was an increasing sense of struggle over which values the middle-class home should represent. For example, in mid-Victorian Britain, gilded and highly ornamented French furniture became fashionable, offering the middle class an opportunity to signify their status to the outside world (Sparke 1995). However, to their critics, these styles represented a betrayal of middle-class values. Rather than signifying the values of domestic moderation that were central to the middle class's claims to distinction, the taste for gilded furniture suggested that members of the middle class were trying to emulate the aristocracy. Similar concerns about this French-style furniture surfaced in the USA where gilded furniture became associated with feminine vanity and deference to aristocratic tastes (Gordon and McArthur 1985). In both countries there was a conscious attempt to reinstate a domestic style that symbolized the moral distinction of the middle-class home and legitimated their claims to 'good taste' (Sparke 1995: 64; Leavitt 2002: 27).

Struggles about 'appropriate' domestic cultures did not only occur within the middle class: middle-class reformers also set out to 'improve' the morals of the working class by transforming their domestic life. In late nineteenth-century Britain, commentators drew attention to the dire housing conditions in working-class slums that provoked concerns about unsanitary, overcrowded and unhealthy living conditions. It was claimed that such conditions not only produced immorality but also the threat of insurrection (Hall 1996). For example, in one sensationalist piece of reporting, newspaper editor W.T. Stead wrote of 'The horror of the slums' as 'the one great domestic problem which the religion, the humanity, and the statesmanship of England are imperatively summoned to solve' (cited in Hall 1996: 14). Middle-class reformers set out to use improved housing in order to 'improve' the morals of the working class – 'a particular form of planning based on segregation and privacy' was used to reduce the perceived threat of sexual depravity and revolt caused by overcrowded slum conditions (Matrix 1984: 63).

Middle-class reformers in the USA also sought to improve and modernize working-class domestic culture through architectural engineering. By the late nineteenth century middle-class domestic styles became increasingly plain and secular under the influence of scientific discourses: a 'cleaner' aesthetic was not only seen as morally uplifting but also as a way of combating 'household problems of dust, germs and inefficiency' (Cohen 1980: 755). Reformers believed that this aesthetic might also solve the 'problems' of working-class domestic culture and, therefore, built these design ideas – and values – into new housing developments for the working class.

However, just because homes are designed with particular values 'built-in' does not mean that these values are necessarily reproduced by their occupants (Attfield 1995). For example, Lizabeth Cohen demonstrates how the working-class occupants of a late nineteenth-century American urban housing development challenged middle-class ideas about 'appropriate' forms of domestic life. Middle-class reformers installed modern kitchens into these new homes that were supposed to operate as efficient workspaces but their working-class occupants drew on an older rural culture to reclaim these workspaces as spaces for socializing. Reformers believed that soft furnishings were old-fashioned because they attracted dirt and were difficult to clean, advocating the use of simple, hygienic furniture and linens but working-class occupants installed elaborate soft furnishings to signify their 'ownership' of the housing that they had been allocated. As Cohen argues, 'Given alien and institutional housing-facades, curtained windows were often a family's only way to make a personal statement to the world passing by' (Cohen 1980: 765).[3] While middle-class reformers advocated iron beds with simple bedding, claiming that old-fashioned and decorative alternatives were unsanitary, Cohen explains how such advice failed to acknowledge how the bed symbolized marital and family happiness in some ethnic working-class culture. For example, among the Italian-American working classes, the exchange of bed linens played a key role in marriage rituals while the bed also played a pivotal role in rituals surrounding death. As Cohen (1980: 767) puts it, middle-class ideas about rational use of domestic space sat uneasily with an emotional investment in 'fluffy, elaborately decorated beds'.

Cohen's study clearly demonstrates how domestic cultures are differentiated by class and ethnicity. Her research shows how a newly urban working class drew on both rural and ethnic traditions to create a way of 'being at home in industrial America': whereas 'middle-class people viewed the appearance of working-class homes as unsanitary, tasteless and un-American, workers in fact felt that their new material world represented acculturation to American urban ways' (Cohen 1980: 770). In this way working-class homes articulated a distinctive cultural response to modernity that also resisted middle-class experts' claims to cultural authority. This example also demonstrates how modernization generates '**re-embedding mechanisms**': unlike abstract expert systems, re-embedding mechanisms attempt to anchor 'disembedded social relations' in 'local conditions of time and place' (Giddens 1990: 79–80).[4] Cohen's study highlights how working-class households may have had little faith in middle-class domestic experts and instead attempted to combat the **disembedding** effects of modernity through localized practices through which they attempted to make 'modern' homes meaningful. In this way Cohen demonstrates how the working class articulated *both* the traditional and modern to produce a meaningful domestic culture.

As I suggested earlier, nineteenth-century ideas about – and experiences of – domestic femininity were not uniform but were differentiated by class, ethnicity and 'race'. While middle-class femininity was partly defined through its distance from labour both in the home and the public sphere, working-class women were not only responsible for their own domestic labour but were frequently engaged in paid work in factories, as domestics in other women's homes or as piece-workers in their own homes. However, by the late nineteenth century, declining employment opportunities for white working-class women in the UK meant that an increasing number of working-class women started to see themselves as 'housewives' rather than as paid employees (Bourke 1994).

Numerous socialist and feminist critics have identified this as having negative consequences for the female working class, arguing that this caused them to emulate middle-class domestic femininity, descend into idleness and passivity, and become economically dependent on men. Yet, Joanna Bourke argues that working-class women's investment in domesticity should not be seen as an attempt to emulate middle-class women but should be understood as a class-specific response to their limited employment opportunities. Because working-class women received low wages – and because going to work actually costs money – full-time domesticity offered a way of improving the family's standard of living. In particular, it created more time to save money – for example, by making rather than buying clothes (see also Gordon 2004).

Bourke rejects the idea that housework is a degrading form of labour and argues that housewifery could operate as a source of power, pleasure and status. Being a housewife offered working-class women the opportunity to create a meaningful domestic and family life. While it did make these women economically dependent on their husbands, housework could offer a greater sense of power than paid labour: it offered opportunities for authority over domestic life, 'control over one's environment and over one's time' and, Bourke (1994: 182) argues 'power is control as much as ownership'. Being a housewife was also pleasurable because it offered working-class women a sense of pride in their work that came from the ability to produce a good home for their children (Bourke 1994: 180). Rather than emulating the leisured lifestyles that afforded some middle-class women their status, working-class women gained their status by making their labour visible by producing 'good homes' that represented their skill as respectable home-makers. (See Attfield 1995 and Partington 1995 for similar arguments about British working-class women in the 1950s.)

Similar arguments have been made about how working-class women in the USA invested in domesticity to produce distinctive domestic cultures. For example, Sarah Gordon (2004) argues that home sewing offered working-class women a way of both saving money and symbolizing important domestic values such as thrift and maternal love. (For a more developed argument about how feminine consumption practices are still often organized around the ideas of thrift and maternal love, see Miller 1998.) Home sewing offered women a way of living up to the image of the 'good housekeeper' while also affording opportunities to resist or subvert ideas about 'appropriate' femininity by enabling them to customize their clothing to create stylish looks. (See Partington 1993, for a similar argument about the use of clothes by British women in the 1950s.) This provides further evidence of how domestic consumption practices are used to both construct and negotiate the meaning of home and to construct domestic cultures that articulate identities that are both classed and gendered.

If class differences challenge the idea that there was a single monolithic form of domestic culture during the period, 'race' further differentiated women's relationship to home. While African-American women frequently invested in the ideology of separate spheres, this was not because they passively accepted the legitimacy of white middle-class domestic femininity: instead, their investment in domesticity was a response to racism. Because black women had been forced to work under slavery, the opportunity for women to become full-time home-makers was understood as a sign of progress for African-Americans as a whole (Horton 1986): 'for a group of people one generation out of slavery, gender-defined work and domestic responsibilities were symbolic of their new status' (Harley 1990: 347).

However, opportunities to do so were limited: the racial discrimination faced by black men in the job market frequently meant that black women in the late nineteenth century had little option but to work. Nonetheless, as Sharon Harley argues, black women refused to have their identities defined by their position in the labour market. As one woman cited her study comments:

> One very important difference between white people and black people is that white people think that you *are* your work . . . Now, a black person . . . knows that what I am doing doesn't have anything to do with what I want to do or what I do when I am doing for myself. Now, black people think that my work is just what I have to do or what I do to get what I want.
>
> (cited in Harley 1990: 345)

Unlike many feminist narratives that define the search for identity in terms of paid work, this woman identified domestic life as a source of identity and self-worth. The ability to produce and care for a home and family – and to signify the ability to do so to the outside world – 'were major sources of pride and status in the black community' (Harley 1990: 349).

In this section I have tried to demonstrate how thinking about domestic consumption and home-making practices problematizes the idea that nineteenth-century domestic culture and domestic femininities can simply be understood through the idea of separate spheres. While a range of texts such as domestic advice literature show the centrality of the idea of separate spheres in the period, if we also consider the material culture of the Victorian home and how women produced the meaning of domestic cultures through their home-making practices, it becomes more difficult to accept the idea that a monolithic ideology of domesticity was simply imposed on women during the period. While women's movement between spheres challenges the idea that they were confined to the home, women's home-making practices also challenged dominant ideas about domestic culture and domestic femininity. Furthermore, these practices were also mobilized as a resource for articulating distinctive classed, gendered, ethnic and 'racial' identities that could offer ways of coping with oppression and resisting classification.

Rationalizing domestic culture?

This section examines transformations in domestic cultures in the 1920s and 1930s. In both the USA and the UK, the ability to have 'a home of your own', whether purchased or rented, became a reality for far more people (Giles 1995).[5] During this interwar period the values associated with Victorian domestic cultures were challenged by new ideas that promised more 'modern' homes: science, technology and business – which had transformed the public sphere – were increasingly seen as indispensable in the home and promised to improve domestic life. In this section I examine how these discourses created new conceptions of home and also helped to create new figures of domestic femininity based around the idea of a professional and modern housewife. Unlike the nineteenth-century middle-class home-maker, the housewife was not defined by her distance from labour but instead used scientific expertise and new household technologies to do her own housework.

The idea that there was a need to rationalize domestic life in order to make it more 'modern' had its roots in the nineteenth century. For example, there were attempts to apply ideas from capitalist industry to rethink the home in the USA – and women's place within it – from the late nineteenth century onwards. New disciplines such as 'domestic science' and 'home economics' demonstrated how the home could become more efficient if it was run along the lines of the industrial workplace (Matthews 1987: 145–6). While many nineteenth-century home experts such as Catherine Beecher had tried to show how Christian principles could be used to make better homes and home-makers, new domestic experts such as Christine Frederick wanted to use 'the power of science to improve the human condition' and train women to run the home more efficiently (Freeman 2004: 29). For example, Frederick demonstrated how more 'intelligent' design could radically decrease the number of steps women took around the kitchen and reduce the amount of time and energy women 'wasted' in the home. Another key figure, Lillian Gilbreth, demonstrated how the principles of **Taylorism**, which had been used to increase productivity in factories, could also be applied to the kitchen. (For more on Frederick and Gilbreth, see Leavitt 2002 and Matthews 1987.) In the process these women aimed to transform domestic femininity, putting it 'on a standardized, professional basis' (Frederick cited in Freeman 2004: 31).

These ideas were popularized through some women's magazines. Newly launched in the 1920s, the British version of *Good Housekeeping* magazine not only offered new images of domestic femininity to its middle-class readers but also promoted new consumer goods that promised scientific and technological solutions to household problems. The magazine assured its readers that its recipes were 'tried and tested' in a 'modern and properly equipped kitchen' to guarantee predictable and reliable results in a similar manner to a scientific experiment in a laboratory (Anon [1922] 1986; Jack [1922] 1990). Home-making was also professionalized through association with business: a piece on 'The Business of Good Housekeeping' showed how the housewife's role in managing the domestic budget was analogous to that of the business professional and advised readers on how to run the household as a business operation by spending money 'wisely and scientifically' (Wooler and Wooler [1922] 1990). Not only were their readers encouraged to use scientific and business knowledge, they were also encouraged to develop medical expertise so they could use hygiene and cleanliness to combat the 'threat' of germs (Forty 1986; Martens and Scott 2005). In a 1924 edition of *Good Housekeeping*, Florence Jack argued that cooking 'should stand on an equal footing with medicine. To prevent a body becoming diseased by feeding it properly is surely as advantageous to mankind as feeding it with drugs' (Jack [1924] 1990: 38). An advert for the Grape Nuts Company in the same magazine in 1928 confidently stated that 'The Modern mother – above all people – is the family health specialist' (Braithwaite and Walsh 1990: 80–1). In the pages of *Good Housekeeping*, the role of the middle-class housewife was portrayed as being on a par with masculine middle-class work in the public sphere (Hollows 2006a).

Technology entered the home in other ways as electricity came to be seen as a central ingredient in the modern home. In the UK, the number of homes with electricity rose from 6 per cent in 1918 to 60 per cent in 1939 and this created a potential market for new 'labour-saving' electrical appliances such as electric irons, fridges and vacuum cleaners (Forty 1986: 189).[6] Through advertising, the modern and professional housewife was encouraged to understand these appliances as indispensable to her work running an efficient home. Critics such as Ruth Cowan (1983) have questioned whether these appliances really saved labour or whether they created more work as the housewife's job description expanded and standards of domestic perfection intensified. Nonetheless, it is important to remember that hot and cold running water and gas and electric heating also had a profound impact on the nature of domestic labour. As Giles (2004: 20) observes, 'modern water supply systems . . . eliminated the back-breaking work of heating and carrying water to where it was needed for cooking, laundering and bathing'. However, many of these services and appliances were not uniformly available: even for those with access to electricity, the majority of the new electrical appliances were beyond the financial reach of many households. Furthermore, technologies in themselves do not simply transform domestic cultures: to understand their significance, we need to look at how they are made meaningful as they become integrated within everyday practices.

There were also attempts to transform interwar domestic cultures by transforming the built environment. **Modernist** architects such as Le Corbusier and Walter Gropius 'rejected the homey values, national character and decorative aesthetic of the Victorian period and defined modernism against domesticity' (Walker 2002: 827). Sparke argues that modernists not only turned on clutter and ornamentation in the name of hygiene but also aesthetics, and their housing designs were frequently stark, minimal and utilitarian. Furthermore, they imagined houses composed of open spaces: 'they eradicated the idea of gendered spaces in the home and instead opened up the interior to become an extension of the exterior' (Sparke 1995: 108). While these modernist aesthetics have frequently been applauded by design professionals, they were often deeply unpopular with their early residents because they were so 'unhomely'.

The application of scientific rationality to the home, combined with an expanding consumer culture and the influence of modernism, all had an impact on conceptions of domestic culture in the interwar period. Critics such as Glenna Matthews (1987) and Penny Sparke (1995) argue that these changes meant that the discourses and material culture of the public sphere penetrated, and threatened to colonize, the private sphere. They suggest that these changes not only intensified the sexual division of labour but also robbed women of their cultural authority over domestic life and their autonomy in creating a personalized space that expressed their identity. In the role of housewife, they claim, women were no longer responsible for producing domestic culture but simply became consumers of mass-produced domestic goods.

While Sparke is more concerned with how these changes challenged women's autonomy to use the home as an expression of feminine taste, and Matthews with the devaluation of women's domestic role and 'craft' skills, both their arguments tend to essentialize the private sphere as inherently feminine and the public sphere as inherently masculine. Not only does this polarize public and private spheres, it also implies that modernization is imposed on domestic life rather than acknowledging the role domestic cultures played in the process of modernization. In the process, both writers tend to see 'technological innovation in the home as an expression of conspiracy towards a devaluation of essentially womanly activities' (Silva 2000a: 626) and ignore the ways in which 'the modern becomes real at the most intimate and mundane levels of experience and interaction' (Felski 2000: 66). Furthermore, while Sparke takes a more ambivalent approach to consumer culture, Matthews argues that it 'sounded the death knell both for housewifery as a skilled craft and for mother as moral arbiter' (1987: 194), reducing domestic femininity to 'the passive role of spending freely' (1987: 222). Such a position assumes that consumer goods prescribe how they are used and fails to acknowledge the range of complex practices and processes involved in domestic consumption (see Chapter 5).

The idea that women's domestic work was simply deskilled in the interwar period ignores more complex changes in domestic labour. The professionalization of domestic femininity was, in part, a response to the changing role of middle-class women: as the number of domestic servants declined, middle-class women became increasingly responsible for *doing* – rather than *managing* – domestic labour. Middle-class women in the nineteenth century had complained of 'a servant problem', bemoaning the difficulties involved in securing and keeping 'good staff'. However, by the interwar period, a series of changes – not least, the expanding range of employment opportunities for working-class women that provided an alternative to domestic labour – reduced the availability of domestic servants. While there is considerable debate about the extent to which domestic service declined in the period (Taylor 1979; Dyhouse 1986; Dyhouse 1989; Glucksmann 1990), the idea that there was 'a servant problem' undoubtedly framed how middle-class femininity was imagined and experienced. As Giles (1995: 134) argues, 'ideas about the value and worth of home-making and house-wifery; about authority within the home; and about appropriate class and gender behaviours and attitudes within and to the home were shaped, sustained, sometimes resisted and frequently made sense of via the cultural narratives and social experience of domestic service'. Furthermore, evidence from magazines such as *Good Housekeeping* also suggests considerable ambiguity about middle-class women's roles, simultaneously addressing its readers as home-managers who were mistresses of servants *and* as 'modern housewives' without servants (Hollows 2006a).

For these reasons the process by which middle-class women became responsible for their own domestic labour cannot simply be thought of in terms of deskilling but is best thought of in terms of processes of skilling and reskilling. With the decline of domestic servants, many middle-class women had to acquire domestic skills they would not have previously possessed. Furthermore, as Elizabeth Silva (2000a) suggests, new technologies such as electric cookers did not reduce their users to passive consumers but demanded invention, skills, knowledge and assessment by cooks as they were put to use. As I discuss in Chapter 6, new technologies can initially appear alien but they are re-embedded as they are inserted into household routines and become 'domesticated'. At the same time, new technologies frequently demand the renegotiation of domestic practices and relationships.

Moreover, while Sparke and Matthews identify a decline in both women's aesthetic role within the home and their involvement in forms of 'craft' production, the reality is again rather more complex. The idea that a housewife's labour involved a degree of creativity remained crucial to maintaining class distinctions between women. Even with the help of 'mechanical servants', middle-class women's identity was dependent on distinguishing their labour from that previously done by working-class domestic servants. Therefore, while British women's magazines envisaged the 'housewife' as a modern woman engaged in professionalized domestic work, they also emphasized some aspects of her work over others. As Giles (1995: 151) argues:

> Women's magazines focused on personal care, cooking, sewing, interior design and childcare rather than how to whiten steps or scrub a scullery floor. Thus those tasks which were potentially creative ... were highlighted as acceptable and indeed fulfilling activities, while 'the rough' remained unspoken – degrading work, hidden and suppressed in these respectable and 'modern' conceptions of housework.

Middle-class women were encouraged to see their work as both creative and modern in order to distinguish their work from that of domestic servants and working-class women more generally. Women's magazines such as *Good Housekeeping* presented activities like cooking as an opportunity to employ both scientific knowledge and feminine creativity. Cookbooks not only provided the middle classes with information about culinary technique but also encouraged people to use food in artistic, even avant-garde, ways (Humble 2005; Hollows 2006a). In the next chapter I consider how distinctions *within* the middle classes became more important in the interwar period. Evidence from novels and cookbooks suggests that the established members of the middle classes were encouraged to see home-making as an artistic rather than scientific endeavour to distinguish themselves from both working-class domestic labour and the lower middle-class modern housewife (Humble 2001: 130).[7]

The interwar period witnessed a shift in how domestic cultures and domestic femininities were conceptualized. While the Victorian middle-class home was represented as a retreat from modernity, in the interwar period the home was meant to become more 'modern' to catch up with the public sphere (Reiger 1985; Giles 2004). However, just as nineteenth-century domestic culture wasn't really outside modernity so the interwar home wasn't totally remodelled in the image of the public sphere. Furthermore, as Giles (2004: 116) argues, 'the demise of residential domestic service did not seamlessly give way to the labour-saving "modern" home, ruled over by the middle-class consumer housewife, beloved of advertisers and commentators'. Interwar domestic culture wasn't just 'modern' in the same way that the Victorian home wasn't just 'traditional' (and for more on these issues, see Light 1991 and Humble 2001). Domestic cultures of the interwar period attempted to reconcile seemingly contradictory meanings of home as home-makers were addressed by both a 'culture of domesticity' inherited from Victorian constructions of home and 'a culture of science' (Bennett 2002: 14). Indeed, these seemingly contradictory pulls towards modernity and tradition continue to exert a strong influence on how domestic cultures are negotiated and lived today.

Conclusions

This chapter has demonstrated how contemporary meanings of home were shaped by transformations in domestic culture from the late eighteenth century onwards. However, I have also shown how the meanings attached to domestic culture are not fixed but go through processes of historical transformation. Moreover, even within a historical period, the meaning of domestic culture will be differentiated by ethnicity, 'race' and class, and across national contexts. While the opposition between public and private has been central in structuring what values are associated with domestic culture, my discussion has also made it clear that distinctions between public and private are frequently far more fluid in practice. Furthermore, while domestic life has often been imagined as 'outside' of – or antithetical to – modernity, in this chapter I have tried to demonstrate how domestic cultures are in fact central to our understanding of modernity.

Women's relationship to domestic culture has also been a central concern of this chapter. Some critics have argued that separation of spheres signalled a retrograde step in the history of women, arguing that women were transformed from active producers, who worked alongside men, to passive consumers, confined to the home and economically dependent on men. Such arguments tend to represent pre-industrial societies as a kind of 'golden age' for women, neglecting the extent to which women were defined as the inferiors of men by religious and legal institutions (J. Williams 2000: 22–3). Furthermore, these critics tend to see paid labour in the public sphere as the only socially and culturally valuable form of labour, devaluing the contribution that domesticity has made to the modern world. Moreover, as I have demonstrated, the separation of spheres was never quite as complete as some critics have assumed.

Writers such as Matthews and Sparke suggest that women's domestic roles gave them new forms of cultural authority in the nineteenth century. However, they suggest that this cultural authority was challenged in the interwar period when science, technology, commerce and architecture – which expressed the values of a masculine public sphere – penetrated the home, devaluing feminine domestic skills. Not only do these ideas essentialize masculinity and femininity – and public and private – but they also underestimate the extent to which domestic consumption practices have been used to resist or renegotiate ideas about home. The values embedded in domestic cultures are not simply imposed from outside; indeed, domestic values have been used as the basis for a critique of the public sphere.

Further reading

Cohen, L. (1980) Embellishing a Life of Labour: An Interpretation of the Material Culture of American Working-Class Homes, 1885–1915, *Journal of American Culture*, 3(4): 752–5.

Davidoff, L. and Hall, C. (2002) *Family Fortunes: Men and Women of the English Middle Class, 1780–1850, 2nd edn*. London: Routledge.

Giles, J. (2004) *The Parlour and the Suburb: Domestic Identities, Class, Femininity and Modernity*. Oxford: Berg.

Leavitt, S.A. (2002) *From Catherine Beecher to Martha Stewart: A Cultural History of Domestic Advice*. Chapel Hill: University of North Carolina Press.

Ryan, M. (1981) *The Cradle of the Middle Class: The Family in Oneida County, New York, 1790–1865*. Cambridge: Cambridge University Press.

Vickery, A. (1993) From Golden Age to Separate Spheres? A Review of the Categories and Chronology of English Women's History, *The Historical Journal*, 36(2): 383–414.

Notes

1 Indeed, Hewitt (2002) suggests that it cannot even be applied to all women within this group.

2 This also included interventions by first-wave feminists who, from the mid-nineteenth century onwards, offered alternative visions of domestic life that challenged the division between public and private (Hayden 1982).

3 Theoretical debates about consumption as appropriation are discussed in more detail in Chapter 5. For similar arguments about different historical periods, see Miller (1988) and Attfield (1995).

4 As Steve Jones argues, Giddens is rather more interested in how re-embedding mechanisms are used by large institutions and businesses than their use in everyday, local practices. However, he suggests, localized re-embedding mechanisms that draw on residual forms of knowledge and practice are widespread (Ashley et al. 2004: 115).

5 For example, in the UK, the home took on a new significance in national life in the aftermath of World War I. Faced with a housing shortage that had been exacerbated by the war, government policy supported a building boom, with 4.6 million new homes built in the 1920s and 1930s (Savage et al. 1992: 82).

6 However, the future of electricity remained unclear at this point: gas was cheaper in the UK and Adrian Forty (1986: 192) argues that for much of the interwar period, gas was used to fuel 'more efficient and better designed appliances'.

7 Indeed, as I have argued elsewhere, tensions between science and aesthetics in *Good Housekeeping* can also be understood in terms of struggles for legitimation between fractions of the middle classes (Hollows 2006a), struggles also identified by Humble (2001, 2005). For more on creativity in relation to the housewife's 'leisure time', see also Langhamer (2000).

3

HOME-CENTREDNESS: SUBURBIA, PRIVATIZATION AND CLASS

Introduction

The chapter examines why an investment in domestic life has been seen as a political problem. Many people aspire to live in decent housing and create a nice home, although their definitions of 'decent' and 'nice' may vary. However, as I intend to show, some critics have seen these aspirations as a political problem and claimed that it leads people to adopt a home-centred and privatized existence, and to withdraw from their roles and responsibilities in the public sphere. As I explained in Chapter 1, many theorists of modernity privileged the public sphere as the site of 'real' politics and 'real' history. They saw 'the longing for home, the longing to attach oneself to a familiar space . . . as a regressive desire' (Felski 2000: 86). In this chapter I explore how, for a range of twentieth-century critics, being home-centred is, at best, to settle for the trivial and mundane; at worst, an investment in domesticity is seen as an investment in capitalist ideology and a retreat from social responsibilities. For all these critics, domestic culture is not really culture at all.

In reviewing these debates, I analyse how some critics have not just been anti-home but have produced a 'negative consensus' (Hebdige 1988) against a particular form of home, focusing their attacks on suburban domestic culture. While nineteenth-century social reformers concentrated on the economically impoverished material conditions of working-class slums,[1] twentieth-century critics of suburbia concentrated on what they believed were the culturally impoverished ways of life of the relatively affluent. In this chapter I explain the reasons why numerous critics, in both the UK and the USA, continually characterized suburban domestic culture as conformist, standardized, privatized and conservative. Indeed, the idea that both suburban housing and its residents are a uniform 'mass' has become so established that it can be endlessly recycled with little need for explanation. To give one recent example, the title sequence for the

American TV show *Weeds*, consists of aerial shots of an apparently homogeneous suburbia, accompanied by 'Little Boxes', the well-known musical critique of suburban living, on the soundtrack. The programme itself sets out to partly subvert the view of suburbia by demonstrating how, once up close, suburbia is a rather more complex phenomena: indeed, the narrative of the show focuses on the exploits of a dope-dealing suburban mom. In this chapter I take a related (although clearly not identical!) strategy and demonstrate that – up close – suburban domestic culture looked rather different than it did to critics who approached suburbia from a distance. Throughout this chapter I also attempt to explain why suburban domestic culture – and suburban home-makers – have been represented as so pathological.

My primary interest in this chapter is why the allegedly home-centred culture of the suburbs has been seen as a political problem at different moments in both the UK and the USA. However, this isn't just of historical interest and recent cultural studies has been guilty of reproducing the assumptions of past critiques. For example, while Roger Silverstone (1997) acknowledges that critics in cultural studies have neglected suburbia because they have been more interested in 'authentic' cultures associated with marginalized groups, he nonetheless claims that 'politics in and of the suburb is still, mostly, a domestic politics of self-interest, conformity and exclusion undertaken within political structures which are, mostly, barely recognized, let alone challenged . . . It is a politics of defence' (Silverstone 1994: 77). In this way Silverstone condemns the suburban and the domestic through association with each other. Homi Bhabha (1997: 299) also reiterates how suburbia is inherently uniform, conformist and politically suspect in his claims that 'the conservative suburban attitude is founded on the fear of difference; and a narrow minded appeal to cultural homogeneity. It is a kind of national paranoia that draws the boundary between what is acceptable and unacceptable even more tightly around the norm of the "known"'. As I go on to discuss, there is a wealth of evidence to support the claim that the history of suburbia is partly built on exclusion and, specifically, racial exclusion and segregation, a trend exacerbated more recently in the rapid rise of **gated communities**, particularly in the USA (see Low 2003). However, if the 'defensive' politics of suburbia is built around fears that are projected onto the urban 'other', then both Silverstone and Bhabha are equally guilty of projecting their own fears onto the suburban 'other'.

This chapter, therefore, traces the fears that have been projected on to suburban domestic cultures. The first section charts the rise of suburbia in the USA and examines fears about suburban domestic culture as a form of mass culture. The second section moves to the UK and explores British critics' concerns about the impact of suburban domesticity on British culture. In particular, they believed that suburban domestic cultures brought about a new lower middle-class culture that threatened cultural traditions. If both these sections deal with fears that suburban domestic cultures were privatized and represented a retreat from the public sphere, then these issues come to the fore in the third section. In this section I discuss critics who were worried that the British working class would lose their distinctive culture and their political identity as they moved into the suburbs in the post-war period. I also examine debates about the impact of home-ownership on domestic cultures.

In many of the arguments I consider in this chapter, home-centredness is assumed to simply reproduce capitalism. It is certainly true that the places in which the majority of people live in the USA and the UK are the product of a building industry that wields extensive economic and political power, increasingly on a global scale (Moran 2004). Hayden (2004: 4) identifies how, in the USA alone, there were 1.5 million new housing units built per year between 1994 and 2002. (American Commerce Department figures suggest that this had fallen to 1.4 million by 2007.) However, just because housing is the product of corporate capitalism does not mean that the meaning of home is simply determined by these relations of production. As Miller (1988: 354) suggests, most of us live in places that are the product of an impersonal system of production but we develop a sense of home and take ownership of these properties through consumption practices that may challenge or renegotiate the meanings that were 'built-in' to them. Put simply, while the ways in which housing is produced – and the form which that housing takes – may shape the meaning of home, the construction industry and house-form alone do not *determine* the meaning of domestic cultures.

Suburban domesticity and mass culture

Suburban domestic cultures are now the dominant form of domestic culture in the USA: as Dolores Hayden (2004: 10) observes, 'by 2000, more Americans lived in sub-urbs than in central cities and rural areas combined'. Although suburbanization has taken place in a range of locations, suburbia is understood by many to be a quintessen-tially American form; indeed, elsewhere, suburbanization is frequently read as a sign of Americanization (Moran 2004). This section introduces a historical perspective on the process of suburbanization in the USA and, in the process, addresses two key debates about the significance of suburban domestic cultures. First, I explore how and why suburban domestic culture was seen as a problem by cultural critics. As Morley (2000: 130) notes, 'suburbia is often held to symbolize the lamentable decline of the body politic, as part of the process in which the urban, informed, rational public sphere proper is undermined and corrupted by the rise of suburban, commercial, commodity culture'. In this way, the move to suburbia was associated with a retreat into a privat-ized, home-centred world of domestic culture and away from the public sphere of 'real' politics. Second, I examine how critiques of suburbanization frequently portray this retreat from the public sphere as a retreat from 'otherness' into the 'familiarity' of suburban domestic culture. As a result, it is claimed, these cultures were built on a desire for homogeneity and conformity.

As I suggested in Chapter 2, nineteenth-century suburbanization was shaped by – and helped to produce – ideas about separate spheres. In the USA, the city was not only associated with the world of work but also with the working class. The middle-class suburb offered a way of creating a physical distance from the urban working class and a symbolic distance from the public sphere. Domestic cultures were identified with the values of the 'rural' and the 'natural'. By the 1870s the suburbs not only represented a separation from urban, public life but also from other people. This sense of privatized living was symbolized by large front lawns that operated as a 'verdant moat' (Jackson 1985: 56–8). Yet not all of these middle-class suburbs were based on the values of privacy and some late nineteenth-century suburban developments pursued very different principles; some of the middle class built 'picturesque enclaves' based on **communitarian living** and the idea that 'shared open space was essential to a new kind of community life' (Hayden 2004: 45). Therefore, from the outset, not all of suburbia was centred around privatized living.

In the late nineteenth and the early twentieth century, the suburbs expanded as developers saw the opportunities for profit in building residential developments around new transportation systems such as railways, boats and streetcars. The expansion of the suburbs was also aided by developments in housing manufacture that not only reduced building costs but also enabled people to assemble their own homes from prefabricated kits that were available via mail order (Hayden 2004). During this period the relative ease of building combined with cheap land enabled a surprisingly high proportion of the working-class and immigrant populations to own their homes in some areas (Jackson 1985). Far from being inward-looking and privatized, self-building could be used to generate a sense of community as people traded skills and worked collectively to build a locality (Hayden 2004). These self-build communities were far from contemporary images of immaculately lawned suburbia: many started with no access to sewerage or running water. While self-builds only accounted for a third of house building before World War II, these developments complicate the portrait of suburbia as a middle-class project.

Self-builds also challenge the ideas about the whiteness of suburbia. Andrew Wiese's study of African-American suburbanization in the first half of the twentieth century demonstrates how 'the suburban dream' didn't just appeal to white Americans.

> Like many other Americans, early black suburbanites internalized images of ideal places to live, and these drew upon black history and culture in the South, as well as the experience and aspirations of black migrants in northern cities. They desired home-ownership in fulfilment of long-held dreams in the black South. They preferred living in family-based communities, although the family of emphasis was extended rather than nuclear. They rejected city-living, and they re-created rustic landscapes reminiscent of the region from which most had come.
>
> (Wiese 1999: 1497)

Wiese argues that African-American suburbs exhibited a strong sense of community spirit that both helped their residents cope with racism and reinforced a sense of racial identity. Therefore, while black and white suburban developments were certainly racially segregated, this work challenges the idea that suburbs are an inherently white, middle-class housing-form.

This also complicates the portrait of interwar suburbia frequently found in cultural criticism of the period (and later). While suburban living is frequently characterized as homogeneous – and found lacking compared to the diversity and energy of urban life – interwar suburban forms were diverse, although they remained socially segregated. While compared to overcrowded urban living, suburbs offered the promise of privacy, this did not mean that suburban domestic cultures were necessarily privatized – indeed, surburban developments were sometimes the product of a community project. Furthermore, there wasn't a uniform suburban experience, although the form of prefabricated housing gave the superficial appearance of standardization. Yet this appearance of standardization became a central motif in critiques of suburbia. For example, **Frankfurt School** critics Theodor Adorno and Max Horkheimer railed against the 'flimsy bungalows' built 'in praise of technical progress' which have a 'built-in demand to be discarded after a short while like empty food cans'. The 'small hygienic dwelling', they claimed, made the individual 'all the more subservient to his adversary – the absolute power of capitalism' (1979: 120). These themes would gain the status of a 'truth' in post-war debates.

The period after World War II witnessed a massive building boom. With the increasing domination of building by large construction companies, this period represents a fall from grace in the more sympathetic histories of suburbia. For example, Hayden (2004: 128) argues that post-war suburbs were 'deliberately planned to maximize consumption of mass-produced goods and minimize responsibility of the developers to create public space and public services'. It is the idea that suburbia was mass-produced for profit – combined with the idea that suburban living created an ideal vehicle for the promotion of a mass consumer culture – that underpinned, and continues to underpin, many critiques of suburban domestic cultures. In these arguments, **Levittowns** – mass-produced, quickly constructed and relatively affordable large-scale suburbs built by Levitt and Sons – frequently acted as a synecdoche for everything that was wrong with suburbia as a whole.

One of the most extended critiques of suburban living in the period can be found in the work of architect and cultural critic, Lewis Mumford. In the suburbs, he argued, 'a multitude of uniform, unidentifiable houses, line up inflexibly, at uniform distances on uniform roads, in a treeless communal waste, inhabited by people of the same class, the same income, the same age-group' (cited in Giles 2004: 29). Furthermore, Mumford claimed that standardized, uniform housing developments produced standardized, uniform people who were part of a **mass culture**. The post-war suburbs, he argued, were 'places in which class distinctions dissolved and ethnic attachments evaporated . . . [and] the notion of uniformity accorded well with the belief that America was itself in the process of becoming increasingly homogeneous' (Polenberg 1986: 139). Mumford, like many other critics, also accused suburbanites of retreating into the private sphere and jettisoning any sense of public and political responsibility. The reason for this increasing privatization, he argued, was not simply the form of suburbia but also the appeal of suburban domesticity. For Mumford, 'the suburb served as an asylum for the preservation of illusion. Here domesticity could flourish, forgetful of the exploitation on which so much of it was based' (cited in Jackson 1985: 156).

In post-war America, suburban domestic culture was linked to a whole range of other social and cultural ills. As the suburbs sucked men into their homes, it was claimed, men became 'emasculated' as they became locked within feminine domestic space with the result that US society became increasingly feminized. (Wylie 1942 provides a good example of this kind of argument while Ehrenreich 1983 and Spigel 2001b offer useful commentary on debates about feminization and suburbanization in the period.) Other critics such as David Riesman (1961) argued that suburbanites became increasingly conformist as they regulated their own behaviour to become more like the lives they assumed were led by their suburban neighbours. Opponents of suburbia also alleged that, with an increasingly privatized existence, '**mass man**' became cut off from other people and became increasingly dependent 'on the media as his sole source of emotional stimulation and social contact' (Pells 1989: 220; see, for example, Anders 1957).

Indeed, TV – frequently seen as a quintessentially suburban medium – was frequently implicated in attacks on suburban domesticity (Medhurst 1997; Silverstone 1997). Many critics believed that TV diverted suburbanites from 'real' issues and promoted the suburban way of life as the norm. (For critiques of TV, suburbia and consumer culture during the period, see Mills 1956, Packard 1957, 1961, Boorstin 1962 and Macdonald 1963.) Not only did these critics frequently draw on exactly the same terms as critiques of suburban domesticity, but also TV and domesticity were damned through their association with each other. As Lynn Spigel (2001b: 4) observes, 'debates about media, privacy, and public life are rooted in a set of cultural beliefs that see the home and the outside world as essentially separate and antithetical spheres of action. Critics who worry about the media's erosion of the public sphere typically describe public life as a realm of active citizenship and useful labour, while they represent home as a space of trivial pursuit.' As Spigel makes clear, the assumption that domestic culture represents a retreat from public life rests on the idea that rigid separations exist between public and private spheres.

If the TV was one of the quintessential consumer goods of the 1950s, TV shows and adverts were also seen to promote a suburban domestic culture organized around consumption. Indeed, many critiques of suburbia centre on the idea that consumption was the central organizing feature of suburban domestic culture. New homes were sold on the promise that they came complete with the latest consumer goods while suburban developments were often built around centres of commerce such as shopping centres (Silverstone 1997; Hayden 2004). Some feminists argued that the suburbs spatially segregated women from all aspects of public life except consumption so that the role of housewife became synonymous with that of consumer (Friedan 1963). Other critics claimed that suburbanites judged each other's worth by what they consumed rather than what they produced, becoming engaged in status competitions as they attempted to 'keep up with the Joneses'. As Scott Donaldson notes, 'the suburbanite clearly can't win, if he leaves his home as he found it, he is accused of standardization and conformity; if he attempts to alter his home, he is accused of a shallow competition for status' (cited in Clarke 1999: 124).

In a fairly typical portrait of the suburban domestic culture of the 1950s, John Cheever – in his 1957 novel *The Wapshot Chronicles* – portrays how the unrelenting boredom of the suburban housewife's life was punctuated only by the trivial distractions offered by 'telephone calls, visits from the vacuum cleaner salesman and trips to shopping centres and supermarkets' (cited in Polenberg 1986: 137). However, studies of the period demonstrate that domestic consumption did not necessarily contribute to privatization and isolation but instead helped produce a sense of community within the suburbs. For example, Herbert Gans's classic sociological study of one of the Levittowns shows how consumption was a key means of producing sociality and neighbourliness. He found that when residents first moved into the new developments, door-to-door 'salesmen became social intermediaries, telling people about their neighbours, and pointing out ones with similar backgrounds or interests' (Gans 1967: 45). Likewise, Alison Clarke (1997: 144–5) identifies how Tupperware parties enabled women to produce 'support networks' in suburbia. Therefore, domestic consumption could be used to build a sense of community and place. There is also considerable evidence to suggest that suburban domestic culture was not only based around consumption but could also become part of 'informal economies' based on swapping anything from home-grown vegetables to skills and labour (Saunders 1990; Clarke 1999; Wiese 1999). This highlights how suburban domestic cultures were not simply privatized and how domestic activities form the basis for blurring the boundaries between public and private.

Therefore, there is considerable evidence to dispute the idea that post-war suburban domestic cultures were simply conformist, standardized and privatized (and further evidence of the complexity of domestic consumption practices is discussed in Chapter 5). However, while it is a mistake to claim that standardized and homogeneous housing-forms produced standardized and homogeneous cultures, arguments about the social homogeneity of the suburbs are less easily dismissed. On the one hand, claims that suburbia is simply a white middle-class cultural form that eradicates difference ignore the extent to which specific suburban spaces have been used to build a range of distinctive suburban communities that articulate a range of class, 'racial' and ethnic identities and cultures (Cohen 2003; Hayden 2004). Yet, on the other hand, suburbanization is clearly implicated in a wider history of racial segregation in the USA. 'White flight' from the city has been increasingly interpreted as a flight from urban cultures that are associated with the black working class and underclass.

Racial discrimination in awarding home loans combined with disinvestment in black neighbourhoods increased racial segregation in patterns of residence. The practice of 'redlining' by mortgage lenders was central to these processes. This practice underpinned decisions about whether to award home loans based on an assessment of how 'risky' a neighbourhood was deemed to be, with 'black neighbourhoods' being seen as particularly 'risky'. This not only helped to produce and maintain racial segregation in housing but low rates of home ownership among African-Americans also became exacerbated by low levels of economic investment in these areas (Jackson 1985; Hayden 2004). Therefore, while institutional and legal forms of racial segregation were being challenged in the 1950s, suburbanization enabled unofficial forms of segregation to flourish. As Polenberg (1986: 163) argues, this offers 'a classic example of how demographic trends could work at cross-purposes with constitutional, political and social change'. Suburbanization undoubtedly had enormous consequences for American cities. As the middle classes fled the city, so did business investors and large urban centres became increasingly associated with crime and decay by the 1960s and 1970s, with profound consequences for those who, because of class and/or 'race', remained trapped there.

Nonetheless, as I have shown, while suburbs remain segregated by class and 'race', suburban culture as a whole is not simply white and middle class. Many critics have seen an investment in suburban domesticity as inherently conformist and conservative – and a retreat from any sense of public or political responsibility. However, these arguments rest on the assumption that a move to the suburbs automatically results in the adoption of a privatized domestic culture that is based on a total disengagement with the public sphere. It is such assumptions that mean that white or black urbanites who make the move to the suburbs are frequently accused of 'selling out', despite the fact that they did not create the forms of decay that can make urban living unappealing. As Pells (1989: 199) has argued, the intellectuals who criticized post-war suburbia were frequently unable to comprehend 'how emotionally gratifying the purchase of a ranch house could be to a generation haunted by memories of immigrant slums, cramped apartments, and the feeling of claustrophobia that marked the impoverished 1930s. Open spaces and residential mobility symbolized freedom as well as privacy'. Indeed, to characterize the desire for a nice suburban house with a garden as a sign of political and cultural irresponsibility is a sign of a profound arrogance on behalf of intellectuals.

Suburban domesticity and the lower middle class

Although British critics in the interwar period shared many of the concerns of their American counterparts, they also identified suburbia as a threat to British culture. The suburbs were seen as 'out of place' in the traditional fabric of British life because they were neither urban nor rural (Matless 1998). The suburbs, claimed Clough Williams-Ellis, sprawled 'like lice upon a tape-worm' (cited in Hall 1996: 80); they followed, argued Thomas Sharp, 'no enlightened guidance or correction from authority' (cited in Hall 1996: 83). If the suburbs were seen as 'out of place' in the British landscape, then many critics suggested that the form of suburban housing, with its 'half-timbered', mock-Tudor exteriors, also showed little respect for British cultural traditions (Oliver et al. 1981).[2] However, for many intellectuals of the period, an even more dangerous threat to British culture lurked in the suburbs – the people who lived there. The expansion of the suburbs was linked to the expansion of the lower middle class who, it was claimed, developed their own distinctive domestic cultures that showed little regard for traditional cultural values. In this way the 'spatial encroachment' of the suburbs on the countryside was linked to the 'cultural encroachment' of the lower middle class on established middle-class values and tastes (Felski 2000: 38). In this section I examine these critiques of lower middle-class domestic culture in more detail, identifying why the suburban home came to be seen as a place *without culture*. The section identifies how these critiques of domesticity not only had a class basis but were also attacks on women's cultural authority within the home.

The expansion of suburbia in the UK was partly a result of the housing boom that occurred in the interwar years. In the aftermath of World War I, the home gained a new significance in British national life (Light 1991) and the government saw decent housing as a way of increasing both the health and the stability of the nation. Between 1920 and 1940 4.6 million new homes were built, giving many people their first opportunity to have a home of their own. Before World War I, the majority of people rented accommodation off private landlords. In the interwar period, an increasing proportion of the middle class became home-owners, with the number of people purchasing their home rising from 10 per cent to 33 per cent between 1914 and 1939 (Savage et al. 1992). Some of the working class had the opportunity to rent properties off the state with the introduction of **council housing** (Savage et al. 1992; Hall 1996).

The growth of new suburban housing coincided with a significant expansion of middle-class occupations – in particular, lower middle-class occupations. Home-ownership was a key way in which the newly middle class could signify their position as 'properly' middle class (Oliver et al. 1981; Savage et al. 1992). The individuality of their suburban homes became a way of representing their class status to both themselves and the outside world; residents valued the ornamental windows, mock-Tudor exteriors and elaborate gardens that were features of suburbia (and were mocked by critics for their pretentiousness and lack of architectural merit). These individual features were particularly important as they also signified their owners' difference from council residents; council developments were often uniform and standardized, offering little scope for expressions of individuality.[3] Given that there was frequently little difference between the social origins of lower middle-class home-owners and 'respectable' working-class council tenants, the individuality of newly purchased houses took on a particular significance and represented 'individualism, private ownership and social mobility' (Oliver et al. 1981: 114). However, this emphasis on individuality should not be confused with privatization: Oliver et al. (1981) document how residents moving into new suburban areas sought out ways to build a sense of community through sports clubs, societies, churches and, most crucially, children.

If their suburban homes represented pride and achievement to the lower middle class, they also signified a cultureless wasteland to many intellectuals in the period. In one of the most damning critiques, George Orwell characterized lower middle-class suburban domesticity as 'a rather restless, cultureless life, centring round tinned food, *Picture Post*, the radio and the internal combustion engine' (cited in Humble 2001: 87). For Orwell, suburban domestic culture is not a 'real' culture because it centres around mass-produced consumer goods. 'Orwell's characters are not waving but drowning in the accumulated detritus of lower middle-class life: stewed pears, portable radios, false teeth, lace curtains, hire-purchase furniture, teapots, manicure sets, life insurance policies' (Felski 2000: 37). The objects and practices of everyday domestic life were used to signify the cultural poverty, inauthenticity and triviality of lower middle-class suburbia.[4]

These scathing attacks on lower middle-class domestic cultures had a class basis. As Judy Giles (2004: 43) argues, these new suburban lifestyles were 'a form of modernity that was not of middle-class making'. In this way, these *lower* middle-class domestic cultures represented an affront to the cultural authority of the established middle classes. Indeed, with the expansion of the middle classes during the interwar years, there was a growing preoccupation with what cultural forms and practices qualified as 'properly' middle class (Light 1991; Humble 2001). Therefore, the attacks on lower middle-class domestic cultures can be understood as an attempt by the cultural middle classes to reassert their own cultural authority. They aimed to achieve this by pathologizing and trivializing lower middle-class domestic culture and representing them as 'singularly inauthentic and uniquely conservative' (Felski 2000: 44).

Suburban domestic cultures were not just attacked because they were lower middle class but also because they were seen to be feminized cultures. As we saw in Chapter 2, ideologies of separate spheres identified home as the sphere of feminine responsibility and influence. However, in the interwar period, critics were concerned that women might have *too* much influence over domestic life. Why did this shift take place? First, domestic culture was seen as increasingly important during the period; as Alison Light (1991: 218) observes, 'questions of the conduct of home life [were] made public property like never before'. Second, while British identity had been associated with 'heroic' masculinity during World War I, in peacetime there seemed to be little place for men to assert their authority in a country that was allegedly becoming more domesticated (Light 1991; Giles 2004). This fear that men were becoming more 'emasculated' was also linked to the decline of the British Empire (which was seen as a threat to ideas of British 'superiority' and, hence, to British national identity). As British life became more home-centred, it was claimed, the country became increasingly feminized and subject to women's authority.

The attacks on lower middle-class domestic culture were frequently aimed at women and critics claimed that feminine domesticity was 'emasculating' men. For example, George Orwell claimed that 'every man you can see has got some blasted woman hanging around his neck like a mermaid, dragging him down and down – down to some beastly semi-detached villa in Putney, with hire-purchase furniture and a portable radio and an aspidistra' (cited in Felski 2000: 48). In Orwell's work, male surburbanites were portrayed as the victims of their wives' desire for the suburban dream. He describes 'a line of semi-detached torture-chambers where the poor little five-to-ten-pound-a-weekers quake and shiver, every one of them with the boss twisting his tail and his wife riding him like the nightmare and the kids sucking his blood like leeches' (Orwell 1983: 435–6). Across a range of critics and discourses, the consumption-obsessed, materialistic suburban woman came to represent 'the most despised aspects of suburbia' (Giles 2004: 42) and a threat to British culture.

What these critiques fail to acknowledge or explain is why a home-centred existence in a semi-detached suburban house was quite so appealing to women (and men) in the interwar period. For many of the new suburbanites who had previously lived in over-crowded urban accommodation, acquiring a home of your own was the realization of a dream. As Giles argues, for many people, their suburban homes offered their first opportunity to live with a proper bathroom with running hot and cold water and an indoor toilet. Not only did these 'modern' conveniences represent a dramatic change in these women's 'quality of life' but they also signified a break from a past in which these women had been judged as inferior 'to those who had never had to empty chamber pots or boil up water for baths' (Giles 2004: 49). Furthermore, whereas intellectuals identi-fied new consumer goods as symbols of feminine greed and materialism, 'the carpet and the three-piece suite, the Hoover and the new gas-oven' operated as 'icons of hope and dignity' to these new suburbanites (Light 1991: 219). While interwar intellectuals might have the ability to have a home of your own taken for granted, Giles (2004: 49) argues that suburban semi-detached modernity offered many people 'the pride of being, at last, worthy of citizenship' which, she suggests, was 'as significant as the vote in enabling people to see themselves as full members of modern society'. Rather than being a political problem, for these new suburban residents, the opportunity to experi-ence home-centredness was more likely to represent a sense of entitlement to a better life (and it may have been this sense of entitlement that generated so much venom from cultural critics).

In the UK suburban domestic culture and lower middle-class culture continue to be condemned through association with each other. Their home-centredness is read as a sign of their political conservatism and lack of social responsibility. (For more on critiques of the lower middle class, see Hartley 1997 and Felski 2000.) Critics continue to represent lower middle-class domestic culture as materialistic and artificial and condemn it for its 'ordinariness' and concerns with 'respectability'. Yet, while ordin-ariness and respectability may appear trivial and petty to suburbia's critics, these values have a distinctive logic within lower middle-class cultures; as Savage et al. (2001: 899) have argued, 'ordinariness is a strategy that people can draw on to try and evade social fixing'. An investment in domestic culture offers opportunities – however tem-porary – for people to imagine themselves as outside class structures. While these investments have been read as a sign of **false consciousness** by Marxist critics, they also demonstrate how domestic cultures can also operate as a defence against the injuries of class. Nonetheless, a desire for respectability and to be seen as ordinary can lead to a defensive identity that seeks to 'other' those whom they do not classify respectable or ordinary. The protests against asylum seekers in some British suburbs and towns provide a contemporary example of such practices of 'othering'.

Home-ownership and the working class

In the mid-1950s British critics found a whole new set of problems with suburban domestic culture. This time they turned their attention to the working class who, they claimed, were becoming more home-centred – and more like the lower middle class – as opportunities for home-ownership and council tenancy expanded and the growth of suburbs continued. In this section I start by explaining why, for many critics, this represented a full-blown political problem. These critics argued that as the working class became home-centred, they increasingly adopted middle-class values and turned their back on the public realm of politics. In the process, it was claimed, the working class lost any sense of their class culture and started to shift political affiliation. Second, I identify how a similar set of debates surfaced in the UK in the 1980s as academics and politicians attempted to explain why the working class continued to vote for a right-wing Conservative government. In both cases, increasing home-ownership within the working class was identified as a key source of the problem. Finally, I look more critically at some of the arguments about privatization and question the assumption that an economic, cultural or emotional investment in domestic culture automatically changes people's political beliefs and relationships to the public sphere.

The idea of home was central to post-war British culture. Alongside a massive programme to build new homes, the family was at the heart of government plans to rebuild the nation. Women's roles as wives and mothers were given a new prominence as domestic life was seen as central to the nation's social, economic and cultural health (Riley 1983; Walkerdine and Lucey 1989; Webster 1998). Despite the persistence of slum conditions – and the racial discrimination faced by new immigrants as they searched for decent housing – many people's housing conditions did improve during this period. Between 1947 and 1961 council housing provision nearly doubled and the number of people who owned their own home rose from 29 to 41 per cent (Laing 1986; Webster 1998). Many of these new homes were located in the expanding suburbs.

These new suburban estates were seen as the breeding ground for a new 'classless' culture. In the mid-1950s, a large section of the working class appeared to be enjoying increased 'affluence' due to a rise in 'real' income (although there was no corresponding decline in class *inequalities*). This meant that home-ownership became an option for these **'affluent workers'** and this transformed the housing market in the UK. In 1956, T.R. Fyvel claimed that:

a generation ago, the English suburban house – and garden – still belonged to a middle-class way of life beyond the reach of the mass of workers. Today the whole nation feels entitled to this privilege; hence you have the sprawling suburban housing estates.

(cited in Laing 1986: 17)

As they bought suburban semis and started to invest in a home-centred form of domestic culture, it was claimed that these working-class home-owners underwent a process of **embourgeoisement** and began to adopt (lower) middle-class values. Furthermore, many critics argued that these new home-owners – like the lower middle class before them – built a domestic culture centred around consumer goods. 'We find manual workers ready to describe themselves as middle class', observed Mark Abrams in 1959, 'because they already own or soon will own a car, a house with a garden, a refrigerator, a washing machine, a vacuum cleaner, and, of course, a television set' (cited in Laing 1986, 20–1). Although the working class who ended up on new suburban council estates were less 'affluent', it was claimed that they also became forced into adopting home-centred lives. Slum clearance broke up working-class communities, and families who were relocated in new suburbs felt 'cut off from relatives, suspicious of their neighbours, lonely', leaving them little option but to turn to the home for a meaningful life (Willmott and Young 1960: viii; see also Young and Willmott 1962).

Why was home-centredness among the working class seen as such a problem? Many commentators believed that the move to a privatized suburban existence caused the working class to lose any sense of cultural and political identity. Traditional working-class culture, it was argued, was based on masculine solidarity and togetherness; this sense of collective identity was fostered by institutions like the pub and trade union. Critics such as Richard Hoggart produced nostalgic accounts of a 'traditional' working-class domestic culture that wasn't home-centred. In *The Uses of Literacy*, Hoggart provided a vivid description of a working-class home presided over by the powerful figure of 'our mam' and based around the extended family and the warmth of the hearth. This traditional working-class culture may have been held together by a powerful woman, he argued, but it wasn't 'whimsical or "feminized"' (Hoggart 1958: 26); this culture may have been family-centred but it wasn't privatized. Instead family members were 'a gregarious group' and the living-room opened directly onto the narrow street and straight into the local 'life of the neighbourhood' (Hoggart 1958: 22, 41).

A similar nostalgia for traditional working-class culture ran through the '**social realism**' of films such as *The Loneliness of the Long-Distance Runner* (1962), *A Kind of Loving* (1962) and *Saturday Night and Sunday Morning* (1960) (Brooke 2001). These films were concerned with 'the corrosive effects of a modern, mass, commercialized culture' and the ways in which 'modern mass production, increasing geographical mobility and urban redevelopment were breaking the traditional working-class communities' (Hill 1986: 150; see also Daniels and Rycroft 1993). In these films home-centredness threatened to 'emasculate' the (male) working class as they became domesticated and trapped in a feminine, privatized and consumption-dominated world. Indeed, social realist films frequently seemed to blame women for producing the new domestic cultures that threatened to feminize working-class men: as Terri Lovell (1990: 367) argues, these films 'persistently portrays the status-conscious woman as the vulnerable point of entry for seductions which might betray a class and its culture'.[5]

Although critics were concerned about working-class women's investment in domestic consumer goods, they weren't concerned about women's investment in home more generally. It was assumed that domestic culture was a feminine responsibility. In his description of the 'myopic' and 'turned-in-upon-itself' life of 'our mam', Hoggart (1958: 27) saw nothing inherently problematic in the identification between working-class femininity and domestic culture. Concerns about the increasing home-centredness of the working class were in fact concerns about the working-class *man*. As Wendy Webster (1998: 74) points out, critics were worried by the arrival of a 'new man' who wanted to spend time in his home with his family, push the pram, help his wife around the house and do DIY rather than spend time down the pub with his friends. (For more on the DIY boom during this period, see Segal 1988 and Brunsdon 2004.) Isolated from his workmates, it was claimed, working-class men lost their working-class political identity, turning their backs on the wider class struggle, and became more conservative.

These debates are frequently underpinned by the assumption that where you live – and what type of house you live in – determines your culture, identity and politics. To residents on new suburban developments, the significance of their new homes may have had little to do with changing their class identity. As Stuart Hall argues, for many people, the key thing offered by their new homes might have been the 'sense of security' that comes from having a place to call your own (cited in Laing 1986: 29; see also Attfield 1995). Like the lower middle classes in the interwar period, one of the most important features of these houses was the sense of relief at having a home with an indoor bathroom. As one woman put it, 'No more chamber pots under the bed and the treachery of having to toil up and downstairs with slop pails to empty the wretched things' (Joyce Storey cited in Webster 1998: 171). Furthermore, while housing forms do come with ideas about culture and identity 'built-in', these are not necessarily reproduced when houses are consumed and 'lived in' by their occupants. For example, Judy Attfield's (1995) study of Harlow New Town demonstrates how the early working-class occupants rejected the architect's ideas of how they should live; instead they drew on the working-class domestic culture that they had grown up in and modified their homes to make them meaningful.[6]

If critics in the period worried about the impact that privatized suburban living had on working-class political affiliations, they were far more concerned about the impact home-ownership had on political attitudes. When the affluent working class bought their own homes, it was claimed, they transferred their allegiance from Labour (the traditional party of the working class) to Conservative (the traditional party of the middle class). Socialist critics suggested that ideologies of home-ownership persuaded the working class that they had a stake in capitalism and prevented them from realizing that socialism represented their best interests as an exploited and oppressed class. Successive election defeats for Labour certainly suggested to some commentators that this must be the case. In *Must Labour Lose?*, Abrams and Rose (1960: 46) posed the question in none-too-subtle terms: 'Does buying one's house turn one into a Conservative, or are Conservatives the sort of people who want to own the house they live in?' While Labour's failure to lose the following election casts doubt on the idea that there was an intrinsic relationship between home-ownership and Conservatism, this line of argument did not disappear for good.

In the 1980s the relationship between home-ownership and political values resurfaced after successive election victories for the Conservative government led by Margaret Thatcher. Home was central to **Thatcherism** in two key ways. First, Thatcherite ideologies advocated a return to Victorian 'family values': it was claimed that families should both take responsibility for instilling moral values in its members and take responsibility for their own welfare needs (Segal 1983). Second, Thatcher's government promoted the importance of home-ownership. This was manifested most clearly in policies that gave council tenants the 'right to buy' their homes. These policies were a direct attack on Labour's philosophies of state control and public welfare provision (Hall 1983).[7] The sale of council houses proved to be popular: an estimated one-third of council tenants exercised their 'right to buy' and 2.2 million properties had been sold by the time Labour regained power in 1997 (Walker 1999). This attack on the State's responsibility to provide housing not only reduced the stock of public housing but resulted in increased dependence on private landlords and increasing rates of homelessness.

It was frequently assumed that the working class who opted to buy their council properties also bought into the whole Thatcherite project. More generally, the home-owning affluent working class and lower middle class were blamed for continued Conservative successes at the ballot box. For example, Charlie Leadbetter (1989: 143) argues that, under Thatcherism, the 'protection of the private space of the home-owning consumer incorporates people within a defence of private ownership and control in the economy. It also incorporates people within exploitative economic relations'. If this were the case, then it would be fair to assume that those working-class voters who bought their council houses have supported Thatcherite policies with their vote but there is insufficient evidence to support this (Walker 1999). However, the figure of the suburban, privatized home-owner continued to be blamed for Conservative successes and was epitomized by 'Essex Man', somebody who had supposedly bought their own council house in Basildon and whose life focused on his home and family (Felski 2000; Gilbert and Preston 2003; Walks 2005).[8]

Therefore, commentators in the 1980s – like those in the late 1950s – assumed that home ownership made people more politically conservative. But did buying a house necessarily imply an acceptance of Conservative policies? In a related context, Frank Mort (1989: 166) has argued that there was:

nothing innately Thatcherite about consuming, just as there is nothing intrinsic-ally socialist about the state. A reductionism which collapses the lived experiences of consumerism with the official version of Tory popular capitalism, is blind to the fact that what people actually *do* when they go shopping may be quite differ-ent from the official script.

As I have demonstrated earlier in this chapter, observing that someone invests in their home – economically, culturally or emotionally – does not tell us about the meaning or significance of that investment. Home-ownership and home-centredness do not only signify conservatism.

Following a study of what home-ownership meant to British people during the Thatcher period, Peter Saunders (1990: 99) concluded that one of the most significant appeals of home-ownership was that it offered the '*inherent* right of use, control and disposal which many people appear to want'. People who own their own homes felt able to 'take control' of their environment because they believed that owning their property gave them the right to do what they wanted to their home. People in privately rented properties are often forbidden to make even minor changes that might personal-ize their housing and make it more 'homely': for example, putting up pictures and posters that leave behind marks on the wall can result in financial penalties. Although council tenants have more freedom, Saunders argues, they frequently feel that they have little control over their housing because it is the property of the State (see also Miller 1988). Therefore, home-ownership may signify the ability to construct a meaningful domestic environment. Such a position does not suggest that home-owners are inher-ently conservative and, Saunders (1990: 290) argues, neither does it mean that home-owners are any more privatized than anyone else. Indeed, he offers evidence to suggest that home-owners have rather more outside interests and activities in the wider com-munity than council tenants.

Saunders suggests that the key meaning that people attribute to the experience of home ownership is what Giddens calls '**ontological security**'. Giddens argues that people seek out a sense of ontological security in response to the conditions of mod-ernity. Modernity appears as unstable and impersonal, beyond people's control, so they search for a sense of rootedness and stability. For Saunders (1990: 293), 'home ownership is one expression of the search for ontological security, for a home of one's own offers both a physical (hence spatially rooted) and permanent (hence temporally rooted) location in the world' (1990: 293). The ability to choose where to live, and how to live in it, offered by home-ownership, he argues, offers greater opportunities for the 'expression of self and identity' that are central to a feeling of ontological security (Saunders 1990: 302).

However, as home-ownership becomes more widespread, it becomes 'normalized' as the key means of acquiring ontological security. This not only makes it difficult to conceptualize other ways of achieving this sense of belonging and rootedness, but it also means that those who are economically excluded from home-ownership are also excluded from this experience of security (Gurney 1999; Ronald 2004). Furthermore, it is questionable whether all home-owners – or people who live in privately owned homes – can achieve this sense of ontological security. Saunders' position rests on an idealized view of home that tends to ignore the constraints, tensions, inequalities or fears that may accompany people's experience of domestic life (ideas I explore in more depth in the next chapter).

The meanings of home-ownership and rental are culturally, nationally and historically specific rather than universal (Dupuis and Thorns 1998; Ronald 2004). Just as it is unwise to make generalizations that equate the meaning of home-ownership with privatization and conservatism, so the concept of ontological security may not travel well, in time or space. Nonetheless, the differences between renting off a private landlord, renting off the State and owner-occupation are significant and these different forms of tenure may contribute to the formation of specific relationships with domestic culture.

Conclusions

The pursuit of profit by large builders (for example, Barratt and Persimmon in the UK, and D. R. Horton and Lennar in the USA) undoubtedly has a profound effect on what types of housing gets produced for whom, and where it is located. Furthermore, relationships to the housing market – and different systems of housing provision – undoubtedly produce and reproduce inequalities between different social groups. Moreover, as Joe Moran (2004: 625) argues, 'carefully refurbished or shinily modern homes are achieved not only at the expense of the homeless or poorly housed, but also other everyday spaces'. For home-owners, especially in inflated housing markets such as that in the UK, their place of residence will often be the largest economic investment they ever make; practices of home maintenance and home-making must to some extent take into account the fact that home represents a huge financial investment. As Moran (2005b: 162) suggests:

> even rich people are spending an extraordinary amount of their incomes on old, cheaply built, overpriced properties. The cultural meanings that accrue around the home – as a space of nostalgia, belonging and security, both existential and financial – conceal this inconvenient fact.

However, at the same time, the meaning of domestic cultures cannot simply be deduced from studying the economics of housing production and distribution. Just because homes are the product of a capitalist system, it does not follow that home-making strategies simply reproduce capitalist values. Furthermore, as I have demonstrated in this chapter (and explore in more detail in later chapters), the meanings of domestic culture – and home-ownership – are complex, diverse and contingent on a range of historical, social and cultural contexts. This is neatly dramatized in property TV shows such as *House Doctor* and *Selling Houses*. These programmes focus on the home as an economic investment: experts offer advice to people who are having difficulty selling their residence and perform a makeover where homes are transformed into desirable properties. However, a central feature of most of these narratives is that the expert admonishes the residents for making their home too personal, too representative of their own everyday life, too much to their own tastes. This would seem to suggest that the need for a 'house doctor' is predicated on the fact that the work that many people perform on their residences is not simply geared towards the idea of home as an economic investment.[9]

In this chapter I have considered how some critics have assumed that it is possible to read the meaning of domestic cultures – and to 'know' the people who live and make these cultures – from the *form* of housing. While architects and planners have some-times believed that it was possible to engineer and 'improve' domestic culture through their designs, other critics have assumed that all people living in three-bedroomed suburban semis must be living identical lives. While the form of the buildings we occupy – and the relationship between our residence and other spaces and places – undoubtedly *influences* how we live, this does not *determine* how we live. As I have demonstrated in this chapter (and go on to discuss in more detail in Chapter 5), people adapt, rework, negotiate and transform the places in which they live to construct meaningful domestic cultures. Therefore, just because suburbia may appear to be full of pseudo-individualized but standardized houses does not mean that their occupants are uniform and conformist; nor does it mean that the domestic cultures they create are identical. As Peter Hall (1996: 303) argues, critiques of 'ordinary' housing are fre-quently elitist: critics who attacked suburban living 'were simply expressing their own class prejudices' against domestic cultures that were not of their own making.

This chapter has also reviewed arguments that suggest an investment in domestic culture leads to a more privatized form of living. While these arguments sometimes assume that investing in housing as a form of private property leads to an investment in the capitalist system, they more generally assume that being home-centred involves a retreat into private space. However, as I suggested in the last chapter, the assumption that home is simply 'cut off' from the public sphere ignores the web of relationships that make distinctions between public and private extremely blurred. Furthermore, by equating privatization with a retreat from the 'real' world of politics in the public sphere, these arguments ignore the extent to which the home is also a site of politics. This idea is explored in more detail in the next chapter.

Further reading

Hayden, D. (2004) *Building Suburbia: Green Fields and Urban Growth, 1820–2000*. New York: Vintage.

Moran, J. (2004) Housing, Memory and Everyday Life in Contemporary Britain, *Cultural Studies*, 18(4): 607–27.

Oliver, P., Davis, I. and Bentley, I. (1981) *Dunroamin: The Suburban Semi and its Enemies.* London: Pimlico.

Saunders, P. (1990) *A Nation of Home Owners.* London: Unwin Hyman.

Silverstone, R. (ed.) (1997) *Visions of Suburbia.* London: Routledge.

Webster, W. (1998) *Imagining Home: Gender, 'Race' and National Identity, 1945–64.* London: UCL Press.

Notes

1 Although nineteenth-century social reformers in the UK documented the effects of material deprivation on working-class domestic culture in the slums, many linked this to what they saw as the morally and culturally impoverished ways of life in working-class homes. Attempts to reform working-class housing were frequently attempts to 'improve' working-class culture through social engineering (Tagg 1981; Tolson 1990; Hall 1996). Since this period, while some commentators have tried to document the effect of poverty on domestic life, there have also been continued attempts to represent working-class domestic culture as pathological because it deviates from (white) middle-class conceptions of domestic culture.

2 While suburbia is a resolutely modern form (Ravetz 1995), interwar suburbia is frequently characterized by its ambiguity, found in its articulation of elements of both tradition and modernity and 'in the vocabulary that was employed: *half* timbered walls of "*semi*-detached" homes for the "*middle*" classes set on *sub*urban estates' (Oliver et al. 1981: 78).

3 The emphasis on uniformity and coherence in council developments not only fitted with ideas of 'good design' in the period but also architects' assumptions that 'communal' ways of life were central to working-class culture (Oliver et al. 1981; Boys 1995).

4 For further illustration, see Carey's (1992) discussion of the period. Although the objects change, more recent critics continue to be preoccupied with the lower middle class's use of consumer goods in their homes to represent their cultural and political poverty – Mike Leigh's films provide a useful starting point here.

5 More recently, in American films and some hip-hop and r'n'b, the 'status-conscious woman' has operated in a similar way in relation to black culture.

6 Attfield (1995: 234) also argues that these Harlow residents didn't attempt to demonstrate their status as respectable housewives through conspicuous *consumption* but by making 'their *work* conspicuous': their identities as respectable working-class housewives were made visible to the outside world by using shining white sheets on the line – and dust-free arrangements of ornaments – to demonstrate their labour.

7 As Hall (1983) explains, 'Thatcherite policies were underpinned by free market economics and linked to anti-statism and anti-collectivism.'

8 More recently, while Labour has managed to capture a less geographically specific but largely homogenized home-centred 'Middle England' – associated with new private estates and the consumption of specifically middlebrow consumer goods and often characterized as 'Mondeo Man' (after his car) – the policies that have been used to woo these voters have frequently rested on the assumption that this 'unknowable' group is still innately conservative (McKibbin 1999; Moran 2005a).

9 Even *Property Ladder*, which focuses on the practices of would-be housing developers,

continually finds people getting 'too personal' in doing up properties to sell for a profit. At the same time it should be noted that there is frequently a struggle between class tastes at play in shows such as *House Doctor* and *Selling Houses*: as both Holliday (2005) and Moran (2005b) point out, working-class home-owners are frequently advised to improve their homes in line with middle-class tastes if they want to make their properties sell.

4 | HOME-*WORK*: FEMINISMS, DOMESTICITY AND DOMESTIC LABOUR

Introduction

Domestic cultures have not only been seen as a problem in terms of class politics but they have also been understood as playing a central role in the reproduction of gendered inequalities. Some critics have viewed home as a place in which women perform hard work for no pay and where they are trapped in conditions that render them powerless against male authority. As we have already seen, the ideology of separate spheres allocated women responsibility for domestic life. For many feminist critics, this associ-ation between women and home has played a central role in reproducing gender inequalities – indeed, some suggest, that this is even the root cause of women's oppres-sion. This chapter explores some key feminist ideas about why domestic cultures are a problem for women.

Before looking at these debates in more detail, it is important to understand that feminism was never a monolithic movement. It is far more useful to think about a range of *feminisms* and crucial to acknowledge that there is considerable disagreement between feminists about the causes of gender inequality. Nonetheless, the idea that 'the personal is political' was central to the historical development of **second-wave femi-nism** in the late 1960s and the 1970s. This challenged the kind of political thinking that we explored in the last chapter, in which the public sphere was seen as the only site of 'real' politics. One of the key legacies of feminism is the idea that the private sphere is also deeply political. Drawing on their own experience (although this was frequently the 'experience' of white middle-class women), women who became involved in the feminist movements of the late 1960s realized that problems they had endured in the private sphere of the home were in fact common problems faced by numerous women. (For more on the idea that 'the personal is political', see Brunsdon 1978.) For these reasons many feminists came to see their everyday lives within the home – and family life, in particular – as a key source of their oppression. Nonetheless, feminist politics did not simply focus on the private sphere: as Sheila Rowbotham (1996: 7) argues, 'the desire to change personal life coexisted with a strong pull towards public political action'.

Second-wave feminists played a key role in challenging many taken-for-granted assumptions about domestic life. For example, many feminists challenged the idea that the existence of gendered, separate spheres was a 'natural' way of organizing social life. The existence of separate spheres, it was argued, shouldn't be seen as a reflection of men's 'natural' predispositions towards ambition and competitiveness and women's 'natural' predisposition towards caring. Instead, some feminists argued, the idea of gendered spheres produced and reproduced cultural differences between masculinity and femininity rather than reflecting what men and women were 'naturally' like. Furthermore, many feminists identified how the very idea of separate spheres for men and women created wider forms of gender inequality. Not only did the identification of men with the role of the breadwinner limit women's opportunities to participate in paid employment on an equal basis to men but it also reproduced women's economic dependence on men. Moreover, it was claimed, the idea that the home was a 'haven' from the world of work obfuscated the extent to which women's activities within the home *were* work, helping to justify the fact that women received no financial reward for their household labour. The idea of home as haven or sanctuary from the outside world, many feminists argued, also masked the extent to which the home could be a site of violence and abuse for both women and children. As Laura Goldsack (1999: 126) observes, 'The home is the most common site of assault, its very fixtures, fabrics and furnishings . . . [are] in reality the most frequent weapons utilized in the violence.' (See also Dobash and Dobash 1980, 1992; Stanko 1985.)

This chapter focuses on three key debates within feminist work on the home. In the first two sections I focus on debates about housework and how it contributes to the production and reproduction of domestic cultures. The first section examines feminist debates about how the **sexual division of labour** within the home is a major source of gender inequality. In the process I also explore empirical studies that document continuing patterns of inequality in men and women's level of contribution to maintaining domestic life, and theories that seek to explain why the sexual division of labour is so resistant to change.

The second section focuses on cooking as a particular form of domestic work. In this section I explore how household tasks play a crucial role in home-*making*: cooking isn't simply about preparing something for people to eat but also plays a crucial role in creating the meanings associated with domestic cultures. In this section I examine debates about why cooking is still closely associated with femininity. I also consider how the meanings of particular forms of household tasks are frequently context-dependent, exploring how cooking can be thought of as both leisure and labour.

In the third section I focus on feminist debates about the relationship between femininity, domesticity and 'the housewife'. Although many feminist critics have seen domesticity as an ideology imposed on women that naturalized their roles as housewives and helped to reproduce gender inequalities, other critics have suggested that women's investment in domesticity can act as the basis for a form of resistance to a male-dominated public sphere. I identify the uses and limitations of both these positions and argue that feminism still needs to develop a more complex position on our relationship to domesticity.

Domestic culture as work culture

The idea that modern societies are organized into separate spheres underpins debates about the sexual division of labour. According to the ideology of separate spheres, the meaning of home is created through its difference to the public sphere of work. Therefore, despite the fact that domestic management and labour are essential for creating homes, the ideology of separate spheres hides the extensive labour required to produce the physical, cultural and emotional elements of home as a refuge and sanctuary. Feminism made a crucial intervention in how we think about domestic cultures by showing the sheer amount of work that goes into producing and maintaining home.

This section explores feminist critiques of a sexual division of labour in which men are seen as responsible for paid work within the public sphere and women are seen as responsible for unpaid work within the private sphere. These critiques also show that while men may make a contribution to the labour involved in producing and reproducing domestic cultures, a sexual division of labour still also underpins what are seen as appropriate tasks for each gender within the home. Feminist activism in the 1970s resulted in women gaining a higher degree of *legal* (if not necessarily *actual*) equality in the paid labour market and, for a wide range of reasons, women now participate at far higher levels in the workplace than they did in previous generations. However, this does not necessarily mean that domestic labour in the home is now equally shared between male and female partners. This section also opens up debates about the politics of housework, considering some of the problems in studying who performs domestic labour and its relationship to gender roles. Finally, I also explore how responsibility for doing domestic labour is not simply a question of gender but also one of 'race', ethnicity and class.

However, it is important to acknowledge that while second-wave feminism has made a major contribution to our understanding of how domestic cultures reproduce gender inequalities, feminist critiques of domestic labour have a far longer history. As Hayden (1982) has argued, the **first-wave feminism** of the late nineteenth and early twentieth centuries challenged ideologies of separate spheres and highlighted how unpaid female domestic labour within the home was a root cause of gender inequality. While these feminists were often privileged white women who paid others to do domestic labour, they introduced the idea that home-makers should receive wages for their housework (just as men received wages for the work that they performed in the public sphere).

Other feminists of the period took this further, attempting to produce new forms of experimental living in which housework and childcare became communal responsibilities and were performed by paid workers. For example, some experimented with new forms of housing design in which domestic tasks were no longer privatized but were taken care of in communal laundries, kitchens and nurseries.

As Hayden argues, these debates were largely forgotten in the following decades: during the interwar and post-war periods, the idea of the privatized nuclear family based on a male breadwinner and female housewife became increasingly hegemonic. However, from the early 1960s onwards, a new wave of feminist critics identified this form of family life as merely a justification for – or even the cause of – gender inequalities. While it should be stressed that there was significant disagreement among feminists about how the family maintained male dominance, some key themes emerged from these debates. First, as I suggested earlier, many critics argued that there was nothing natural about women's responsibility for domestic life. While it might appear that women were more biologically suited to the roles of wife, mother and home-maker because they were more nurturing, many feminists claimed that women's 'nurturing nature' was not a product of biology but culture. Second, for many critics, the nuclear family maintained male dominance because it made women economically dependent on male breadwinners and this made it difficult to challenge male power within the home. Third, because the labour women performed in the home was not recognized as 'proper' labour, it was not seen as worthy of payment and this maintained women's economic dependence on men. Fourth, for some feminists, housework was degrading work: women had been relegated to performing those tasks that were boring, invisible, monotonous and mundane drudgery and that were carried out in isolation. Fifth, the roles of wife and mother taught women to sacrifice their own sense of personal identity and to put the needs of their husbands and children before their own, living through others. Sixth, numerous feminists pointed out that while the home was frequently represented as a haven from the world of work and a site of leisure, domestic leisure was in fact only an option for men: for women, the home was the workplace. Finally, it was argued that the roles of wife and mother taught women to sacrifice their own sense of personal identity and to put the needs of their husbands and children before their own.

Housework does not just involve a series of tasks such as hoovering, ironing, cooking and childcare, it also involves overall responsibility for producing and maintaining domestic life. The role of housewife ascribes women responsibility for producing and maintaining domestic life (although financial control of domestic life has frequently been in the hands of a male breadwinner) and this means that women's ability to be 'properly feminine' may also be judged by their ability to keep a 'good home'. As Pauline Hunt (1995: 302–3) explains:

At first glance a houseworker, especially a full-time houseworker, would seem to be largely free of social pressure in the performance of her highly privatized job.

> The main influence on her performance would seem to come from the recipients of her labours – her own family members. Certainly a large part of her job is geared to the accommodation of her family's needs and desires. Yet the wider community makes itself felt, and not only through the pressure of expectations exerted on her by her neighbours [etc.] . . . There is also a more general pressure resulting from her perception of her domestic role in society, which tends to be reinforced through cultural images and messages relating to domestic practice.

Not only are images of 'good housekeeping' reinforced through cultural forms such as women's magazines (see, for example, Winship 1987), but, as Hunt suggests, women may feel themselves judged by others' perceptions of what makes a 'good home' and a 'good home-maker'. These pressures are less likely to be experienced by men because 'the roles of wife and mother are intimately tied to expectations for doing housework . . . and displayed through outcomes such as a clean house' (Bianchi et al. 2000: 194). Furthermore, as I explore in more detail in the next section, these ideologies are not simply imposed on women but are also reproduced through their own practices. A number of studies reveal how women refuse help around the house because they believe that male partners lack the appropriate skills and dispositions to carry out domestic tasks up to 'feminine' standards (Hunt 1995; Madigan and Munro 1999).

One of the central issues that emerged in second-wave feminist debates about the sexual division of labour was about whether women should receive wages for housework. Many feminists agreed that it was essential to recognize that housework was actually a form of labour comparable to the productive work carried out by men in the public sphere. Furthermore, many feminists agreed that 'the principle of the wage-earner and his dependents, of the husband who contributes cash while the wife contributes household labour, is not a division of labour between equals but an unequal exchange in which men's interests predominate' (Barrett and McIntosh 1982: 65). However, critics and activists disagreed about whether giving wages for housework was a solution. For proponents of wages for housework, a wage would not only give social and economic recognition to a housewife's labour as proper work, but it would also make women less economically dependent on men and, therefore, reduce men's power over women. However, other feminists criticized the idea of wages for housework, arguing that this simply reproduced women's position within the sexual division of labour. The point, they claimed, was to recognize that women were equal to men and give them equal opportunities to earn equal wages in the paid labour market rather than maintain their isolation and responsibility for boring, monotonous work within the home (Malos 1980).

Since then, the idea that full-time home-makers should receive a wage for their work has declined, not least because of married women's increasing participation in paid labour. However, this does not mean that housework has disappeared, although there is evidence to suggest that dual-income families are outsourcing domestic labour, whether this consists of buying ready-prepared meals, buying childcare in a crèche or employing other people to do domestic labour within the home (a point I return to below). Furthermore, it is important to note that many social and economic systems still operate *as if* households contain a full-time home-maker. For example, the timing of school days and school terms presume that there is someone in a household who is not in full-time employment while the fact that women's earnings remain less than their male counterparts suggests that female wages are in some way 'supplementary'.

Therefore, more recent research has focused on whether married women's increased participation in paid labour has resulted in a more egalitarian division of labour within the home or whether women carry the 'dual burden' of paid labour and unpaid domestic labour, taking on board what Hochschild et al. (2003) call 'the second shift' when they return home from a day of paid work. While it is frequently difficult to identify precisely the extent to which there has been a transformation in the sexual division of labour, a range of studies suggest that while there has been a shift towards a more egalitarian division of domestic labour in dual-income households, housework is still not shared equally by male and female partners (Warde and Hetherington 1993; Warde 1997; Bianchi et al. 2000; Sullivan 2000; Oates and McDonald 2006). Furthermore, research suggests that women frequently remain responsible for ongoing, mundane, repetitive, everyday tasks while men are more likely to perform larger but more 'episodic' household work such as DIY or cooking a meal for a special event (Bianchi et al. 2000; Nordenmark and Nyman 2003). As Bianchi et al. (2000: 218) conclude from their study of gendered divisions in domestic labour in the USA, although men are doing more housework and women are doing less housework, 'the someone doing housework today is still usually female'.

Significantly, relatively new domestic tasks such as recycling are still accommodated within existing divisions of labour (Oates and McDonald 2006: 428). Some critics have suggested that unequal divisions of gendered labour are not only the result of men's disinclination to take on what has traditionally been seen as feminine work but also women's perceptions that domestic life is still, ultimately, a feminine responsibility (Baxter 2000; Sullivan 2000). This is because 'housework does not have a neutral meaning but rather its performance by women and men helps to define and express gender relations within households' (Bianchi et al. 2000: 194). Furthermore, women may often feel 'morally obligated to care' for others, especially children, because this is so closely connected to the cultural expectations of motherhood (Duncan et al. 2003: 310).

Many critics increasingly acknowledge that some of the premises that have underpinned studies of housework are problematic. 'Housework' is not simply a neutral term within second-wave feminism but, as I go on to explain later in the chapter, is frequently associated with trivial, boring or unskilled domestic tasks performed by women in unequal power relations. For example, in a classic second-wave feminist study, Christine Delphy (1984) argued that unpaid housework is work done on behalf of others. However, this leaves no space for conceptualizing the position of the single person who understands cleaning the toilet as a form of housework (Pink 2004). In another classic second-wave feminist study, Ann Oakley (1974) defines housework as the labour performed by the housewife on behalf of other members of the nuclear family. As Sarah Oerton (1997: 425) points out, these ideas imply 'that *only* women/ wives can engage in personal servicing of other household members and *only* men/ husbands can indirectly "help out", since a husband's contribution is *necessarily* assigned the status of "gift" or "favour"'. Because second-wave critics such as Oakley assume that the relationship between gender and domestic labour can only be under-stood in terms of the power relationships between men and women in a heterosexual couple, Oerton argues, then it becomes virtually impossible to think about how people who live outside of heteronormative relationships organize domestic labour without thinking about them as somehow 'outside' gender.

Some of the early feminist studies of the sexual division of labour neglect the fact that housework takes place in all kinds of homes, not just in nuclear families. Indeed, housework is a fundamental part of everyday life for the vast majority of households and, for many people, it is a key home-making practice. However, if a range of prac-tices such as cooking, cleaning, laundry and childcare are simply subsumed within the concept of 'housework', it is easy to miss the variety of meanings that might be associated with these 'domestic practices' in everyday life (Chapman 2004). For example, Jo VanEvery (1997) points out that some people might experience cooking as leisure while others may experience it as domestic labour; likewise, the same person might experience cooking as either leisure or labour depending on the context. For this reason, knowing who does the cooking tells us little about the meanings that people bring to this practice. Furthermore, VanEvery suggests that rather than assuming that certain domestic practices are already sexed or gendered – for example, cooking is women's work or feminine – it is necessary to consider how the meaning of domestic tasks are not necessarily fixed (although, at the same time, their meaning is not neces-sarily open as well). Moreover, the meaning of masculinities and femininities may be produced, performed and negotiated through domestic practices. Therefore, we need to think about how domestic practices do not take place within a pre-given entity such as 'the family', 'household' or 'home', but instead how the meanings of home and family are produced, reproduced and negotiated through domestic practices. These ideas are explored in more detail in the next section.

However, before moving on, it is important to remember that the politics of domestic labour are not just about gender but also about 'race', ethnicity and class. While there was a significant decline in the use of domestic servants in the interwar period (see Chapter 2), the use of paid domestic labour is again on the increase with an estimated 2.7 million British households employing some form of domestic help within their own homes at the beginning of the twenty-first century (Cox 2006). The increasing use of domestic help is both a product of middle-class women's experience of 'time poverty' as they pursue career success, and of limited employment opportunities for working-class and migrant women. However, Nicky Gregson and Michelle Lowe (1994: 232–3) argue that middle-class women increasingly use domestic labour to create more 'quality' time for family togetherness and leisure, and to enable them to invest in the more rewarding aspects of domestic labour such as childcare and baking while delegating 'the messiest aspects of daily household reproduction' to working-class women (see also Hochschild 2000 on the USA).

Thinking about paid domestic labour not only highlights how 'employer-employee relations have been re-established between the middle class and working classes around domestic labour' (Gregson and Lowe 1994: 231) but also demonstrates how domestic cultures intersect with processes of globalization. There is a long history of both forced and voluntary migration and domestic work, including the forced movement of people as slaves. Amid wider forms of globalization today, migrant female labour from nations like the Phillipines and Sri Lanka are encouraged to earn foreign currency abroad as domestics in order to help pay off the national debt back home, being employed to care for families in wealthy nations in insufficiently regulated working conditions, while having to leave their own families behind (Cox 2006: 4). As dual-career families in the West become increasingly dependent on labour from elsewhere to help manage their time, 'the space and time of home in the Western world is intimately connected to the work of women from poorer countries' (Johnson and Lloyd 2004: 157; see also Ehrenreich and Hochschild 2003). This also reconfigures the relationship between public and private in new ways on a global scale.

Home is not only a site of work for household members but is also for those who are employed to work in other people's homes. Many first- and second-wave feminists tended to see the politics of domestic labour primarily in terms of gender inequalities. As I explained earlier, many first-wave feminists believed that paid working-class domestic labourers would enable them to reorganize housework so it was not simply identified as women's work (Hayden 1982; McFeeley 2001). Some second-wave feminists also suggested that paid domestic labour might help resolve the sexual politics of the home: 'For those who can afford it, paying someone to clean the house or cook meals is preferable to making it a duty of one household member' (Barrett and McIntosh 1982: 144). What such solutions fail to address is the extent to which the politics of domestic labour have not only been structured by gender but also 'race', ethnicity and class.

Housework and home-making

In this section I examine how cooking is both a form of gendered domestic labour and a gendered home-making practice. In the process, I want to explore three interrelated issues that develop some of the themes introduced in the previous section. First, I use the example of cooking to think about how seemingly routine domestic practices are also practices through which people *make* homes. While cooking is not the only form of domestic labour that is a home-making practice (see Pink 2004), it does provide a particularly rich example of how everyday household tasks produce the very experience of home and family. This allows us to see how housework plays a crucial role in producing domestic cultures. Second, I consider how 'feeding work' (DeVault 1991) is also very often feminine work. In the process I go beyond studies that document continuing inequalities in the amount of cooking that men and women actually do, and think about how gendered identities are created and practised through feeding work. Cooking practices do not simply reflect pre-existing gendered identities but actively contribute to the ways in which gendered identities are constructed, experienced and lived. Finally, I explore how domestic practices cannot straightforwardly be classified as labour or leisure and use the example of cooking to explore how the meaning of domestic practices needs to be understood in relation to specific contexts and social relations.

The meaning of cooking and eating is frequently intimately bound up with ideas of home and family. The formally recognized start of a new family home through marriage is frequently marked with gifts of items for preparing, serving and eating meals, and these items often figure on wedding lists (Bugge 2003; Purbrick 2007). In social policy governing the allocation of state benefits in the UK, the existence of shared meals is seen to indicate that a couple are cohabiting (Charles 1995). Conversely, a lack of shared meals between partners can be used as an indication of the breakdown of a marriage in divorce proceedings, and mealtimes are often used as a way of maintaining a sense of a 'normal' family life for children following a divorce (Burgoyne and Clarke 1983).

As Moisio et al. (2004: 361) argue, home-made 'food stands as a metonym for the family and marks family roles and relationships in material form' (see also Lupton 1996). Ritual meals associated with religious days and national holidays are also seen as a way of bringing together dispersed extended family members, affirming the connection between home, family and food. Films focusing on the preparation and eating of Thanksgiving dinner in the USA – for example, *What's Cooking* (2000) and *Pieces of April* (2003) – also represent the way in which these ritual feasts are not only privatized culinary celebrations of home and family but also connect together many families across a nation through a common temporal experience of cooking and eating. Ritual forms of eating also connect homes and families with a wider community in other ways. For example, the Jewish *Seder* ritual enables a **diasporic** community to experience a sense of togetherness between homes through domestic food consumption.

However, its not only ritual meals that evoke and embody home and family. Research into the meaning of domestic cooking documents how people understand their everyday practices in relation to ideas about what constitutes a 'proper meal'. Conceptions of the 'proper meal' are largely cultural and emotional rather than nutritional and are closely entwined with images of home and family. While the notion of the 'proper meal' is frequently tied to particular foodstuffs – and in the UK frequently is epitomized by the 'traditional' roast dinner – there are also particular forms of domestic social relations that are integral to its production and consumption. Research demonstrates that people believe that 'proper meals' bring the household members together around the dinner table to participate in the collective experience of family (hence, the phrase 'the family that eats together, stays together'). Research also demonstrates that people equate a 'proper meal' with a 'home-cooked' meal. Home cooking is central to many people's very understanding of the meaning of home: unlike commercially produced food, home cooking is understood to be personal, and laced with intimacy and warmth provided by the cook (Murcott 1983; Charles and Kerr 1988; Warde 1997; Mitchell 1999; Ashley et al. 2004; Moisio et al. 2004; Bugge and Almås 2006).

It is the intervention of the cook that provides the final ingredient that is absolutely central to many people's conception of what makes a 'proper meal'. A home-cooked meal is seen as emotionally as well as physically nourishing because it is the product of female labour – and, more specifically, motherly labour – in which food is an expression of care and love (Moisio et al. 2004). The significance of women's responsibility for cooking within the sexual division of labour, therefore, goes beyond simply producing meals that other people consume, and involves the production and reproduction of a whole range of cultural and emotional qualities and entities such as home and family.

In her research into the relationship between cooking, femininity and family, Marjorie DeVault (1991) suggests that providing meals for the family isn't just about the practice of cooking but involves a whole range of feeding work. 'Feeding the family', she argues, is comprised of a wide range of tasks such as planning and shopping. It is also geared towards a complex range of outcomes: for example, giving family members pleasure, producing 'interesting' and 'proper' meals and producing the experience of family life itself by creating mealtimes as a family event. She also demonstrates how feeding work involves a vast amount of mental, manual and emotional labour that remains largely invisible. This is captured in Luce Giard's (1998: 200) description of the practices involved in 'doing-cooking':

> One has to organize, decide and anticipate. One must memorize, adapt, modify, invent and take into consideration Aunt Germaine's likes and little Francois's dislikes, satisfy the prescriptions for Catherine's temporary diet, and vary the menu at the risk of having the whole family cry out in indignation.

Likewise, DeVault (1991: 90) documents the amount of feminine labour that goes into producing the 'quality time' that is necessary for people to experience family life:

> Feeding work . . . reconciles the diverse schedules and projects of individuals so as to produce points of intersection when they come together for group events. Within the group that this kind of scheduling creates, attention to individual needs and preferences establishes the family as a social space that is personalized.

Feeding work needs to be understood as a form of domestic labour that is also central to everyday domestic life and an ongoing home-making practice. By providing food that is imbued with values associated with domestic cultures such as intimacy, warmth and the personal – and by scheduling time for household members to come together as a group – cooking is also about creating and reproducing the experience of home. Home-making practices such as feeding work do not just produce the material and social aspects of domestic life, they also produce the emotional experience of home. An integral dimension of these home-making practices is the activity of 'caring for' which creates the experience of 'being cared for' that is a central element of the meanings that many people associate with home.

However, as DeVault's work makes clear, the creation of home as a 'care-full' environment is the result of an extensive amount of female labour. For DeVault (1991: 4), caring is an invisible activity performed by women on behalf of their families. Indeed, she suggests that caring work is 'undefined, unacknowledged activity central to women's identity'. By thinking of feeding practices as caring practices, she demonstrates the complex relationship between gender and domestic labour. She suggests that women's responsibility for domestic caring is not created by 'an extraneous gender ideology' that is imposed on women (Warde 1997: 130). Instead, domestic caring work is one of the primary ways in which women perform and inhabit their gendered identity. DeVault (1991: 18) argues that 'it is not just that women do more of the work of feeding, but also that feeding work has become one of the primary ways women "do" gender . . . By feeding the family, a woman conducts herself as recognizably womanly.' This is not because women are more 'naturally' caring – as nineteenth-century ideologies of separate spheres suggested – but because of the ways in which femininity and caring have become so culturally intertwined. As Beverly Skeggs (1997: 67) suggests, 'the link between femininity, caring and motherhood contributes towards naturalizing and normalizing the social relations of caring'.

DeVault's work also offers a way of understanding why the sexual division of labour is relatively resistant to change. While research suggests that men are increasingly contributing to home cooking, and while domestic cooking is no longer straightforwardly coded as feminine, caring remains a feminine competence and disposition. In her study of domestic cooking practices in the UK, Frances Short (2006: 78) found that it was assumed that women did the cooking but men could *choose* to cook. She argues that 'there is an implicit understanding that, whilst men can "take on" cooking and being a cook, women have to reject or "offload" it'. In a similar vein, in their recent study of domestic dinners among young families in Norway, Annechen Bahr Bugge and Reidar Almås (2006: 210) found that women took responsibility for managing feeding work while men were delegated the role of assistant. While these women did not see their cooking practices as a means of subordinating themselves to their husbands, they understood these practices as a way of 'caring for children' and producing both home and family.

Therefore, while men may be taking on an increasing amount of feeding work, the successful performance of masculinity is not dependent on their 'success' in caring for the family. Indeed, research demonstrates that women are frequently responsible for everyday domestic cookery whereas men are happy to contribute to elaborate meals that become a 'special event' and are associated with leisure rather than labour (DeVault 1991; Bell and Valentine 1997; Kemmer 1999; Roos et al. 2001). This masculine disposition towards cooking is often reaffirmed in TV cookery. For example, in *The Naked Chef* series, Jamie Oliver is often shown doing domestic cookery for special events such as parties and celebrations in his 'free time', offering his guests a culinary performance in his kitchen and presenting dishes that are 'real theatre' (Oliver 2000: 153; see Hollows 2003a. For more on representations of masculinity and cooking, see also Moseley 2001 and Hollows 2002). Likewise, because the men interviewed in Short's (2006: 78) study 'saw themselves as having a real choice of whether to cook or not', they also had the ability to view cooking as a leisure experience.

This provides further evidence that the meaning of domestic practices is contextual. Studies of the extent to which men and women cook tells us little about what these practices *mean* within the home. Cooking can be experienced as a leisure activity or as labour and an obligation to others. Cooking may be about expressing care for others and the creation of a family identity but it can also be about expressing creativity. While it would be rash to claim that any of these meanings are straightforwardly gendered – or that it was impossible for the same person to experience all these meanings of cooking in different instances – research does suggest that men's contribution to cooking does not incur the same anxieties as it does for women. This is because domestic femininities are associated with providing food for others in a way that domestic masculinities are not.

However, while feeding work is often oriented towards producing the 'ideal' experience of home, ideas of 'the proper meal' create ideas about 'normal' practice that relatively few women can live up to. Domestic femininities – like domestic masculinities – are multiple and cross-cut by class, 'race', sexuality, ethnicity, religion, nation and generation. For example, for women living in financial poverty, the act of putting food on the table may be an 'achievement' in itself (DeVault 1991: 201). Likewise, while convenience foods are frequently pathologized – and linked to everything from the decline of family life to child obesity – they are not only often relatively inexpensive foods but also respond to an increasing experience of time scarcity (see Chapter 7). Furthermore, there is little research on the relationship between cooking and home in single-person households or same-sex relationships and theories of 'feeding the family' frequently identify domestic femininity with the position of mother.[1] Therefore, while domestic practices such as cooking need to be understood as home-*making* practices, more research is needed on the range of ways in which potentially diverse notions of home are created through these everyday activities.

Feminism and the politics of domesticity

As this chapter has made clear, feminists have made an invaluable contribution towards understanding domestic cultures. They have demonstrated that home is a place of labour not simply leisure; that home can be a site of conflict and danger rather than a sanctuary; and that the organization of domestic life is frequently predicated upon – and works to reproduce – gender inequality. However, there remain problems with the ways in which home has been conceptualized within feminism.

In this section I explore these problems by examining debates about how feminists have conceptualized the value of domestic practices. I begin by exploring a series of key arguments within second-wave feminism that condemn the home as a problem and which are predicated on the assumption that there is little of value to feminism in domestic life. I then move on to a second set of arguments that celebrate the domestic as a female-centred space that might offer a model from which to improve the public sphere. After an examination of why both these positions are problematic, I finish the section by exploring the work of feminist critics who refuse to simply condemn or celebrate home and who attempt to develop a more complex understanding of the relationships between feminism, gender and domesticity.

Giles (2004: 141–2) observes that, in many second-wave feminist narratives, ' "leaving home" . . . is a necessary condition of liberation' (see also Felski 2000; Johnson and Lloyd 2004).[2] Within second-wave feminism, the home was frequently represented as a place in which women are confined, isolated and powerless, where they are sentenced to a life of drudgery and lose all sense of identity. Likewise, these conditions were associated with a specific form of feminine identity embodied in the figure of the housewife. As I go on to explain, second-wave feminists frequently represented domesticity as 'something that must be left behind if women were to become "modern", emancipated subjects' (Giles 2004: 142). In this way, second-wave feminism frequently drew on the assumptions of other theories of modernity that privileged the public sphere as the site of politics, identity and history and found little of value in either private life or the housewives whose lives were defined by domesticity.

One of the clearest articulations of such a position can be found in Betty Friedan's *The Feminine Mystique* (1963), one of the foundational texts of **liberal feminism**. Like many other American critics in this period (see Chapter 3), Friedan's critique centred on the suburbs, which were identified as conformist and claustrophobic, and organized around a mass-produced consumer culture. Speaking as a suburban housewife herself, Friedan set out to reveal a further unspoken problem with suburban life: in the suburbs were thousands of educated middle-class women who had turned their back on the world of work to invest in domestic life.[3] Instead of making them happy, she claimed, domesticity was making them ill – suburban women were suffering from 'the problem with no name' characterized by feelings of failure, of nothingness, of 'is this all there is?'

Friedan argued that this 'problem' was caused by 'the feminine mystique' that was promoted through women's magazines and advertising and which equated being a fulfilled woman with being 'healthy, beautiful, educated [up to a point], concerned only with her husband, her children and her home' (Friedan 1963: 13). Taking on the role of 'the happy housewife heroine', Friedan argued, did an immense amount of psychological harm to women: the drudgery involved in doing housework produced fatigue and breakdown. Furthermore, because women were encouraged to see themselves as wives and mothers, they lost any sense of their own identity. For this reason, Friedan believed that the only solution was for women to reject their investment in domesticity and understand that it would never bring them any sense of fulfilment. Instead, she advocated that they try to find their 'real' identity by pursuing higher education, getting a rewarding career and staking out a place in the public sphere.

Friedan clearly values the qualities associated with the public sphere over those associated with the private sphere. However, while she claims to speak 'as a housewife', she also clearly has very little sympathy or regard for them or their work. The feminine mystique, she claims, produces a particular mode of feminine identity – 'the housewife' who:

> stunts her intelligence to become childlike, turns away from individual identity to become an anonymous biological robot in a docile mass. She becomes less than human, preyed upon by outside pressures, and herself preying on her husband and children. And the longer she conforms, the less she feels as if she really exists. She looks for security in things . . . she lives a vicarious life through mass daydreams and through her husband and children.
>
> (Friedan 1963: 296–7)

Housework also occupies a paradoxical role in Friedan's argument. It is represented as labour – and this is manifested in countless references to housework as 'drudgery' – but it isn't 'real' or 'socially valuable' labour because it is organized around consumption rather than production. Furthermore, she frequently conflates the identity of the housewife with what she regards to be the boring, degrading and monotonous nature of housework, suggesting that it is labour that is best suited to 'the mentally retarded' or an eight-year-old child (Friedan 1963: 244–5).

There are numerous problems with Friedan's work but, in this context, I want to concentrate on two key issues. The first problem is that she ignores how the experience of femininity is cross-cut by 'race' and class. Friedan's housewife is profoundly middle class and the solution that she presents to 'the problem with no name' is that women should claim the same rights and entitlements in the workplace as (middle-class) men. At one point she comments that 'hundreds of able educated suburban housewives . . . apply for jobs as receptionists or saleswomen, jobs well below their actual abilities (Friedan 1963: 34). In this way Friedan tends to see work as an identity project rather than a means of earning money: for many working-class women, the jobs that Friedan dismisses would have represented a move upwards in the job market. Indeed, she also neglects the number of women who would have been employed as 'domestics' to help out with middle-class women's housework. Furthermore, if being trapped within the home caused white middle-class women problems, the idea of being a full-time suburban mother may have seemed like an impossible dream to many African-American women (hooks 1991).

The second problem is that Friedan clearly 'disidentifies' with the housewife, her work and domestic culture as a whole.[4] While highlighting the boredom that might be induced by the repetitive nature of housework, she also represents the 'modern housewife as a subject rather than object of boredom' (Johnson and Lloyd 2004: 121). In this way Friedan constructs a feminist identity as anti-home and anti-housewife. Women who invest in domestic femininity and domestic culture are implicitly represented as antifeminist and, in the process, Friedan helps to set up an opposition between the feminist and the housewife that would continue to haunt much feminist theory (Brunsdon 2000).

Friedan is certainly not the only feminist critic to condemn both the housewife and domestic work as lacking little value. Studies of the sexual division of labour have not only questioned the unequal division of domestic tasks between men and women but have frequently represented housework as boring, monotonous, laborious, degrading and isolated drudgery. A good example can be found in the work of British **socialist feminist** Ann Oakley (1974: 1) who also denied that housework was 'proper' work. Like Friedan, she also believed that the role of housewife denied women any real sense of identity – 'housework is directly opposed to the possibility of human self-actualization' (Oakley 1974: 222). Furthermore, Oakley (1974: 225) argued that people who claimed that housework could be creative were misguided in their attempt to make 'housework into something bigger, better, more difficult and more rewarding'. Such claims, she argued, hid the fact that there could be no creativity when housework consisted of 'the frenetic pursuit of goals outside oneself'.

While Oakley's analysis is certainly more reasoned and theorized than that of Friedan, she also reinstates the opposition between the identities of the feminist and the housewife. The housewife, she argues, has an 'emotional investment in continued subordination' because she has married her oppressor and because she has no right to any status of her own (Oakley 1974: 233). Furthermore, Oakley (1974: 233) claims that 'An affirmation of contentment with the housewife role is actually a form of antifeminism, whatever the gender of the person who displays it. Declared contentment with a subordinate status – which the housewife role undoubtedly is – is a rationalization of inferior status.'

The legacy of these arguments is important in understanding feminist theories of domestic culture. First, by seeing the role of housewife as 'antifeminist', Oakley reproduces an opposition between 'the feminist' and 'the housewife' so that the roles appear mutually exclusive and antagonistic. From such a position there is no way of thinking about how the two identities can be articulated because, as Johnson and Lloyd (2004: 90) observe, the housewife is seen as 'an inflexibly gendered *identity*' rather than 'a form of gendered *labour*'. But the housewife is not simply a monolithic form of domestic femininity and nor does housework have a fixed meaning. There is considerable diversity between – and there have been significant changes in – 'what it means to "run" homes and "do" families' (Martens and Casey 2007: 226). Furthermore, whether housework and caring is 'feminist' or 'antifeminist', it still needs to be actually done by someone. By associating the identity of the feminist with someone who works full time outside the home, critics such as Friedan risk 'alienating women whose lives are defined by caregiving' (Williams 2000: 145).

Second, as this suggests, housework doesn't have a single meaning. Despite Oakley's assertion that there can be no 'real' sense of creativity or identity as a result of doing housework, as Chapter 2 demonstrated, other studies have emphasized how housework can be used as a source of demonstrating skill or a source of pleasure or power. Furthermore, the opportunity to have a home might well be experienced as a privilege that offered the right to claim a full identity for working-class women who had been denied this opportunity due to inequalities of both 'race' and class. As Joan Williams (2000: 157) argues, 'Feminists' imagery of the family as the locus of subordination seems most convincing to women otherwise privileged by class and race; to working-class women, it may seem instead (or as well) a haven against the injuries of class'. Moreover, 'domestic practitioners' (Martens and Scott 2005) have used their skills, experience and knowledge to build collective identities and take action within the public sphere (Johnson and Lloyd 2004). The home itself can be an important site of politics: as bell hooks (1991: 42) argues, 'it has been primarily the responsibility of black women to construct household spaces of care and nurturance in the face of the brutal harsh reality of racist oppression, of sexist domination'.

Finally, by homogenizing the range of tasks that contribute to the creation and maintenance of domestic life, these second-wave feminist arguments reproduce the assumption that domestic practices are of little social or cultural value. Rather than revaluing women's contribution to modernity through their domestic work, these arguments challenged the gendering of spheres while rarely 'question[ing] the separation of work and home life' (Johnson and Lloyd 2004: 154). In these second-wave arguments, 'the feminist resolves the tension between domesticity and public achievement by leaving the former at home for the latter' (Johnson and Lloyd 2004: 17).

If these arguments condemn both domestic life and women's work within the home, there was an alternative second-wave feminist position – particularly within American feminism – which celebrated the values of domestic culture, drawing on elements of nineteenth-century **domestic feminism**. Victorian domestic feminists reproduced the idea of gendered spheres, arguing that women were 'naturally' more suited to domestic life than men because they were best suited to being moral guardians as they had a 'natural' connection to virtue and self-sacrifice. From this perspective it was women's separation from the immoral world of commerce and industry that contributed to their higher virtue. As a result, domestic feminists claimed, women should be given authority to arbitrate on matters in the public sphere because their investments in domesticity made them morally superior to men (Hayden 1982; Matthews 1987).

Some second-wave feminists would draw on this relationship between feminine virtue and self-sacrifice in order to develop theories that celebrated women's domestic role. For example, the cultural feminism of the 1970s celebrated women's difference from men and saw the home as a site for nurturing 'a female counter-culture' in which domestic skills and crafts could be mobilized as a way of challenging a society organized around patriarchal values (Echols 1989: 51). In the 1980s a related position emerged among a diverse range of second-wave feminist critics who shifted towards 'a "pro-family" stance' that echoed aspects of domestic feminism in its celebration of 'traditionally feminine qualities, particularly those associated with mothering' (Stacey 1986: 222).

However, one of the most developed cultural feminist positions that drew on elements of domestic feminism can be found in the work of Carol Gilligan (1982). Gilligan argued that women possess 'an ethic of care' and their 'moral development is distinctly different from that of men . . . They display greater compassion and empathy' (Segal 1987: 145–6). Gilligan implies that it is women's position as mothers that make them inherently more selfless, caring and self-sacrificing – and hence, more virtuous – than men. While the public sphere is governed by masculine self-interest, she argues, domestic cultures nurture more humane values, values that have been lost in the pursuit of individual achievement in the public sphere (J. Williams 1991). Elements of this position have been reproduced more recently within some strands of ecofeminism (see Mies and Shiva 1993).

These feminist positions that focus on women's essential *difference* from men seek to revalue women's contribution to social life through their role as caregivers within the home. Furthermore, they do not simply associate domestic cultures with stasis and conservatism but demonstrate how they are the basis for a vibrant and rich feminine cultural tradition that counters the values of self-interest and competition that characterize the public sphere. However, these arguments are also deeply problematic because they assume that there is a universal feminine identity tied to women's position as mothers. Furthermore, these arguments frequently locate women's difference to men in terms of biological differences between the sexes. For example, Gilligan claims that women have a universal feminine 'voice' based on their role as mothers that reveals their 'real' femininity. However, this argument rests on the assumption that feminine identities are 'natural' rather than cultural. Such ideas are deeply problematic because they naturalize differences between men and women and, in the process, can work to legitimate the existing sexual division of labour. For example, these ideas can support the idea that women are best suited to caregiving roles within the home and are ill-suited for the competitive world of the professional workplace (J. Williams 1991).

So far in this section I have identified two key theoretical approaches to domesticity within second-wave feminism and demonstrated how there are problems with each approach. These two approaches attempt to offer different solutions to what Johnson and Lloyd (2004: 16) call 'the tension between domesticity and public achievement' that has haunted feminist thought. In the first approach, feminists such as Friedan suggested that women should leave domesticity behind in order to pursue public achievement. In the second approach, Gilligan suggests that women are better suited to the valuable work of caregiving in the home and psychologically unsuited to the ways in which public achievement has been defined in a patriarchal culture.

More recently some feminist critics have returned to the question of how to address this tension in more productive ways by arguing that it is necessary to rethink the relationships between public and domestic life and the ways in which these relationships are gendered. Rather than condemning domestic life as a site of degradation and boredom – or celebrating domestic cultures because they express feminine virtue – some critics have suggested that it is crucial to demonstrate that domestic life is the site of important cultural values, and that responsibility for the maintenance of these values should not simply lie with women.

In thinking about the important social and cultural work that is performed within the home, Iris Marion Young (1997: 151) seeks to revalue what has traditionally been women's work within the home. She criticizes the idea that home is simply a site of reproduction, stasis and monotonous work and explores how home-making is an ongoing process through which personal lives are given meaning and identities are created and anchored.[5] As Johnson and Lloyd (2004: 156) observe, 'in the making of home, developing its rituals and daily practices – including how and when the dishes are washed, the house is tidied and belongings are arranged – individuals and families are making meaningful lives for themselves' (and I explore how home-making practices create meaning in more detail in the next chapter). Furthermore, as I have already suggested, it is through the practices of meaning-making within the home that people may 'address the political issues that most affect our daily lives' which can form the basis for 'subversion and resistance' (hooks 1991: 48).

With the separation of spheres, domestic life became associated with cultural values such as caring that many people see as worthy of preservation. Johnson and Lloyd (2004: 160) suggest that, rather than abandoning these values, 'feminism has a responsibility to reassert the importance of these values in the public world in a way that challenges the separation of home and work life and the relegation of humane values to the home.' For Joan Williams (2000: 198–9), feminism should not abandon domestic traditions but instead think about how domesticity could be made to mean in different ways, 'bending domesticity into new configurations'. Drawing on the work of Judith Butler, she argues that domesticity is associated with important cultural values but these need to be used 'self-consciously' to destabilize the ways in which relationships to public and private spheres continue to be gendered and frame the way both men and women can live their lives. She suggests that 'we need to offer not a fated assault on domesticity but a new interpretation of it . . . identifying the parts of domesticity that must be left behind if we are to move closer to our ever-elusive ideals of equality' (J. Williams 2000: 160).

This argument is useful in thinking about how we conceptualize and theorize domestic cultures because it demonstrates how asserting the value of domestic life does not need to be tied to the maintenance of traditional gender roles (see also Silva 1999). Furthermore, in asking feminists to 'bend domesticity into new configurations', Williams opens up space to think about how domesticity is mobilized outside 'conventional' families. Many feminist theories of domestic life frequently assume that people continue to live in nuclear families when contemporary living arrangements are far more diverse than this. Furthermore, these theories often conflate women's experience of home with the experience of motherhood. By 'destabilizing' domesticity, it becomes possible to think how some of the values associated with domestic cultures can be used as a resource for not only rethinking gendered relationships to – and between – the public and the private, but also rethinking how domesticity can be made to mean in a diverse range of domestic living arrangements.

Conclusions

This chapter has explored feminist arguments about how home is a problem for women. Although the number of households organized around a full-time male breadwinner and a full-time female home-maker has decreased since the second-wave feminism of the 1960s and 1970s, the sexual division of labour within the home has proved far more resistant to change. As Joan Williams (2000: 27) argues, 'The shift of women into the workforce has undermined neither domesticity's linkage of women with caregiving nor its association of men with breadwinning.' However, as I argued above, this does not necessarily mean that home is an intrinsically negative space for women – the challenge that remains is to think about how the organization of domestic life might be transformed to make it more egalitarian while still recognizing that the activities associated with home have social and cultural value. This kind of transformation can only take place if the relationships between the public and private sphere – and the nature of both home and work – are also reconceptualized. However, as I go on to explore in more detail in Chapter 7, current social and cultural changes are transforming the relationships between public and private in ways that may reinforce inequalities based on class, 'race', ethnicity and gender.

This chapter has also highlighted how household tasks need to be also thought of as home-making practices. As I suggested in the previous section, these practices involve an active process of giving meaning to our everyday lives and creating an 'affirmation of personal and cultural identity' (Young 1997: 156). In the next chapter I explore these issues in much more detail by focusing on domestic consumption practices as home-making practices. However, while these ideas have been developed in much more depth in studies of consumption, it is important to remember that mundane household chores also play a crucial role in the process of making homes. Indeed, while the organization of chapters in this book suggests that domestic labour and domestic consumption are separate issues, this separation is largely artificial. Although academic research on domestic labour and domestic consumption has often been shaped by different questions and agendas, it is crucial to make connections – and identify the relationships – between these two fields of study.

Further reading

DeVault, M. (1991) *Feeding the Family: The Social Organization of Caring as Gendered Work*. Chicago: University of Chicago Press.

Friedan, B. (1963) *The Feminine Mystique*. New York: Dell.

Johnson, L. and Lloyd, J. (2004) *Sentenced to Everyday Life: Feminism and the Housewife*. Oxford: Berg.

Oakley, A. (1974) *The Sociology of Housework*. London: Martin Robertson.

Williams, J. (2000) *Unbending Gender: Why Family and Work Conflict and What to do about it*. New York: Oxford University Press.

Notes

1 There is little research on the meaning of cooking practices among households and families that do not conform to 'conventional' nuclear family structures. Ideas of 'normal' family meals work to 'other' those who live outside of 'normal' families (Bell and Valentine 1997). Nonetheless, feeding work is used to create a sense of 'family' outside nuclear and extended family patterns: for example in recent films that centre on gay relationships such as *Big Eden* (2000) and *Latter Days* (2003), preparing and sharing meals is represented as performing a crucial function in cementing relationships and establishing expanded notions of family.

2 This narrative is also central to many 'popular' novels associated with second-wave feminism. For more on these, see Coward (1980) and Whelehan (2005).

3 Friedan's claims to speak as a suburban housewife have been seen as deeply problematic by a number of critics: see, for example, Giles (2004), Johnson and Lloyd (2004) and Meyerowitz (1994). For more discussion of the problems with Friedan's work, see also Bowlby (1992), Hollows (2000, 2007) and Knight (1997).

4 For more on how processes of 'disidentification' have been used to think about the generational politics of feminism, see Brunsdon (2006).

5 However, her analysis rests on a problematic categorical distinction between housework and home-making in which the creative work of home-making is valued over 'merely instrumental' household tasks (Young 1997: 149). As I have already suggested, the meaning of these activities is frequently context-specific. Furthermore, as Pink (2004: 41) argues, 'housework and home creativity are not absolutely separate sorts of activity; both are performative activities and creative processes'.

5

HOME-MAKING: DOMESTIC CONSUMPTION AND MATERIAL CULTURE

Introduction

This chapter focuses on how people produce the meaning of domestic cultures through their consumption practices. As we saw in the last chapter, Young (1997) uses the concept of home-*making* to think about the ways in which people are actively engaged in creating and recreating the meaning of home – and the identities of the people who live there – through everyday practices. The meaning of home is also created, maintained and renegotiated through our engagement with material culture. These consumption practices do not simply involve the selection and purchase of goods: as Young (1997: 151) argues, 'homemaking consists in the activities of endowing things with living meaning, arranging them in space in order to facilitate the life activities of those to whom they belong, and preserving them, along with their meaning.' This chapter examines a wide range of studies that contribute to our understanding of these home-making practices.

The concept of consumption is crucial in understanding our relationships to the places we live. As Miller (1988: 354) observes, 'a theory of housing . . . has to be largely a theory of consumption'. Few people in the West build their own houses or apartments and so our primary relationship to the places we rent or buy is established through consumption rather than production. As we saw in Chapter 3, some critics have assumed that consumption involves little more than passively reproducing the meanings that are built-in to goods, whether these are houses, curtains or TV sets. However, more recently, many theorists have employed a more expansive understanding of consumption as an active process through which people engage with the world of goods. As Peter Jackson (1993: 209) argues, 'artefacts are not simply bought and "consumed" [that is, used up], but given meaning through their active incorporation in people's lives.'[1] In thinking about domestic culture, I draw on this understanding of consumption to think about how people use consumer goods to make homes and identities, and to establish relationships within – and beyond – the home (Clarke 1997). In the process I demonstrate how home-making practices aren't simply inward-facing and privatized but are also frequently 'stretched' to incorporate people or ideas that extend beyond the place of residence (Rose 2003).

Many of the forms of household labour discussed in the last chapter contribute to the process of making homes and could be thought of as forms of domestic consumption. However, in trying to show that domestic labour is just as important as paid labour in the public sphere, many feminist critics have approached 'domestic work as a form of production rather than "mere" consumption' (Casey and Martens 2007: 2). (For a more detailed explanation of why feminists have had an uneasy relationship with the concept of consumption, see Casey and Martens 2007, Martens and Casey 2007, Silva 2007 and Hollows 2007.) For second-wave feminists, the aim was to revalue how women's work had been conceptualized rather than revalue how consumption had been conceptualized. Therefore, although feminist research on the home shares much in common with research on domestic consumption, there has often been little dialogue between these two fields (Jackson and Moores 1995: 1). While the organization of this book does reproduce this division, it is crucial to recognize that consumption practices are frequently also a form of domestic labour. For example, while cleaning the toilet or reheating a can of beans or creating a 'family kitchen' might be experienced as leisure activities, they are also undoubtedly experienced as labour by many people. Therefore, despite the association between consumption and pleasure in the work of some theorists, my argument rests on the idea that many domestic consumption practices can also be thought of as domestic labour (Lury 1996).

Although this chapter focuses on the relationships between consumption and identity, it is important to remember that home-making also takes place within a wider context. While the housing and goods that are produced for us do not determine the meaning of domestic cultures, they nonetheless frame how we understand our homes and the ways in which we live in them. Indeed, dominant styles of house-form do no only place limits on how people create homes within nations, but Donna Birdwell-Pheasant and Denise Lawrence-Zúñiga (1999: 28) suggest that the globalization of Western house-forms has strengthened Western hegemony. They argue that global house-forms may have had a greater impact than global TV in their capacity to restructure 'the most intimate lives of people within their domestic settings'. Various forms of regulation also shape how we consume houses and construct the meaning of home, from social workers who may police the boundaries of what is an 'acceptable' domestic environment to building regulations that place limits on what home-owners can do to the physical infrastructure of their housing. Likewise, the ways in which home is represented and mediated also may have a significant impact on home-making strategies and, in the following section, I explore one aspect of how this, examining how the meaning of domestic culture, is constructed in lifestyle media.

In this chapter I explore three key areas of research that offer different ways of understanding how domestic consumption practices are used to create the meaning and experience of home. The next section explores whether the home has become a site in which people seek to construct and display distinctive lifestyles. I identify how the meaning of home is constructed in lifestyle TV and explore whether these dispositions towards home are reproduced in domestic consumption practices. In the process I assess the extent to which home has become a site in which we are free to construct lifestyles that enable us to *play* with identity.

The following section focuses on ethnographic studies of how people use domestic consumption practices to create, maintain and negotiate a sense of home. These studies enable us to understand the meanings people bring to their home-making activities and how the meaning of domestic cultures is frequently sustained through seemingly mundane everyday consumption practices. In the process, I identify how 'home' is an idea that has to be actively maintained. In the subsequent section I explore the relationship between material culture, domestic consumption and identity in more detail. I examine how the ways in which we relate to objects – and how we choose to arrange them – creates the foundations for our everyday practices and the ways in which we relate to a place called home (Young 1997). In the process I identify how the history and accumulated meanings attached to things not only enables home-making but also how they may constrain our ability to create a sense of home. As I go on to discuss, the places we live – and the things we use within these places – have a history that may shape the ways in which we interact with them.

Show homes? Lifestyle and consumption

Across a range of contemporary representations, the home is often imagined as a site for creating and displaying a lifestyle. The 2007 catalogue for the home furnishings giant IKEA opens with the invitation to 'Reclaim Your Own Way of Living' suggesting that:

> the best way to create a living home is to do it your way. Furnish it your way. Decorate it your way. Forget the expected or accepted look or style of the moment. It's your life, your home, your mind. And with IKEA, you can create a home that's as unique as your own family.

If IKEA promises that we can express our individuality and create new ways of living through our homes (if we buy their products), then similar approaches to home are found across a range of advertising for household products from air-fresheners to snacks. Likewise, the marketing of new homes increasingly draws on the language of lifestyle. Urban Splash, developers of upscale urban apartments in the UK, draw on a similar rhetoric to IKEA, offering their affluent customers 'SPACE TO LIVE. It's your life. Live it your way'. Other developers promise potential buyers the opportunity to buy into a more clearly defined lifestyle. For example, the MiCasa Group offer Harrow apartments that are 'more than just a home, but also a lifestyle choice' based around 'the ultimate "metropolitan" lifestyle' in a 'vibrant cosmopolitan setting'.[2] These marketing strategies share – and sometimes draw on – the discourses used by lifestyle media that promise to give us the knowledge and skills to transform our homes – and, in the process – our identities.

In this section I examine the argument that areas of everyday life have become lifestyled as a result of a series of wider social, economic and cultural changes, and explore how these arguments help us to understand how the home is represented in lifestyle media in terms of aesthetic choices and self-expression. However, I go on to argue that this emphasis on lifestyle does not mean that people primarily understand their homes in terms of lifestyle choices. Drawing on studies of domestic consumption, I suggest that not only do home-making activities offer limited opportunities for 'playing' with identity but also that, despite aesthetic differences, people frequently construct very similar conceptions of home through their domestic consumption practices.

Some theorists have suggested that the idea of lifestyle became increasingly important because of a shift from a **Fordist** to a **post-Fordist** consumer culture. Under Fordist methods of production, it was argued, there was little scope for lifestyle differentiation through consumption because industry was geared towards the mass production of similar goods. However, for a variety of reasons, by the early 1970s, mass production was no longer seen as a way to secure profits and industries increasingly diversified their product lines and aimed them at *niche* – rather than *mass* – markets (see Lee 1993 and Slater 1997 for a much more detailed account of these changes). Under post-Fordism, it has been argued, goods were now targeted at specific lifestyle groupings that were identified (and created) by advertising and marketing professionals. Design, packaging and advertising highlighted the differences between goods and how they could be used by people to *differentiate* themselves from others through their lifestyle (Mort 1988; Hebdige 1989). An increased emphasis on the aesthetic differences between goods also meant that an expanding range of commodities became subject to ideas of fashion. People were encouraged to replace objects that were 'out of fashion' – or 'aesthetically obsolescent' – rather than when they were worn out or broken (Lee 1993: 136). With a proliferating number of goods on offer, there was the potential for anxiety over what – and how – to consume goods to construct a distinctive lifestyle. As a result, it has been suggested that consumers became increasingly dependent on 'expert' advice from advertisers, women's and men's magazines, and lifestyle media.

Arguments about the shift to post-Fordism suggest that domestic cultures are increasingly characterized by a concern with questions of fashion, style and aesthetics and claim that people use their homes to construct and display a distinctive lifestyle and identity. There is plenty of evidence to suggest that we are encouraged to understand home in this way through the ways in which products are advertised and marketed. For example, the home furnishings store Habitat, launched in the UK in the mid-1960s, aimed to change the ways in which people understood their homes. The store invited its customers to use their fashionable and stylish furnishings to adopt a more playful approach to home as a lifestyle space. Likewise, even a relatively mundane commodity such as paint has become thoroughly linked to lifestyle choices. People who want to paint their homes are not only faced with choices about what kind of colour and finish they want but also what kind of lifestyle associations they want to construct through their choice of paint. Consumers must choose whether they want to make a cosmopolitan identification with 'Swedish' or 'Umbria', 'California' or 'Cotswolds', or whether they want to make an imaginative association with 'Edwardian', 'Georgian' or 'Victorian' eras.[3] However, while there is certainly an increasing invitation to think of homes in terms of lifestyle in the ways in which goods are promoted, as I go on to discuss below, this does not mean that this has necessarily changed the meaning of home.

Other critics have examined how the idea of lifestyle is linked to wider social and cultural changes. For example, Mike Featherstone (1991) suggests that aesthetics are increasingly important in the way people construct and experience everyday life. Consumer culture promotes the idea that our identities are no longer the product of traditional social identities such as class and encourages us to make self-conscious choices to construct distinctive lifestyles through an 'assemblage of goods, clothes, practices, experiences, appearance and bodily dispositions' (Featherstone 1991: 86). Similar themes can be found in Giddens's (1991) argument that there has been a 'detraditionalization' of established modes of modern life. In place of fixed identities that are 'handed down' to us, people are encouraged to reflexively make and remake their own identities. 'The more post-traditional the settings in which an individual moves', Giddens (1991: 81) suggests, 'the more lifestyle concerns the very core of self-identity, its making and remaking'. These arguments would suggest that home has lost any fixed meaning and is increasingly seen as an arena through which we undertake lifestyle projects by using consumer goods to create living spaces that construct a sense of self.

If creating our identity through lifestyle seems a daunting task, then lifestyle media promise to offer an education in how to use material culture to create a coherent sense of self. While lifestyle had a growing prominence in theoretical debates in the 1980s and 1990s, it also had an increasing presence in magazines and newspapers, and on TV. For example, new TV formats gave advice on how to 'inject lifestyle' into our domestic life by offering advice on how to 'improve' our interiors, gardens and cooking – and, in the process, 'improve' the self. While there is a longer history of TV programmes that offer advice about aspects of domestic life, these new lifestyle shows are distinguished by the type of advice they offer. Rather than demonstrating how 'amateur enthusiasts' can gain new skills to achieve transformations, lifestyle TV addresses an audience of consumers and focuses on the results of a transformation or 'makeover' (Brunsdon 2001: 54; see also Brunsdon 2004. For more on some of the key generic features of contemporary makeover television, see Moseley 2000). In the process, home-making was no longer represented in terms of practical skills but in terms of the spectacular transformation of domestic lifestyles. Furthermore, these shows make 'the private space of the home . . . a public spectacle' (Attwood 2005: 90; see also McElvoy forthcoming).

However, this is not to suggest that the representation of home in terms of lifestyle leads to deskilling. In addressing the audience as consumers rather than amateur artisans, some lifestyle shows emphasize the importance of acquiring design skills and, in the process, contribute to an aestheticization of home. As Feona Attwood (2005: 96) argues in her analysis of the UK show *Home Front*, domesticity is reconfigured as 'a design issue' (see also Taylor 2005). Indeed, Ruth Holliday (2005: 67) suggests that home and property TV offers the pleasure of 'consuming a design idea'. These forms of lifestyle media encourage the audience to understand – and work on – the aesthetic dimensions of domestic life through the application of design principles.

Many types of lifestyle TV demonstrate how the improvement of our homes will also effect an improvement of our lives and even 'the self' (Holliday 2005). In many ways the representation of home in these shows seems to support theories that suggest that lifestyle has become a dominant way of constructing the self and practising everyday life. Within the world of lifestyle TV, everyday life becomes aestheticized: these programmes encourage us to play with different domestic styles and different styles of life through our use of consumer goods. Indeed, given that TV is a visual medium, it is perhaps unsurprising that home interiors shows are preoccupied with the representation of home as an expression of a visual idea. However, as I go on to discuss below, this does not necessarily mean that the meaning of domestic culture has necessarily undergone a fundamental change.

The idea that people are free to reflexively construct their own lifestyle through 'projects of the self' rests on the assumption that traditional sources of identity – for example, gender and class – no longer play a key role in structuring everyday life, including domestic life. Suzanne Reimer and Deborah Leslie's (2004) study of domestic consumption demonstrates that people who live alone can often experience the home as a place in which they have the freedom to define and express their identity outside the constraints of the workplace. However, they suggest, this does not mean that domestic consumption is best understood as a self-reflexive and individualistic activity because consumption practices are frequently oriented towards the negotiation of 'a (collective) household identity' (Reimer and Leslie 2004: 192–3). Furthermore, DeVault (1991) and Miller (1998) suggest that women's consumption practices are not organized around the self but around caring for others. As should be clear from earlier discussions in the book, the ability to experience the home as a site to 'be yourself' – or create 'the self' – is constrained by power relations within the home and by wider expectations about the performance of 'appropriate' identities.[4]

An increased emphasis on the aesthetic dimensions of domestic culture does not necessarily signal the erosion of traditional class divisions either. Pierre Bourdieu's (1984) influential work on taste in France in the late 1960s demonstrates how aesthetic dispositions are strongly related to class positions and identities. For Bourdieu, while the unequal distribution of economic capital between classes shapes what people can afford to consume, people's class position and consumption practices are also shaped by the amount and type of **cultural capital** they acquire through their families. During childhood we learn to discriminate, classify and make sense of the world through what Bourdieu calls the 'habitus', a 'system of dispositions' through which we distinguish between what is – and isn't – our kind of thing. In this way, our dispositions towards consumption are classed because they are shaped by our family's class culture. Therefore, Bourdieu suggests, our lifestyles are shaped by our class background rather than freely chosen.

The relationship between economic and cultural capital becomes much clearer if we explore how different classes have different dispositions towards domestic consumption. Bourdieu identifies how working-class domestic meals are a cultural response to the material position of manual labourers. He argues that the French working class have a preference for cheap cuts of meat (a response to their scarce financial resources) and substantial portions (to sustain them in manual work) but they also celebrate their ability to acquire the resources to put food on the table by serving generous quantities of food eaten in an informal and convivial atmosphere. Members of the bourgeoisie who are rich in both economic and (legitimate) cultural capital share a very different disposition towards food: 'a person who has been brought up with the abstractions of education and capital, and who is certain of obtaining daily necessities, cultivates a distance from these needs, and affects a taste based in the respect and desire for the abstract, distanced and formal' (Miller 1994: 150). For these reasons the bourgeoisie have a preference for 'light' and 'refined' meals that deny the biological functions of food and that are eaten in a restrained and formal manner. In this way Bourdieu demonstrates how lifestyles and domestic consumption practices are not only shaped by how much economic capital people have but also by the cultural dispositions that arise from – and contribute to – their class position.

From such a perspective domestic consumption practices offer few opportunities to play with identity but instead both produce and reproduce class identities. These ideas are supported by a number of studies of domestic consumption in the UK. For example, Dale Southerton (2001) found that people's choice of kitchen – and their ideas about what kitchens should be like – was shaped by their class. Whereas working-class households tended to see the kitchen in functional terms, middle-class professionals and managers saw the kitchen as a site for expressing their identity, displaying originality through design and investing with 'personal meanings' about the nature of family life. His findings suggest that the middle classes did see the kitchen as a lifestyle space in which they could express their design ideas. However, this suggests that a preoccupation with lifestyling the home is consistent with middle-class dispositions rather than indicating lifestyles are no longer shaped by class.[5]

Indeed, there is evidence to suggest that there are significant class distinctions in the forms of lifestyle that are represented within lifestyle media. Domestic interiors magazines do not address a mass market but frequently present lifestyle ideas that are consistent with the class and gender identities of their target markets. Lisa Taylor

(2005) has demonstrated that newspapers in the UK offer very different ideas about what constitutes an aesthetically pleasing garden depending on the assumed class identity of their readers. While national newspapers that are aimed at a middle-class audience represent the garden as a 'lifestyle space' where readers can use their cultural capital to 'play' with aesthetic codes, gardening supplements in the local press that are aimed at a working-class audience favour 'an aesthetic ethos of plain orderliness based on conserving the respectability of traditional garden elements' (Taylor 2005: 117–20).

While there is little evidence to suggest that class-based lifestyles have been replaced by the pursuit of individualized lifestyles, this does not necessarily suggest that the meanings people ascribe to their home-making practices can simply be reduced to the differences between classes. Indeed, the meanings that people associate with home are often remarkably consistent across class groupings. Even in Bourdieu's study, while there are some significant differences in the attributes that different class fractions associate with the 'ideal home', nearly all class groupings valued 'comfort' above all other attributes of the home (Bourdieu 1984: 248).[6]

Likewise, while Ian Woodward (2003: 394) found that some middle-class Australians concentrated on design in their home-making practices as a way of demonstrating their class distinction, many of his middle-class interviewees eschewed pursuing design ideas and sought to create homes that were 'comfortable and relaxing'. Indeed, Woodward questions whether ideas about home as a site for aesthetic self-expression are important even within the middle classes. He suggests that while the middle classes may experiment and play with style and acquire designer goods in other aspects of their lives, domestic consumption may be underpinned by a different logic. As he suggests, 'there is a moral component which underpins the organization and presentation of domestic space and which relates to matters of decorum, respectability and presentation of a protocol of domestic welcoming' (Woodward 2003: 407). Indeed, everyday life in family homes often sits uneasily with the pursuit of distinctive aestheticized lifestyles. As Martens et al. (2004: 169) observe, 'the presence of children . . . changes the materiality of living space, with household organization, style and design all being compromised by the presence of kids' stuff and the functional requirements of (especially young) children.'

This is not to deny that ideas about lifestyle inform contemporary discourses of home and home-making practices. Consumers are encouraged to understand their homes in terms of design and fashion and to see their home-making practices in terms of aesthetic choices. However, these lifestyle discourses compete with other discourses of home that associate domestic culture with ideas such as privacy, morality, family and care. Domestic consumption practices may be influenced by questions of lifestyle and design but, as I explore in the next section, domestic consumption practices are frequently geared to the creation of meanings and ideas that have little to do with lifestyle. Furthermore, the emphasis on the 'spectacular' dimensions of domestic consumption in lifestyle discourses tends to obfuscate 'the mundane, routine, inconspicuous elements of consumption practice' such as selecting an electricity or gas supplier (Warde 2002: 19).

While ideas about lifestyle often promise that our homes can operate as a blank canvas upon which we can create and inscribe individual identities, research demonstrates that class identities and differences still exert a considerable influence on domestic consumption practices. As Bourdieu's work demonstrates, the difference between the homes of different classes are not represented as 'equal differences': the domestic consumption practices of the middle classes have been legitimated as morally, culturally and aesthetically superior to those of their working-class counterparts. As Bev Skeggs's (1997: 89) research vividly portrays, working-class women's ability to find pleasure in the way they construct a sense of home is 'disrupted' by the knowledge that others may judge their homes as inferior. However, as I go on to explore in the next section, the meaning of home-making strategies cannot simply be reduced to the meaning of class differences. By focusing too closely on class, we can often miss the complexity of household consumption practices (Miller 2001a).

Making homes: domestic consumption practices

This section examines how domestic consumption practices are used to create a sense of home within the built environments we inhabit. Indeed, it is frequently these practices that transform housing into homes. Therefore, while the meanings of domestic culture are often produced for us, they are also produced by us through our consumption practices (Furlong 1995). In this section I explore a range of studies that demonstrate the complex ways in which both ideas and experiences of home are created through everyday practice. These home-*making* strategies add layers of meaning to – and also sometimes negotiate and challenge – wider constructions of the relationship between public and private spheres. Furthermore, these practices may also confound assumptions about home as a bounded and fixed space by highlighting how home is not necessarily the place we inhabit but may be located elsewhere.

Many studies of domestic consumption use research methods drawn from **ethnography**. Ethnographic research seeks to understand how people construct their social worlds by understanding the meanings people bring to their everyday lives (Miller 2001a). Classic ethnographies often involved the researcher immersing themselves for a long period in a particular cultural milieu in order to understand the cultural significance of everyday practices. **Qualitative research** within cultural studies has often had more limited ambitions but has drawn on many aspects of ethnographic enquiry in order to understand 'the dynamic nature of social and cultural processes and of meaning production' and 'to respond to the complex ways in which individuals, or agents, or subjects, inhabit their specific formations, identities and subjectivities' (Gray 2003: 18). While few of the studies I discuss below explicitly locate themselves within a cultural studies tradition, they frequently share these aims and seek to demonstrate that we can only begin to understand the meaning of home by coming to terms with 'layers of fractured experience' (Garvey 2001: 66).

Frequently, there are limits to the ethnographer's ability to immerse themselves in other people's domestic lives (short of moving in with them!). Therefore, researchers who are investigating domestic cultures have frequently used interviews – combined with observations in the domestic contexts in which the interviews occur – to gain insights into the meaning of domestic practices. This means that the researcher needs to be sensitive to the fact that they often rely on 'people's representations of their everyday lives' (Pink 2004: 32) and, in interpreting these accounts and writing up their research, researchers themselves add a further level of representation. Nonetheless, the ways in which people represent the meaning of home can tell us a great deal about how people imagine the significance of their domestic practices and give meaning to the ways in which they negotiate particular forms of domestic culture.

As we saw in the last section, debates about lifestyle frequently focus on the *visual* dimensions of home, attempting to read the meaning of domestic consumption from how homes look. In the process, these approaches frequently miss how 'the visible or aesthetic qualities of home decoration (and housework) are the result of complex relationships between the different identities, agencies, resources and relationships in the home' (Pink 2004: 64). Critics who focus on home decoration as a form of self-expression also tend to focus on 'the results of home decoration' and miss the significance of the '*processes*' of home decoration (Garvey 2001: 48). Indeed, Pauline Garvey's study of the significance of moving furniture around demonstrates how the meaning of home isn't just constructed through large-scale redecoration projects but also lies in smaller, everyday consumption practices through which we make homes. Relocating objects in a room, she suggests, has little to do with self-representation or the display of identities but instead involves practices that enable people to temporarily inhabit a different experience of home by rearranging 'the feel of the material' (Probyn 1993: 283).

Approaches that focus purely on the visual in creating the meaning of domestic cultures can also miss the ways in which homes are made through practices that engage with other senses. Sarah Pink's research into home-making practices demonstrates how people also construct a sense of home through sounds, smells and textures. For example, she found that her interviewees often had very strong ideas about how homes should – and shouldn't – smell. They engaged in a range of consumption practices to make their residences smell more 'homely: they were concerned with the smell of their homes and deliberately used plug-ins, air fresheners, fresh air (from open windows), scented oils and candles, and cleaning products' and became 'creative appropriators and mixers of diverse smells' (Pink 2004: 67). Other informants used music and radio to create a personalized and meaningful soundscape that captured their own ideas of home. Indeed, for some people, sounds offered a way of temporarily taking possession of their domestic space that was impossible to achieve through decorative strategies. However, just as sounds, smells, textures and tastes can create a sense of home, they can also mark out other spaces as 'unhomely'. For example, in Liz Kenyon's (1999: 93) research on student housing, one interviewee complained about the 'pub-carpet type' floor-covering in their house because it didn't belong in a place they could call home. Instead, they longed 'for a carpet you can walk on in your bare feet like at home', claiming 'this one's so disgusting that you have to wear shoes at all times'.

As this student's rejection of 'pub-carpet' suggests, the ways in which people experience and understand home are informed by the relationship between the meanings of public and private. Home is shaped by ideas of what is 'not-home': as Giddens argues, in modernity 'the private is a creation of the public and vice versa; each forms part of newly emerging systems of internal referentiality' (cited in Attfield 2000: 180). These relationships are fundamental to the home-making practices of the young working-class couples in Norway studied by Marianne Gullestad. Her interviewees' domestic consumption practices were oriented by the idea that 'a nice home should be literally and figuratively warm . . . A home should be decorated . . . in order not to give off an impression of impersonal emptiness' (Gullestad 1995: 330). Indeed, Gullestad observes, if people call someone's home impersonal or compare it to an institution, this was interpreted as an insult.[7]

Although the architecture of housing and workplaces frequently distinguishes private from public spaces, residential spaces still need to be transformed into homes through domestic consumption practices. These practices are often oriented towards the production of specific values that are understood as fundamental elements of home. Gullestad (1995: 330) identifies how 'home is a rich, flexible and ambiguous symbol' that signifies a wide range of values, relationships and concepts to the people in her study:

> Personal identity; the identity of the family; marital, filial and parental love; closeness . . .; sharing and togetherness . . .; a sense of wholeness . . .; integration and unity in life; independence and self-sufficiency; safety, security . . ., control, order, 'peace and quiet', cosiness . . . and comfort. . . . and decency . . .; practical sense and a realistic outlook; control and mastery; direction in life; and social reference groups.

These qualities are used to continually reaffirm boundaries between public and private. For example, Gullestad's interviewees place great value on making their interiors look 'unique', not because they want to demonstrate their distinction but because this is a way of personalizing domestic space and distinguishing it from public spaces. Furthermore, her respondents' aesthetic strategies are constantly geared to the production of moral values. The moral values of a 'good home' are signified through the aesthetic qualities of a 'nice home': 'through aesthetics a vision of a moral order is created and expressed' (Gullestad 1995: 330).

As I suggested in the last section, 'comfort' is frequently seen as a central component of home. In his history of 'the idea of home', Witold Rybczynski (1987) demonstrates how the idea of comfort was central in the historical development of modern domestic cultures and plays a crucial role in distinguishing the private from the public. While a degree of cleanliness and tidiness may be central to many people's understanding of comfort, 'hominess is not neatness. Otherwise everyone would live in replicas of the kinds of sterile and impersonal homes that appear in interior design and architectural magazines' (Rybczynski 1987: 17).[8] The centrality of comfort to people's understanding of the 'ideal home' is supported across a range of studies. Csikszentmihalyi and Rochberg-Halton (1981: 127) found that many people in the USA believe that home should be 'comfortable', 'cosy' and 'relaxing' while Woodward (2003: 407) suggests that middle-class Australians wanted their home to represent 'comfort', 'relaxation' and a good family life.

Yet, these studies also reveal that comfort is not a natural aspect of domestic spaces (and, as Rybczynski points out, it was actively opposed in modernist interiors). People understand comfort as a value that has to be worked at through their domestic consumption practices. Gullestad (1995: 323) shows how the young couples in her study selected and arranged objects to create a sense of 'polished and almost sumptuous comfort', and how these values were reaffirmed by the use of domestic labour to maintain 'a spotless order'. In Liz Kenyon's (1999: 92–3) research, it is the absence of comfort that leads students to conclude that their term-time residence is not a 'real home'. Their student houses were described as 'uncomfortable and basic' and 'lacked aesthetically pleasing and comfortable décor'.

In many studies, the meaning of home is closely related to the experience of communal life (which is often equated with the family) and the value of intimacy. Indeed, the students in Liz Kenyon's study identified the lack of communal space within their student housing as an obstacle to creating the experience of home. The strategies people employ to personalize domestic space can also be used to represent those friends and family that they associate with home, and also the sense of intimacy that people associate with these close relationships. As I go on to discuss in more detail in the next section, photographs are frequently used to personalize the home, create a sense of intimacy and represent those people who are identified with a particular domestic space. Likewise, as I explained in the last chapter, idealized images of domestic cookery link home-cooking with intimacy because meals are created for the tastes of household members and because the experience of eating affirms a sense of communal life. This is reinforced in some British studies of notions of the ideal kitchen. June Freeman's (2004: 155) research demonstrates how the idea of a 'living-kitchen' was valued by her interviewees and was seen as 'a potential means of creating material conditions conducive to and supportive of domestic solidarity'. The live-in kitchen enabled people to come together in a communal space around shared activities such as eating, enabling household members to experience being a member of a household unit. Elizabeth Silva (2000b: 12) identifies a similar point in her research. She identifies how women saw creating a kitchen as a means of practising care for their families by producing 'a space for family intimacy'. The kitchen also offers a space in which the practical aspects of care – cooking, cleaning, and so on – could be intertwined with the emotional aspects of care in order to produce 'a nourishing family life' (Silva 2000b: 23).

This research also provides a useful reminder of the work that goes into creating the meanings of home as a caring environment. As we saw in the last chapter, women's domestic labour is often oriented towards providing the experience of being cared for, an experience that frequently is understood as an indispensable element of home. Not only is home often seen as a caring environment, but values such as comfort and intimacy are also produced through caring practices associated with feminine domestic labour. As I suggested earlier, there is no clear dividing line between domestic labour and domestic consumption. However, the domestic consumption activities through which care is practised – from creating a healthy environment for household members by cleaning the toilet to organizing photos to create a sense of family identity – are frequently performed by those people who are culturally predisposed to invest in caring practices (Silva 2007: 143). As I suggested in Chapter 4, although 'caring practices' can be performed by both men and women, 'caring dispositions' are often associated with the performance and experience of femininity.

However, in thinking about how domestic consumption practices produce the meanings and experience of home, it is important to remember that home is a complex entity. For a start, numerous studies demonstrate that the meanings ascribed to 'ideal homes' do not necessarily accord with the experience of home. For example, while comfort may be valued, this does not necessarily mean that people have the economic, social, cultural and even political resources to create a comfortable home. Further-more, as I have made clear throughout this book, notions of what constitutes home – and how we going about making home – are not universal. Although some of the keywords associated with home may reoccur across time and place as they are con-structed through both representation and practice, differences between the meaning of domestic cultures are often equally significant. As I demonstrate at various points in this book, the meanings that people bring to home-making are shaped by class, gender, generation, sexuality, ethnicity, 'race' and age. Moreover, it is crucial to remember that the place we call home will not necessarily be the place we reside – it may be another residence or another location altogether (hooks 1991).

Moreover, even when concepts such as care, comfort and intimacy are invoked when people explain their home-making practices, this does not mean that they necessarily understand these terms in the same ways. For example, while the idea of home as a caring environment is usually associated with the feminine practice of caring for others or the experience of being cared for within a family, Pink (2004: 48) identifies how single people in her study saw home as a place in which they could care for themselves. Some of her interviewees saw seemingly mundane practices such as washing-up as 'a type of "therapy" that they would engage in when faced with a problem when working from home'.

Domestic consumption practices are not only just oriented towards constructing 'ideal homes' but are also oriented towards idealized relationships and identities. While much of the research I have discussed so far is concerned with how domestic practices produce 'the family', other critics have tried to show how domestic consumption practices enable people to negotiate and construct a range of identities. For example, when couples first move into a place together, their negotiations about how to furnish it, what home means and how to organize domestic life play a key role in creating their identity as a couple (Clarke 1998; Reimer and Leslie 2004; Gorman-Murray 2006c). These practices cannot simply be thought of as reflections of pre-existing subjectivities but instead create the identity of a particular couple.

The complex ways in which identities are produced through home-making practices is illustrated in Alison Clarke's (2001) research on domestic consumption on a London council estate. She argues that households work through their identities through their consumption practices: 'consumption, in the form of home decorating, is seen as a focal point, rather than a "reflection", of the construction and negotiation of "household philosophies"' (Clarke 2001: 32). For Clarke, people do not simply reproduce dominant ideas of what an ideal home might be but instead use their domestic consumption practices as part of an ongoing process through which they imagine and re-imagine what an ideal home would be like. For example, Lola uses the process of decorating her children's bedrooms to imagine an identity for her children that is both British *and* Chilean, using her consumption practices as a means of 'easing the way of her first generation British-Chilean children into their new social worlds' (Clarke 2001: 39). Another resident, single-mother Kelly, invests her energy and money into producing a highly designed and polished living room. Through the process of home decoration, she creates a home in which she not only has an 'artistic' identity but also in which she might establish a relationship with a man who would appreciate this particular conception of both her and her home. In this way, Clarke (2001: 32) demonstrates how people use domestic consumption practices to 'establish relations with an outside and ideal social world'. Although the women in her study received few visitors, they 'used "home" . . . to project themselves beyond their immediate surroundings'.

As Liz Kenyon's (1999) study of students reminds us, the places we inhabit – and the domestic cultures we produce and practice – are not necessarily the same as home. For these students, neither their term-time accommodation nor their parents' residences were associated with a domestic culture they equated with home: the values they associated with home were located in an imagined 'future home' where they hoped to one day live. A different relationship to domestic culture is identified in Elia Petridou's (2001) study of the home-making practices of Greek students in London. These students disliked their student accommodation and rejected the values they associated with British domestic cultures. They created a sense of home in this alien environment by adopting their native domestic practices and by 'tasting home' via food parcels that were sent by friends and family 'back home' in Greece, asserting their Greek identity through an identification with Greek domestic culture.

As Karen Fog Olwig (1999: 83) argues, home has two key meanings: 'first, it can refer to a site where everyday life is lived, often surrounded by close family, and second, it can mean a place associated with a notion of belonging, of "feeling at home"'. In both Kenyon's and Petridou's studies, these meanings of home do not coincide. The same is true in Fog Olwig's (1999) study of the home-making practices of migrants from the Caribbean island of St. Nevis. Economic conditions in St. Nevis caused these migrants to move to the UK to earn money, much of which was sent back home to the Caribbean to help maintain and support the family home. Despite establishing residences and families in the UK over a long period of time, these migrants 'continued to devote themselves, emotionally and economically, to their home in Nevis, while living in another place' (Fog Olwig 1999: 83). In this way, the home-making activities of Nevisian migrants produced a home – and contributed to domestic consumption – that was geographically remote from their own place of residence.

Therefore, home may be created though a range of practices but we do not necessarily reside in the place we call home. Alternatively, people may use their home-making practices to connect different understandings of home across a range of scales and locations. As Katie Walsh (2006: 138) observes in her study of British ex-pats in Dubai, migrants use domestic objects to 'imaginative[ly] travel to other space-times'. However, these objects were not simply used to transport these ex-pats back to a domestic and national home in the UK, but were also used 'to contribute to current homemaking and future projections'. In a world where geographical mobility is increasingly common (whether this mobility is on a local, national or global scale), domestic cultures may well be increasingly characterized by 'the multiplicity and fluidity' found in the homes of transnational migrants (Walsh 2006: 138). While I return to the migrant experience of home in Chapter 6, the following section discusses the place of material culture in home-making practices in more detail.

Haunted houses: consumption and material culture

So far in this chapter I have explored how people use domestic consumption practices to create a sense of home. In this section I focus more explicitly on the relationships between people and objects in producing domestic cultures. As Donna Birdwell-Pheasant and Denise Lawrence-Zúñiga (1999: 8) remind us, 'the materiality of domestic life is a central factor in forming and reproducing the family biologically, socially, economically and morally'. They suggest that rather than focusing simply on what people do with their residences and domestic objects, it is also essential to consider how these places and things exert an influence over how we live. While earlier in the book I considered how architectural forms can shape domestic cultures, in this section I explore some of the more complex ways in which material culture may limit our ability to appropriate, or claim 'ownership' of, the places where we live. Therefore, this section examines both how people interact with material culture to build and maintain a sense of home and how material culture may also place constraints on home-making practices.

As we have already seen, people use material culture in the home-making practices in an attempt to create meaningful domestic cultures. However, certain objects can come to be seen as indispensable to our very understanding of what home is. In their study of domestic symbols, Csikszentmihalyi and Rochberg-Halton (1981: 15) argue that things do not just simply express the self but certain objects also become 'essential elements' of us. Their research identifies how cherished domestic objects can convey a range of meanings to people, from values such as 'comfort' through to 'important memories, relationships and past experiences' (Csikszentmihalyi and Rochberg-Halton 1981: 60–1). For example, as I suggested earlier, photos play a central role in many domestic interiors, not only 'preserving the memory of personal ties' but also giving 'a tenuous immortality to beloved persons' and providing 'an identity, a context of belonging, to one's descendents' (Csikszentmihalyi and Rochberg-Halton 1981: 69). For many people, the presence of treasured photos of significant people, times or places is indispensable to their conception of home. Indeed, as Gillian Rose (2003: 12) suggests, the practice of arranging photos can bring friends and family together in groups within the home even when they are physically absent. 'Family snaps are seen as a trace of a person's presence; but they are also taken, displayed and circulated in awareness of the pervasiveness of absence and distance . . . Photos bring near those far away'. Rose notes that this doesn't just involve integrating people who can't be co-present but it also performs a kind of temporal integration in which different moments in time are given order.

The centrality of certain objects to our identity and to our sense of home is highlighted in the experience of household burglary. Not only may people feel that their homes have been invaded and are no longer 'their own' (Chapman 1999), but separation from our belongings 'often equates with getting separated from that which appears to be stable and familiar' (Marcoux 2001: 80). As Walter Benjamin (1992: 69) suggests, the identities of objects aren't just defined by their owners but our identities often 'live' in the objects we surround ourselves with. Without certain objects, we may feel that our sense of who we are no longer exists. Jean-Sebastien Marcoux explores this relationship between objects, identity and home in his study of the process of 'sorting' that accompanies moving house. As people decide what to take with them, and what to leave behind, Marcoux (2001: 85) argues, certain things 'come to matter': 'the "essential" does not necessarily pre-exist the move. It is something to be achieved.' However, domestic objects also have an agency. Some things 'refuse' to get left behind when we move while others appear to influence how we organize our lives. For example, in property TV, house-buying experts are frequently infuriated by how people's decisions about whether to buy an extremely expensive property are determined by seemingly 'irrational' considerations about whether a relatively inexpensive dining table or bed will fit into the space. Yet the objects which we surround ourselves with are often:

> more than mere 'things', they are a collection of appropriated materials, invested with meaning and memory, a material testament of who we are, where we have been . . . They are what transforms our house into our *home*, a private cosmos

that houses our memories of bygone times, as well as our hopes for what is yet to come.

(Hecht 2001: 123)

Of course, buildings themselves are also a form of material culture and exert an influence on the kinds of home that people can make. The meanings and identities of the places we inhabit have not only been shaped by architects and planners but also by the practices of previous occupants, practices that were themselves influenced by changing ideas about the meaning of domestic life. A useful way of thinking about houses as a form of material culture – and the ways in which their meanings change over time – is offered by Arjun Appadurai. He distinguishes between the 'cultural biography' of individual things (for example, a particular house), 'as they move through different hands, contexts, and uses, thus accumulating a specific biography' and the 'social history of classes or types of thing' (for example, the Victorian terrace), which involves looking at 'longer-term shifts . . . and larger-scale dynamics that transcend the biographies of particular members of that class or type' (Appadurai 1986: 34; see also Kopytoff 1986).

For example, we could study the 'cultural biography' of a particular Victorian semi-detached house and identify the transformations that have taken place as residents have made changes and lived in the place, and how the meaning of the house has also been shaped by changes in the street and the locality in which it is situated. Indeed, Julie Myerson's book *Home: The Story of Everyone Who Ever Lived in Our House* (2005) provides a vivid example of how previous owners and residents performed a series of transformations on her Victorian house as they modified it, lived in it and established identities in relation to it within a locality that itself went through a series of changes. The individual cultural biography of her Victorian house was also shaped by a wider social history of Victorian houses as a 'class of things'. For example, by the middle of the twentieth century, this nineteenth-century housing was increasingly seen as old-fashioned because it failed to be easily adapted to more modern conceptions of home. Indeed, home-owners in the 1950s were advised on how to make these homes more contemporary. For example, DIY experts suggested that people should rip out old Victorian fireplaces and install central heating, and they offered advice on how to make these houses look less Victorian by covering up 'old-fashioned' panelled doors with hardboard in order to achieve a more sleek, streamlined interior. However, in more recent decades, nineteenth-century housing has become fashionable as 'traditional' Victorian features have become desirable because they are seen to signify authenticity, craftsmanship, heritage and individuality, in contrast to contemporary mass-produced housing.

The meaning, identity and feel of the places we inhabit are, therefore, not only shaped by architects and planners and by representations of ideal homes but also by the practices of previous residents. All these factors mean that buildings have a form of agency that new residents must interact with: as Ivan Illich observes, 'to dwell means to live in the traces that past living has left' (cited in Birdwell-Pheasant and Lawrence-Zúñiga 1999: 9). Indeed, the first thing many people do on moving into a new home is decorate it in order to establish a sense of 'ownership' by expelling traces of 'past living'. On property shows, people who want to sell their homes are often advised to create a 'blank canvas' by depersonalizing their property to enable prospective buyers to imagine how they would establish their own identities within the space. Yet, such strategies not only rely on contemporary ideas about what a 'blank canvas' should look like; they also risk making a place feel impersonal, a quality that most people understand as antithetical to home.

The idea that buildings can operate as a blank canvas assumes that inhabitants simply inscribe their own identities on their housing. However, as Alan Metcalfe (2006a: 255) argues in his research into the meanings people bring to the process of moving house, the place people choose to move to (for those who have a choice) 'already expresses some of their ideals, it already connects with their tastes, and their senses of identity', even if these are identities that are yet to be fully realized. It is for this reason that people frequently claim to know when they have found 'the one' that they can call home in the process of house-hunting. Therefore, Metcalfe (2006b) suggests that theories which assume that homes express – or should express – their occupants' identity frequently fail to take into account that there are already other identities embedded within the places we live. (See also Winstanley et al. 2002 on the meaning of moving house.)

Indeed, Daniel Miller suggests that our ability to feel a sense of 'ownership' of the places we live depends on how we relate to the traces left behind by past occupants and past modes of domestic culture. For Miller (2001b: 109), ghost stories are one of the ways in which people have tried to come to terms with the ways in which homes are 'haunted' by the past. Ghosts operate as 'a partial anthropomorphism of the longer history of the house and housing relative to its present inhabitants'. Indeed, he argues that the figure of the ghost may be invoked as an 'excuse' for our inability to take 'possession' of our homes by 'positing the agency as belonging to the house itself and its possessions, where these objectify those people who have previously lived within it' (Miller 2001b: 112).

While this might sound fanciful, Miller illustrates his argument with reference to his earlier study of a London council estate in which he analysed the strategies that residents used to appropriate – and take 'ownership' – of housing provided for them by the State. Some of the households he studied used their consumption practices to gain a sense of 'ownership' of their homes to 'develop their self-conception as households' (Miller 1988: 354). They 'exorcized the alien presence of the council and in effect took possession of the place in which they lived' (Miller 2001b: 113–14). However, other residents felt 'haunted' 'by the sense that their apartments belonged to the council . . . and not to themselves. The council was clearly felt by some to be an unwelcome presence objectified in the very apartment itself that haunted and depressed them' (Miller 2001b: 113–14). Because the State owned their home – and signified this through the architecture and fittings of their apartments – these people felt unable to establish any ability to take 'possession' of their residence.

Miller is not alone in demonstrating how housing can have agency and assert its own identity. A woman interviewed by Csikszentmihalyi and Rochberg-Halton (1981: 128) complained that her house would not let her 'be herself'. Unable to take possession of her home, she could only experience a transient relationship to it, claiming that 'I'd like to move and find out where I am going to be next, inside and out'. Likewise, Metcalfe (2006b) discovered that the process of moving into a new house is often accompanied by an encounter with the house's past residents and former lives. For one couple this involved an ongoing struggle with the presence of an elderly woman who manifested herself in lingering smells in hidden corners of their house. However, another couple chose to embrace their house's previous lives and felt that this intensified their relationship with it. As they discovered aspects of the house's histories and traces of previous residents in the layers of wallpaper, 'they began to feel a connection with the house and its own past, a connection with the history of the place and the lives that had been lived here previously' (see also Myerson 2005). Yet, for another couple, whose house refused to become their home despite their labours of transformation, 'the ghosts there were so troublesome' that the couple's only option was to move house.

These studies demonstrate how buildings and domestic objects are not simply a blank canvas upon which people create identities or lifestyles. As Metcalfe (2006b) argues, 'the home is the outcome of a relationship between the inhabitants and the place'. Research demonstrates how the materiality and history of residences can often create a gap between how people would like to live and how they actually end up living; places and things enforce 'an agency of their own' (Clarke 2001: 27). Therefore, in order to understand the meanings of domestic consumption, we have to not only understand the meanings that underpin people's use of buildings and objects but we also have to understand the impact that our homes and domestic material culture has on us.

Conclusions

Earlier chapters have already explored the range of ways in which consumption practices are not only integral to the processes of making homes but also produce, reproduce, negotiate or resist wider definitions of home. In this chapter I have tried to think more widely about how domestic consumptions are integral to processes of home-making and can be used to create and maintain a range of identities. However, as I have suggested, the places we live are not simply a blank canvas upon which we can inscribe our identities. Rather, the way in which we seek to create an identity for ourselves, our households and our homes are not only shaped by wider representations through which home is imagined, but also within the material environment in which our home-making takes place.

Yet, at the same time, consumption practices are often oriented towards ideas of home that may extend beyond our residence. While the idea of home is frequently represented as defensive and inward-facing, objects can act as markers of people, places and times that are absent but whose symbolic presence is necessary to maintain our conception of home (Csikszentmihalyi and Rochberg-Halton 1981; Massey 1993; Hecht 2001). For example, Rose (2003: 15) demonstrates how 'looking at photographs stretches domestic space through a relation with people, places and times that are not in the home at the moment of looking'. In the next chapter, I examine how domestic media also contribute to the process of 'stretching' domestic cultures.

Further reading

Miller, D. (1988) Appropriating the State on the Council Estate, *Man*, 23(2): 353–72.
Miller, D. (2001) (ed.) *Home Possessions: Material Culture Behind Closed Doors*. Oxford: Berg.
Jackson, S. and Moores, S. (eds) (1995) *The Politics of Domestic Consumption*. Hemel Hempstead: Harvester Wheatsheaf.
Pink, S. (2004) *Home Truths: Gender, Domestic Objects and Everyday Life*. Oxford: Berg.
Rose, G. (2003) Family Photographs and Domestic Spacings: A Case Study, *Transactions of the Institute of British Geographers*, 28: 5–18.

Notes

1   Ideas about what we mean by 'consumption' can vary across disciplines: for an introduction to these issues, see Warde and Martens (1998) and the essays in Miller (1995).
2   IKEA catalogue (UK) 2007; 'Space to Live', http://www.urbansplash.co.uk/us.php (accessed 2 April 2007); 'More than Just a New Home at Metro', http://www.easier.com/view/News/Property/article-87232.html (accessed 2 April 2007).
3   Taken from Ecos and Dulux paint charts. Ecos – a UK-based organic paint manufacturer – also raises questions about a further series of lifestyle choices based on environmental considerations.
4   For work on how gender inflects the representation of domestic consumption in contemporary lifestyle media, see work by Rachel Moseley (2001), Hollows (2003a), Bell and Hollows (2007) and Isabelle de Solier (2005) on male celebrity chefs such as Jamie Oliver; Brunsdon (2006) and Hollows (2003b) on femininity and domesticity in relation to female celebrity chefs such as Nigella Lawson; and Attwood (2005) on gender and the role of the male designer in programmes such as *Home Front*. For work on sexuality in relation to the representation of domestic consumption on lifestyle TV, see Gorman-Murray (2006a).
5   Indeed, Bourdieu's work suggests that the focus on using consumption creatively and imaginatively to develop new lifestyle experiences is consistent with the dispositions and lifestyle practices of the 'new middle classes' who emerged from the 1960s onwards. For example, Bourdieu (1984: 366–7) argues that new petit bourgeoisie invest in 'the art of living, in particular, domestic life and consumption' and value the 'amusing, refined, stylish, artistic [and]

imaginative'. Forms of lifestyle advice that accentuate the importance of enriching the emotional and aesthetic experience of domestic life can be seen to legitimate the tastes of the new middle classes. For more on Bourdieu's conception of the new middle classes, see Binkley (2004), Featherstone (1991) and Lee (1993). For work on new middle-class tastes in relation to domestic consumption and lifestyle media, see Hollows (2002, 2003a, 2003b) and Taylor (2005).

6 Out of nine class fractions, only 'craftsmen, small shopkeepers' and 'medical services, cultural intermediaries, art craftsmen' did not rank comfort as the most important attribute of the ideal home (they ranked it fourth and third, respectively, out of nine possible characteristics). These two class fractions are usually seen as having relatively little in common and, indeed, there are very significant differences in the ways in which they rank other attributes of home.

7 Although the importance of warmth to the meaning of home is far from universal, the significance of fireplaces in many Western domestic cultures suggests that home is often associated with warmth. Indeed, in the UK, fireplaces continue to have a symbolic significance that far exceeds their utility in centrally heated homes: fireplaces not only literally symbolize warmth but they also evoke ideas about 'traditional' domestic practices in which the family is gathered around the hearth. However, if warmth isn't a universal value of home, it is also expressed differently across cultures. In his study of France, Bourdieu (1984) finds (perhaps counter-intuitively) that warmth is more positively valued by the middle classes than the working classes. Pink (2004) identifies how carpets may signify warmth and cosiness in the UK but, in Spain, carpet does not have the same symbolic importance; tiled flooring is more common in Spain and Pink suggests that these differences can be explained by cultural responses to different environmental conditions and architectural traditions in the two countries.

8 Although, as Rybczynski explains, it is important to note how elements of domestic comfort were incorporated into the public sphere to domesticate it: for example, in the plush upholstery of Victorian public transport. In Chapter 7, I return to ideas about how comfort is mobilized to create a sense of homeliness in the public sphere.

THE MEDIA IN DOMESTIC CULTURES

6

Introduction

Media technologies are a key form of material culture in many homes. Like other forms of material culture, these technologies are also used in the processes of creating and negotiating the meaning of domestic culture. Although TV and radios may often appear to be 'invisible' because they are taken for granted as a 'natural' element of contemporary homes, this chapter explores the processes involved in domesticating these technologies and making them part of our everyday lives (Moores 2006). However, it is crucial to remember that information and communication technologies (ICTs) differ from many other forms of material culture because they are not simply objects but are also a 'medium' through which a range of texts enter domestic space (Silverstone 1994). Therefore, in thinking about the domestic consumption of media, it is necessary to think about the consumption of both technologies and texts.

In order to theorize how technologies are taken up and used within the home, many critics have focused on the process of *domesticating technologies*. Media technologies (like many other domestic technologies) are produced in the public sphere and often appear to be 'foreign' when they first enter the home. (For work on the domestication of other household technologies, see Bell 2006, Lehtonen 2003 and Shove and Southerton 2000.) It is only through processes of domestication that these technologies come to be *at home* in the places we live. These processes may start before technologies are purchased. For example, Silverstone (1994) explains how production, design and marketing frequently attempt to 'pre-domesticate' technologies so they do not conflict with the values that people associate with domestic culture. However, once they are taken home, further domestication needs to take place to 'bring things under control' and to effect the 'transition' and 'translation' of objects from public to private spheres (Silverstone 1994: 98): media technologies have to become 'house-trained' (Berker et al.

2006: 2). While there are some problems with the concept of domestication that I explore in the conclusion to this chapter, domestication offers a useful starting point because it helps us to understand:

> the capacity of a social group . . . to appropriate technological artefacts and delivery systems into its own culture – its own spaces and times, its own aesthetics and its own functioning – to control them, and to render them more or less 'invisible' within the daily routines of daily life.
>
> (Silverstone 1994: 98)

Drawing on theories of domestic consumption discussed in the last chapter, Silverstone demonstrates how the 'invisibility' of media technologies – the way in which they appear to be a 'natural' element of everyday life – is the product of complex work by household members. In the next section I illustrate and develop these ideas by looking at historical studies of how media technologies undergo a process of **enculturation** after entering domestic space.

In the case of many media technologies, this process of domestication is also consolidated by the content provided through them. For example, the content of radio and TV programming has often focused on domestic life. Furthermore, broadcast professionals have often devised schedules and formats around the imagined domestic activities of audiences. As I discuss in more detail in the following sections, media forms and contents can contribute to the way in which domestic media become embedded within everyday routines and can also give shape to these routines. For this reason it is necessary to consider how both media technologies and media texts are used in the processes of constructing and negotiating the meaning of domestic cultures.

The approaches I discuss in this chapter challenge 'commonsense' assumptions that media texts and technologies have direct 'effects' on domestic cultures. We have already encountered these assumptions in Chapter 3 where I considered the views of some critics who claimed that increasing TV ownership caused people to become increasingly privatized, in the process weakening their involvement in the public sphere. More recent debates also often suggest that the media have direct effects on domestic life. For example, there have been moral panics about how children's use of domestic computers – and, in particular, computer games – causes them to become increasingly isolated from the social. However, Morley (1986: 22) argues, just because leisure becomes more home-centred does not mean that it stops being a social activity. As I go on to explore, media technologies are often used to create the experience of a collective life within a household. Furthermore, the meaning of domestic media consumption needs to be understood in relation to existing roles and relationships within a household and the power relations that underpin these relationships. Therefore, this chapter explores how media technologies and texts are 'embedded within pre-existing routines' within households (Morley 2000: 86): while media technologies and texts contribute to the meanings of domestic cultures, the meaning of the media is also shaped by domestic cultures.

This chapter also examines how media technologies and texts have been used to negotiate relationships between public and private spheres. Raymond Williams's (1974) ideas about '**mobile privatization**' have been influential in shaping how critics have conceptualized this relationship. For example, Williams suggests that while TV could be seen to privatize leisure as people's leisure time becomes increasingly located within domestic space, TV has also made the experience of home more mobile (Moores 1996: 2). Therefore, while TV has often been seen as the domestic medium *par excellence*, it also enables domestic viewers to 'make imaginative "journeys" to distant places and events in the public realm' (Moores 1993: 72–3).

By connecting domestic users to elsewhere, media technologies can often contribute to the processes by which domestic cultures become 'stretched'. Later in this chapter I examine these processes in more detail, considering how media consumption enables people to make connections between their place of residence and other conceptions of home. As Morley and Silverstone (1992: 201) argue, 'Television has to be seen as embedded within a technical and consumer culture that is both domestic and national (and international), a culture that is at once both public and private'. This chapter identifies how radio and TV have not only played a key role in producing a sense of a national home but also how ICTs have been used to create new transnational and **diasporic** identities. However, while media technologies have the potential to make the home a less bounded place, the ability to use media technologies to 'travel' elsewhere is still shaped by power relationships within domestic space (Moores 1993: 74).

The following section examines the processes through which media technologies become domesticated, drawing on historical accounts of the radio and TV and also examining the more recent domestication of the computer. The subsequent section explores debates about the domestic consumption of media technologies, identifying how media consumption needs to be understood within the context of domestic cultures and the power relations within them. In the section that follows I open up the debate to consider in more detail about how media technologies and texts contribute to processes through which domestic cultures are 'stretched', enabling people to create a range of identifications and negotiate relationships between the local and the global. Throughout the chapter I consider how studying the media in domestic cultures adds complexity to our understanding of relationships between public and private spheres.

Domesticating technologies

This section provides an overview of how ICTs undergo processes of domestication by exploring how the radio, TV and the computer came to be *at home* in domestic space. I also examine how these technologies have also been used to rework the meaning of domestic culture and the experience of home. In particular, I consider how the representation, regulation and consumption of media technologies has been bound up with wider questions about the relationship between public and private spheres.

Historical studies of the ways in which new media technologies enter domestic space demonstrate how domestication is a complex process. While the radio may now appear to be a 'natural' element of domestic life, when they first appeared in the UK in the 1920s, they appeared to be foreign objects that disrupted domestic culture. During this period, radios were primarily thought of in terms of their technological properties rather than as a medium for broadcasting media content. As Shaun Moores (1993: 77–8) demonstrates, the early users of radio were usually men who enjoyed playing with the technological capacities of radio as a 'gadget'. However, he argues, other household members often experienced the radio as an ugly and obtrusive invader that looked out of place in domestic space. Furthermore, rather than uniting households and families, early radios fragmented the family groups as 'listening' could only take place by using individual headsets. It is worth noting that many later media technologies have also gone through this 'gadgeteer' phase before later becoming domesticated (see, for example, O'Sullivan 1991 on TV, Klinger 2006 on home cinema and Lally 2002 on computers).

As Moores (1993) argues, a series of factors helped to transform the meaning of the radio from being an 'unwanted guest' to part of the family. First, as radios gained the capacity to transmit to households rather than an individual listener, they also underwent aesthetic changes. They began to resemble other domestic objects and to look at home in the living room. Second, the development of broadcasting helped to domesticate the radio through the content of transmissions: broadcasts attempted to construct the radio audience as a family audience. Finally, broadcasters also created schedules that dovetailed with everyday life within the home and, in particular, 'the imagined daily activities of the housewife' (Moores 1993: 80; see also Spigel 1992 on the USA). In the process, the radio not only became domesticated and increasingly gendered as feminine but also came to be seen as an integral part of British domestic culture and something that helped to enhance the experience of family life.

By the late 1930s the radio was no longer seen as an alien invader in the home but as an object and medium that had 'increased the home's attractiveness' (Moores 1993: 83). Although broadcast schedules were constructed around what were imagined to be 'everyday domestic rituals', both schedules and programming also helped to regulate and restructure temporal rhythms within the home. Indeed, these schedules also 'helped to bring precise temporal measurement into the private sphere' resulting in 'a "domestication" of standard national time' (Moores 1993: 86). In the process radio was used to enable the domestic experience of public life – listeners were not only able to participate in an experience of time that was imagined to be common across households but broadcasts also constructed a common experience of events in the national calendar within the home.

While there are some similarities between the ways in which different media technologies have been domesticated, these processes of domestication are also framed within discourses that are the product of distinctive historical and national cultures. Lynn Spigel's (1992) study of the domestication of television in the USA in the 1950s demonstrates how debates about the relationship between TV and domestic life were also used to work through a series of tensions about the meaning of family life. Representations of domestic culture in the period frequently emphasized the importance of family 'togetherness' and TV was represented as a 'new hearth', a focus for family life and a 'cement' that would hold the family together. Through representations of the 'family circle' clustered around the TV set, TV became domesticated through being imagined as a valued member of the household (Spigel 1992: 37–40).

However, this process of domestication was not automatic. Spigel (1992: 86–91) observes how a number of commentators claimed that TV did not belong in the home and might represent a threat to family life. For example, while TV was often represented as a useful device for persuading children to spend time in the home with the family, children were also represented as potential victims of the power of TV (concerns that have been repeated in relationship to later ICTs such as the Internet). Likewise, while TV viewing was represented as an ideal form of family leisure, it was also represented as a threat to gender relations. Women could listen to radio while doing domestic work in the home, but TV was an audio-*visual* medium that threatened to divert women from their roles as wives and mothers. Still, if women privileged domestic labour over TV viewing, they would be unable to participate in the experience of family togetherness around the TV set.[1] Indeed, some networks took the opportunity to run advertisements that advised women on how they might watch TV and perform domestic labour at the same time. This demonstrates how the entry of new media technologies within the home is accompanied by attempts to work through the meaning of these media within specific cultural formations.

The arrival of TV in many American homes also offered an opportunity to negotiate ideas about the relationships between public and private life. Although many critics argued that the increasing popularity of TV in the 1950s caused people to become home-centred and turn their backs on the public sphere (see Chapter 3), it was also represented as offering the possibility of erasing the distinction between public and private (Spigel 1992: 104).[2] For example, some advocates for TV claimed that it could act as 'a "window on the world" that would imaginatively transport viewers across the globe' (Spigel 2001a: 386). In this way, TV was not represented as a retreat from public life but a means of imagining domestic culture as mobile.[3]

However, although it offers opportunities to explore elsewhere from the living room, TV scheduling and programming strategies have often been preoccupied with everyday domestic life. Just as radio broadcasts were often organized around – and helped to organize – everyday practices in the home and helped to construct a family audience, so TV broadcasting developed along similar lines. Spigel (1992: 78–83) explains how daytime TV in the post-war USA was constructed around the imagined activities and interests of housewives. For example, 'variety' and 'magazine' formats reinforced ideas about 'women's interests' by focusing on domestic life and advising housewives about how to carry out their role more efficiently. Daytime shows were also fragmented into short slots to enable women to watch in a 'distracted' way while performing household chores. Likewise, daytime soap operas also frequently focused on domestic life and used repetition to enable views to watch in a distracted way.[4] Other genres, such as the situation comedy, helped to domesticate TV, naturalizing its role within the 'family circle' by focusing on everyday life in families (Spigel 1992: 136).[5] For these reasons, TV came to be understood as a thoroughly domesticated medium both located within, and concerned with, family life.

While TV's place in domestic space is now taken for granted in the West, the structure, style and scheduling of daytime and early evening programming on network TV continues to frequently reaffirm the connection between TV and domestic culture. In their study of breakfast TV in the UK, the USA and Finland, Wieten and Pantti (2005: 22) explain how breakfast programmes attempt to insert themselves into daily domestic routines by designing their content and form to fit with the imagined 'moods, schedules and activities of the audience'. The use of fragmentation enables the audience to drop into shows for short periods while going about their normal morning routines; presenters adopt an informal conversational style suited to domestic life and sets are designed to resemble the imagined audience's own homes. For Moores (2005: 75) such shows demonstrate a 'will to ordinariness' by presenting themselves as 'nothing special' and 'part of life'. Some more recent generic developments still seek to maintain a connection between TV and everyday life. Reality shows such as *Big Brother* focus on the minute details, the routines and rituals, of everyday life in 'the house' as participants attempt to develop ways of living together as a household. Such shows highlight the extent to which TV as a medium has a long-standing connection with the 'familiar, the everyday and the comfortable – it is an intimate medium closely related to its position within domesticity' (Wood et al. forthcoming). (For more on the relationship between TV and everyday domestic life, see Brunsdon and Morley 1978, Scannell 1996 and Bonner 2003.)

At the same time, while TV as a technology and a medium has been domesticated within the home, it also connects private life with public entities such as the nation. In the UK, **public service broadcasting** was modelled on the idea of a nation of families, where 'all the citizens of a nation can talk to each other like a family sitting and chatting around the domestic hearth' (Keane cited in Morley 2000: 105). Although I discuss in more detail how TV creates a relationship between the domestic and nation later in this chapter, it is worth acknowledging at this point how TV enables people to experience – and participate in – the collective life of the nation within the living room, whether this is through viewing national ceremonies such as royal weddings or engaging in more daily rituals such as watching the national news (Morley 1992: 283–4). Morley (1992: 285) argues that both radio and TV broadcasting have played a key role in shifting our understanding and experience of the relationships between public and private: 'the "public" is thus experienced in the private (domestic) realm; it is "domesticated". But at the same time the "private" itself is thus transformed or "socialized". The space (and experience) created is neither "public" nor "private" in the traditional sense.' Therefore, thinking about the domestication of both radio and

TV also involves reconceptualizing the way we understand relationships between public and private life.

As both radio and TV have become a taken-for-granted part of everyday life, they have also become a key part of the very fabric and *experience* of everyday life. Paddy Scannell uses the concept of 'dailiness' to think about how broadcasting plays an often invisible but nonetheless central role in our everyday routines. He argues that we come to expect that:

> TV will be delivered as a daily schedule, not now and then but continuously, uninterruptedly and indefinitely . . . This dailiness yields the sense we all have of the ordinariness, the familiarity and obviousness of radio and television. It establishes their taken-for-granted, 'seen but unnoticed' character . . . This structure yields the timetables of modern daily life and is fundamental to the ways in which broadcasting appears daily as part of and as for each and every day.
>
> (Scannell 2000: 19)

TV audiences not only frequently use TV as a way of scheduling everyday life and understanding the temporal rhythms of the day but these practices also connect the experience of time in individual homes with those of others across the nation (Silverstone 1994: 20–1; Gauntlett and Hill 1999: 282–3). Therefore, while media technologies such as TV are bound up with what Giddens identifies as the disembedding processes associated with modernity (which involve the stretching out of social relationships across time and space), TV is also part of the re-embedding processes. These processes offer a sense of security through their intimate connections with our daily routines, creating both 'temporal simultaneity' and a sense of belonging to wider collective groupings and identities (Moores 2000: 37–9). The dailiness of TV also creates a sense of 'ontological security'. For example, through fixed scheduling and the strategies that are used to reassure viewers, TV news broadcasts can work to alleviate anxiety and generate a wider sense of trust in the world around us (Silverstone 1994).

However, it is not only broadcasting schedules and programming that help to domesticate media technologies. These technologies are also a form of material culture that are given meaning in domestic space as they are used within home-making practices. Therefore, we need to think about how radios, TVs and – in my final example – computers are combined with other forms of material culture to construct and negotiate the meaning of domestic culture. For example, in her research on the meaning of TV in Brazil, Ondina Fachel Leal (1995: 316) identifies how the TV set as an object can play a key role in symbolizing particular meanings of home. The working-class people in her study surrounded their TVs with an 'entourage' of other meaningful objects. In the process, the TV is 'made' to be watched by both members of the household and passers-by on the street, even when the set is turned off.[6] Indeed, sometimes the consumption of the set itself may be far more significant than the consumption of programming. This is clearly demonstrated in Gell's study of Sri Lankan fishermen who proudly displayed their TV as a status symbol despite having no access to an electricity supply that would enable them to watch it (Morley 1992: 214). More generally, Lally (2002) suggests that when new technologies enter the home they also need to establish relationships with existing objects within the home. A computer may replace an existing technology such as a typewriter, it may compete for attention with other objects within the home and it may give other things a new lease of life (a discarded table might become a 'new' computer desk).

While the majority of this section has focused on historical studies of the domestication of media technologies, the more recent example of the computer demonstrates how similar processes of domestication continue to accompany the entry of new technologies into the home. Unlike TV, computers had a significant 'social life' in the public sphere before being thought of as a domestic technology (Haddon 1992: 86). Before the late-1980s, domestic computers (like radios before them) were primarily used by 'gadgeteers' who were mainly interested in the technological capabilities of the hardware rather than the software (Murdock et al. 1992; Lally 2002). However, in her study of home computing in Australia, Elaine Lally (2002: 51–2) argues that by the 1990s computers were increasingly being sold as a 'domestic appliance' that was an essential component of modern family life. The problem was that computers did not look domesticated at this stage and still resembled technologies associated with the workplace. While some manufacturers attempted to pre-domesticate computers by making them resemble 'brown goods' such as TVs (and many other home entertainment technologies that have often had a wooden or bakelite finish), these were rejected by consumers who were not yet prepared to accept that computers were a leisure, rather than a work, technology (Lally 2002: 61). (Apple's IMac – which 'came in colours' – successfully overcame some of this resistance in the late 1990s.) Nonetheless, it was the representation of computers as an essential household item that helped to pre-domesticate the technology. For example, women's and computer magazines demonstrated how the computer could be integrated into household routines and activities such as collating recipes or budgeting while educational discourses constructed home computing as a form of **rational recreation** (Lally 2002: 55–9; see also Murdock et al. 1992).

Lally's study examines how first-generation users of domestic computers negotiated a place for the technology within the temporal rhythms and spatial patterns of their homes. The position of computers in domestic life was not instantly achieved. They were often subject to a period of novelty use when first purchased before being embedded in 'temporal patterns of everyday routines' and 'cyclical patterns of working weeks and weekends' (Lally 2002: 123). In some households computers became thoroughly domesticated as they became embedded in domestic routines as, for example, people checked their emails with their morning cup of coffee; in other homes, the computer had a far less central place in everyday life.

In domesticating the computer, households used home-making practices to negotiate a place for this relatively immobile technology. Rooms and furniture had to be adapted in order to make the computer at home, while relationships between household members were negotiated through the arrangement of the computer's desktop. Other people tried to domesticate the technology through aesthetic and caring practices, such as making a cover for their computer or decorating it with teddy bears (Lally 2002: 178–9). For others, tidying around the computer and its 'entourage' – or tidying the desktop itself – offered 'a strategy for maintaining control over the domestic ensemble' and establishing 'a sense of proprietoriality' (Lally 2002: 208), although creating a mess around the computer is another strategy for establishing a sense of ownership (Furlong 1995). The idea that people use their consumption practices to establish ownership of a technology – or to negotiate their relationships with other household members – is explored in more detail in the next section.

In this section we have explored the complex processes through which media technologies are made to be at home in domestic cultures. ICTs have been domesticated through their incorporation into the existing values and practices associated with home. Indeed, in the case of radio and TV, these processes of domestication have often worked to reproduce the connection between home and family, working to exclude those who do not watch or listen in 'conventional' families. However, media technologies have also been used to renegotiate the meaning of domestic culture, including new conceptions of 'normal' family life. Furthermore, these technologies have also been used to enable people to be both at home and mobile, and to break down some of the boundaries between public and private spheres.

The media in everyday life

In order to understand how media technologies are incorporated into domestic cultures, we also need to understand how our engagement with media technologies and content is shaped by the social relationships between household members within the home. For example, the place that TV viewing has in our domestic lives is often the result of complex negotiations between household members about how we watch TV, when we watch it, where we watch it and who we watch it with. In this section, I examine studies that demonstrate how the meaning of domestic media use is shaped by wider social relations within the household. These studies suggest that media technologies are frequently inserted into existing power relationships between men and women, and adults and children, within the home. The way in which we make use of the media can reproduce – and sometimes challenge – these power relationships. Furthermore, studying the social relationships within which we use media technologies can also contribute to our understanding of domestic cultures more generally, offering insights into how households organize the relationships between domestic labour and leisure, and into how households negotiate the relationship between public and private spheres.

In his study of the domestic consumption of TV, Morley (2000: 92) argues that family viewing does not occur 'naturally' but has to be orchestrated. Just as family mealtimes are often the result of complex scheduling and organizational activities that enable household members to come together to experience a sense of 'family life', so family viewing is often dependent on similar negotiations. Furthermore, with the increase in multi-set households, it has been claimed that family viewing – like family eating – is under threat and requires more complex negotiations in order to be achieved. However, collective viewing is not only used to build a sense of a family or household identity. Moores (1996) illustrates this point using the example of a group of students who forged a collective identity by sharing a subscription to satellite TV and watching TV together, despite the fact that they did not actually live together.

However, it is not only the simultaneous consumption of domestic media that is used to establish household identities; the ways in which access to these technologies is organized also contributes to a sense of a collective identity and is part of a household's 'techniques of managing their living together' (Lally 2002: 136). Not surprisingly, the results of these negotiations are not always harmonious. For example, Lally observes how tensions can be generated between household members when one person monopolizes the telephone lines – or generates huge telephone bills – through their use of the Internet. (Lally's study was conducted at a time when dial-up Internet connections – rather than Broadband – were dominant.) Likewise, she found that parents were often engaged in struggles to regulate children's access to computers and, in particular, to the type of content that their kids had access to through the Internet. In this instance, organizing media use within a household also becomes a means of managing the relationship between the home and the public sphere.

Tensions around the use of media technologies also need to be located within an analysis of power relationships within households. In *Family Television*, Morley (1986) focuses on how these power relationships are gendered. Although TV viewing is a key leisure activity, he argues, the ability to experience it as a form of leisure – and to exercise choice over what and how to watch – needs to be understood in relation to the way in which gender structures the extent to which the home is experienced as a site of leisure. As we have already seen, the association between masculinity and the public world of work means that home has been constructed as a site of leisure for men, while for women who have primary responsibility for domestic labour, the home is less easily experienced as a site of leisure because it is also a place of work. Morley argues that men's economic and social power deriving from their social roles as 'breadwinners', combined with their ability to experience the home as a site of freedom and leisure, resulted in them asserting their power over the TV set in a number of ways. For example, men used their power to exercise control over what was watched and were able to devote themselves to concentrated viewing because they identified home with leisure. However, for most of the women in his study, the home was a site of work and they found it difficult to claim a similar right to watch TV as a leisure activity; women frequently multi-tasked while watching TV and they would defer to other people's viewing preferences as a way of maintaining family harmony, only able to indulge their own 'solo pleasures' when there was no-one else around. This suggests that there are not 'equal opportunities' to engage with the TV set. Gendered roles and responsibilities shape people's relationship to each other and the TV set.

Morley's study suggests that media technologies are not only inserted into existing power relationships within the home but can be used to extend or reinforce these domestic power relationships. While some critics have argued that Morley's study is now sufficiently dated to have little use in explaining contemporary media use (Gauntlett and Hill 1999), a range of other studies have also suggested that the domestic consumption of ICTs frequently reproduces existing gendered divisions and identities within the home. For example, a number of studies have demonstrated how women use the telephone to enable their gendered role as carers who are responsible for family life by maintaining connections with – and a sense of connectedness to – family members (Livingstone 1992; Rakow 1992; Moyal 1995). Likewise, Lally (2002: 159) demonstrates how women's use of the domestic computer is an extension of the social and cultural requirements of motherhood: 'the mother's role as nurturer, supporter and household manager tends to be perpetuated around the home computer' (see also Wheelock 1992). However, women may also use new technologies to resist their roles as wives and mothers. For example, Ann Gray (1992) found that some women refused to learn how to programme the video recorder because they didn't want to add to their domestic responsibilities. Lally documents how some women found that learning to use the computer was a way of developing their self-confidence and self-esteem, enabling them to challenge masculine authority. Nonetheless, despite the number of years between their studies, Lally's (2002: 157) research reinforces Morley's earlier conclusions about domestic media use. She argues that:

> new technologies arrive into an already gendered setting: with a gendered domestic division of labour, gender-specific household technologies, gendered access to the economic resources of the household, and gendered differences in the right to spare time within the routines of the household.

Media technologies are also used to reflect, construct and negotiate generational relationships within the home. For parents, decisions about the role of media technologies within the home are often negotiated in relation to ideas about both the potential and dangers that these technologies can pose for children, and for family life more generally. Parents often make decisions about what media technologies should be purchased for the home in relation to what is appropriate or 'necessary' for their children (Seiter 1999; Buckingham 2000). For example, research suggests that a first home computer is often purchased 'on behalf of the children' because they have been represented as crucial for educational success and as a form of rational recreation (Lally 2002; Murdock et al. 1992; Wheelock 1992). However, at the same time, parents may often see ICTs as a potential threat to their children and this not only involves negotiating *which* technologies to buy but also *where* they should be placed within the home. Given widespread moral panics about how both TV and the Internet can bring 'unsuitable' content into the home that poses a potential threat to children, parents have to negotiate the extent to which they wish to regulate media use within the home. However, these decisions and negotiations are also effected by material factors: there remain significant inequalities between children's access to media technologies that can compound other forms of inequality and social exclusion (Buckingham 2000). Nonetheless, many children in the West do enjoy a 'media-rich bedroom culture' that can challenge the idea that the family living room is the centre of domestic media consumption (Bovill and Livingstone 2001).

Silverstone (1992) suggests that domestic media consumption also takes place with the distinctive **moral economy** of a household – a framework that is established in constructing what home means within a particular household. However, children may make use of ICTs to challenge their parents' right to define the meaning of home by reworking the boundaries between public and private. A number of studies demonstrate how computer gaming – often a central part of 'boy cultures' – is practised across a network of households (Haddon 1992; Wheelock 1992). For example, Ruth Furlong's (1995) research demonstrates how computer gaming is a social activity that can be used to challenge parental control over 'appropriate' media use. The boys in her study were clearly aware of whose homes would enable them to best indulge their media use, so the activity of 'moving *between* houses' became a means gaining 'spatial freedom' and constructing 'an "alternative" moral economy' (Furlong 1995: 179; for work on the domestication of the gaming console, see Flynn 2003).

Other studies demonstrate how Internet technologies are used by children to create a virtual distance from – as well as privacy within – the home, enabling them to create collective identities with friends rather than physically co-present family members (Livingstone 2005). At the same time these technologies offer ways for households to overcome the tensions produced by family life, enabling people to 'live together separately' (Flichy cited in Livingstone 2005: 21). As Bovill and Livingstone (2001: 17) argue:

> Within the home the multiplication of personally owned media may facilitate children's use of individual, privatized space, as opposed to communal family space . . . At the same time, the nature of such private space within the home may be transformed as the media-rich bedroom increasingly becomes the focus of peer activity, and as the media themselves, through their contents, bring the outside world indoors.

For example, social networking websites such as Facebook and Myspace facilitate children's ability to be both home and away at the same time. In this way children's media use challenges the idea of home can be thought of as either a coherent or bounded entity.

Furthermore, domestic consumption practices are not only shaped within households but also by relationships beyond a household. For example, absent parents in reconstituted families may shape domestic life by playing a role in regulating what media content is suitable for children (Lally 2002). Furthermore, single-parent families often engage within 'extended households' that include former and new partners (Lemor 2006); children who moved between these households 'could experience different rules and regulations, different regimes' (Haddon 2006: 109). Maria Bakardjieva (2006: 66) takes this argument further in her study of the Internet. Internet use within the home, she suggests, doesn't simply reflect pre-existing values within the household but is part of a process through which households engage in a 'constant struggle to manage change' as 'ways of life had to be reinvented and renegotiated almost on a daily basis'.

These debates add substance to Lally's (2002: 38) observation that there are often 'multiple "homes"' within a household. Furthermore, these studies problematize the idea that households are fixed and stable entities with their own specific 'moral economy'. Domestic media consumption not only reproduces power relationships within a household but can also be used to resist, challenge or rework these power relationships. Moreover, as I have already begun to suggest, media technologies have the capacity to blur or rework the boundaries between public and private. It is these issues that I explore in more detail in the following section.

Media homes and homelands

This section focuses on how the sense of belonging that is often associated with home is created at a range of scales, from the domestic to the national and the transnational. In this book, I have explored how a sense of home is constructed within domestic space. However, as I have also suggested, the idea of home cannot simply be equated with domestic cultures and domestic spaces. Instead, we need to think about the relationships between 'material and imaginative geographies of home' that are created locally, regionally, nationally and transnationally and 'the lived experience of home on a domestic scale' (Blunt and Dowling 2006: 198). For example, some of the literature on migration demonstrates how migrants frequently identify a sense of home with a place of origin that is far away from their place of residence. Nonetheless, as I go on to explore in this section, the media frequently play a key role in articulating these distant 'homelands' and domestic spaces, creating complex new conceptions of home. Although large-scale social processes such as globalization and localization may appear to be far removed from the focus of this book, Dave Morley argues that we can only understand the significance of these processes by examining the ways in which people make sense of and experience them within everyday domestic cultures. The local spaces we inhabit are partly produced through 'the "indigenization" (or "domestication") of global or "foreign" resources and inputs' (Morley 1992: 282).

The media play a crucial role in bringing the experience of belonging to a nation into everyday life and, in the process, they enable 'the public' to be experienced within 'the private'. For Benedict Anderson, it is only with the development of the national newspaper that people acquire a sense of consciousness of belonging to a wider collective unity called 'the nation'. Anderson (1991: 66) argues that nations are 'imagined communities': they are 'imagined because the members of even the smallest nations will never know most of their fellow-members, meet them or even hear of them, yet in the minds of each lives the image of their communion'. It is not only the content of newspapers that helps to produce a consciousness of common interests and values that unite the nation but also participation in the ritual act of reading the newspaper that produces a sense of collective experience. The development of national broadcasting systems strengthens this sense of connectedness with other members of the nation and brings the nation into everyday domestic life. While the content of broadcasts can foster the sense of a common culture that members of the nation share, ritual participation in viewing particular broadcasts helps to produce a common sense of temporality across the nation. As Paddy Scannell (2000: 21) argues, 'Day in day out radio, television and newspapers link . . . two incommensurate temporalities: the historical life of societies and the lifetimes of individual social members'.

Morley argues that TV in the UK – like radio in the 1930s – has been imagined primarily as a domestic medium consumed by families and, in the process, constructs a 'nation of families'. (For work on the often complex relationships between nation, TV and the domestic in other national contexts see, for example, Dhoest 2007.) Indeed, familial imagery is central to the way in which the nation is constructed more generally, enabling people to feel a sense of connection with a relatively abstract notion. As Anne McLintock observes:

> The term nation derives from natio: to be born – we speak of nations as 'motherlands' and 'fatherlands'. Foreigners 'adopt' countries that are not their native homes and are nationalized in the 'national family'. We talk of the 'family of nations', of 'homelands' and 'native' lands. In Britain, immigration matters are dealt with at the Home Office; in the United States the president and his wife are called the First Family.
>
> (cited in Morley 2000: 108)

This 'familialization' of the nation also works to legitimate the idea of domestic cultures as family cultures, working to exclude those who do not live in 'conventional' families. Furthermore, as Morley (2000: 107) argues:

> National broadcasting can thus create a sense of unity – and of corresponding boundaries around – the nation; it can link the peripheral to the centre; turn previously exclusive social events into mass experiences; and, above all, it penetrates the domestic sphere, linking the national public into the private lives of its citizens through the creation of both sacred and quotidian moments of national communion.

Therefore, broadcasting not only produces the experience of national life in domestic space but, at the same time, it involves 'a nationalization of the domestic and a domestication of the national' (Morley 2000: 107).

As I have already suggested, the sense of connectedness between domestic cultures and national cultures is not only produced through the content of broadcasting but through the way in which TV is woven into daily routines across households. The most obvious example of this is found in news programming that not only constructs a sense of what a nation has in common but also offers a rarely changing timetable around which individual households can collectively structure their days.[7] In the UK the relatively fixed schedules of prime-time soap operas can also connect individual households in simultaneous common ritual practices and establish knowledge and interests that their viewers share in common. Likewise, 'national festivals . . . become. . . . media occasions' (Chaney cited in Morley 1992: 284) that create a domestic mode of participation in public events and fuse public and domestic life. These 'festivals' may be 'traditional' events such as the Queen's annual Christmas broadcast to British households on behalf of the royal family; they may also be events in the annual media calendar – for example, TV charity events such as Comic Relief and Children in Need that encourage domestic participation as part of a national public event. As a result, Dayan and Katz argue, 'ceremonial space has been reconstituted . . . in the home . . . the huge audience of media events has led to . . . the domestic celebratory form' (cited in Moores 2000: 110).

However, this is not to suggest that there is a harmonious fit between the values of domestic and national cultures. While some people may refuse the power of ICTs to bring public life into domestic cultures,[8] others may refuse to identify with the ways in which national broadcasting constructs a 'common culture'. For example, people may refuse to let a particular classed version of national culture dominate their domestic life. As a respondent in Lofgren's historical study of Swedish broadcasting articulated it, 'when the radio was on, the room wasn't really ours – the sonorous voices with their (metropolitan) accents pushed our thick regional voices into a corner, where we commented in whispers on the cocksure statements from the radio' (cited in Morley 2000: 437). In a similar vein, some of the people interviewed by Moores (1996: 56) in his study of satellite broadcasting, refused the 'paternalistic' address of British TV news and sought out the 'Americanized' sense of the world offered by satellite news channels. This case demonstrates how some people may take advantage of the opportunities to establish new forms of identification that are offered by the proliferation of cable and satellite channels, the rise of **narrowcasting**, and by the expansion of transnational media technologies that cut across national boundaries. However, as Morley (1991) argues, these changes do not simply result in new forms of global culture nor do they simply fragment media audiences; instead, he suggests that we need to understand how people are using domestic media technologies to create complex relationships between the domestic, the local, the national and the global.

While some people may refuse the power of national broadcasting to shape their domestic culture, other people may find themselves excluded by the terms on which broadcasting constructs the nation. The address to a 'nation of families' not only excludes those who live outside 'conventional' family structures but, as Morley (2001:

437) argues, 'British broadcasting principally issues an invitation to participate not simply in an abstract form of "sociality" but in a particular type of white, middle-class, English ethnic culture – an invitation which, by definition, excludes a great many'. However, transnational communications can be used to enable alternative experiences of home for ethnic groups and migrants who feel excluded from the national culture where they physically reside. Satellite TV can be used to create 'transnational and diasporic public spheres' and 'small media' such as letters and emails enable other forms of collective identification with people who are physically distant (Morley 2000: 125). However, such uses of media technologies are not uncontested and national governments may seek to regulate which forms of transnational media can be consumed in living rooms within their boundaries. For example, authorities in Iran have attempted to limit access to satellite TV that have been seen as part of a Western attack on Islam (Morley 2001). Likewise, Morley (2001: 435) notes, French right-wing politicians have attempted to ban the use of satellite dishes in districts with a high North African immigrant population because they claim that it enables these groups to live 'in a world of "Virtual Islam"'. He argues that 'these immigrants' virtual involvement in this transnational cultural space was . . . presented, in effect, as a form of "cultural treason" against the French nation'. In this way the use of media technologies to maintain a sense of connectedness with a 'foreign' culture within everyday domestic practices has been seen as a threat to established relationships between national and domestic cultures.

A useful example of how media technologies can be used to negotiate forms of domestic culture that maintain a connection to distant 'homelands' is provided by Marie Gillespie's (1989) study of the use of video by South Asians in Southall. She identifies how the families in her study scheduled time at weekends for the collective viewing of 'Asian' films on video as a means of creating time for family togetherness. For the parents in Gillespie's study, the content of these films not only offered them opportunities to experience nostalgia for their homeland, but these films were also seen as a crucial way of socializing children into their linguistic, cultural and religious heritage. The parents saw watching these videos as a means of linking children to a distant regional culture within their British homes. Watching videos not only offered a way of overcoming spatial distances and participating within a South Asian diaspora but it also offered a way of creating new British-Asian identities through the consumption of 'Indian' films in a British context. In this way, watching videos enabled these families to construct complex understandings of home that articulated elements from global, national and local contexts within domestic culture. Similarly, more recent work by Shaun Moores and Karen Qureshi (2000: 132–3) has examined how parents in Pakistani-Scottish families used Asian cable and satellite channels to enable their children to have 'a routine and familiar point of contact with their "cultural heritage"'. In both these studies, there were significant generational differences in the ways in which these media resources were used. In Gillespie's study the children use the films they saw on video as a resource in making sense of their own position as both Asian and British, while in Moores and Qureshi's study, the children frequently rejected Asian channels, finding more to identify with in British terrestrial TV channels.

However, studies that focus on migrants' use of media to maintain a connection to homeland have rarely analysed the significance of how the consumption of 'foreign' media impacts on everyday domestic practices. These issues are addressed by Asu Aksoy and Kevin Robins (2002) in their study of Turkish-speaking Londoners who watch Turkish national TV live via satellite. They argue that '*the* key innovation in the lives of Turkish migrants . . . is simply the ability to routinely watch television from Turkey, and to be thereby in synchronized contact with everyday life and events in Turkey' (Aksoy and Robins 2002: 6). While Turkish TV offers opportunities to experience the dailiness of life in Turkey within domestic space in London, the spatial separation between the national contexts in which these broadcasts are produced and consumed transforms these London Turks' relationship to TV. As Aksoy and Robins (2002: 18) argue, 'the world of broadcasting is not seamlessly connected to the world of the street outside, as it would be for viewers watching in Turkey' and this creates a 'dislocated kind of viewing'. Turkish TV broadcasts both become part of everyday domestic life in London and simultaneously also appear to be divorced from their surroundings.

Aksoy and Robins' study demonstrates the importance of understanding how transnational media are consumed in local, domestic contexts. While migrants' use of transnational media may enable them to maintain a romantic attachment to a 'homeland', these media also have to rub up against another sense of home, '*the lived experience of locality*' (Ahmed 1999: 341). The consumption of global media in local domestic contexts involves an interplay in which the meanings of – and sense of identification with – elsewhere is worked upon within domestic cultures. Therefore, as critics such as Morley remind us, transnational forms of identification and community are experienced in concrete and lived domestic cultures. In this way, global flows of ideas, people and communications undergo processes of domestication in our places of residence.

Conclusions

In this chapter I have demonstrated how the concept of domestication provides a useful framework for not only understanding how media technologies undergo processes of enculturation within the home but also how the same media technologies are used to transform domestic culture. While I have used domestication as a value-neutral concept, it is important to be aware that some critics have assumed that domestication is an inherently conservative process. For example, Silverstone (1994: 174) claims that the domestication is ultimately 'a process both of taming the wild and cultivating the tame' (a position reproduced in Berker et al. 2006). The implications of this become clearer in his later work in which he argues that domestication has a 'conservative' side that is organized around 'moral defensiveness': domestication seeks to preserve 'the core of a personal world against all-comers' and can lead to the 'neutralization of potential for real change' (Silverstone 2006: 247). Indeed, he concludes that 'in so far as domestication fully succeeds, it could also be said to be failing' because it 'refuses the claims for a wider sense of responsibility for the world, and for those who share it with us' (Silverstone 2006: 247).

Silverstone's argument reproduces a position in which domestic cultures are represented as inherently conservative and inward-looking, a position that I criticized in Chapter 3. While domestic cultures *can* certainly be conservative, there is little evidence to suggest that the domestication of media technologies results in resistance to change and a desire to withdraw from the world. Indeed, as some of the examples I have discussed in this chapter demonstrate, the domestication of media often results in a renegotiation – and often a weakening – of boundaries between public and private. It brings the outside world into the home and enables forms of transnational identifications that challenge traditional boundaries. Indeed, Silverstone (2006: 244) remains aware of how new media might be used to blur the divisions between public and private, creating new conditions in which 'private conversations . . . occupy public spaces . . . creating new kinds of public cultures, shifting boundaries between public and private'. This can also reverse the flow of communications from the public into the private: for example, webcams can make our domestic cultures into public events (Couldry 2005: 218). While I discuss changing relations between public and private in more detail in the next chapter, it is crucial to remember that the interpenetration of public and private is not just a product of *new* media technologies.

This chapter has also explored a more expansive sense of home that extends beyond domestic space at both national and transnational scales. As Blunt and Dowling (2006: 196) argue, 'transnational homes are shaped by the interplay of both mobile and located homes and identities and by the processes and practices of home-making within particular places and across transnational space'. Thinking about how a sense of home is constructed across a range of scales, therefore, doesn't undermine the significance of domestic cultures: it is frequently within domestic space that our connection to other senses of home is negotiated and lived. This also provides further evidence of the ways in which domestic cultures are not necessarily bounded and defensive but instead are a site for working through a range of relationships to both the national and the global. As Morley (2001: 428) argues:

> The modern home itself can be said to be a 'phantasmagoric' place, to the extent that electronic media of various kinds allow the intrusion of distant events into the space of domesticity . . . Thus, the 'far away' is now irredeemably mixed in with the space of the near, as processes of migration and of media representation bring actual and virtual forms of alterity into jealously guarded 'home territories' of various sorts.

However, inequalities in material and cultural resources can impact on people's opportunities for virtual travel from domestic space. Moreover, unequal power relations within – and beyond – domestic cultures also structure who has the ability to take advantage of these imaginative forms of travel, who they get to travel with and where they are able to go (Moores 1993).

The themes raised in this chapter can also enable us to think about alternative ways of thinking about domestic culture beyond the case of the media. In her argument about how to conceptualize 'a progressive sense of place', Doreen Massey (1993: 66) argues that we need to think about how the 'uniqueness of place' is formed through the 'particular interactions and mutual articulations of social relations, social processes, experiences and understandings, in a situation of co-presence' and how 'these relations, experiences and understandings are actually constructed on a far larger scale'. We can use these ideas to think about how domestic cultures are also never bounded places. Although they are frequently imagined through an opposition to the public sphere and 'the outside world', 'the particularity of the linkage *to* that "outside"' is 'part of what constitutes the place' (Massey 1993: 67). In the next chapter I examine in more detail some of the wider ways in which this linkage between domestic cultures and 'the outside world' are being negotiated and reworked.

Further reading

Berker, T., Hartmann, M., Punie, Y. and Ward, K. (eds) (2006) *Domestication of Media and Technology*. Maidenhead: Open University Press.

Lally, E. (2002) *At Home with Computers*. Oxford: Berg.

Moores, S. (2000) *Media and Everyday Life in Modern Society*. Edinburgh: Edinburgh University Press.

Morley, D. (1986) *Family Television: Cultural Power and Domestic Leisure*. London: Comedia.

Morley, D. (1991) Where the Global Meets the Local: Notes from the Sitting Room, *Screen*, 32(1): 1–15.

Silverstone, R. and Hirsch, E. (eds) (1992) *Consuming Technologies: Media and Information in Domestic Spaces*. London: Routledge.

Spigel, L. (1992) *Make Room for TV: Television and the Family Ideal in Postwar America*. Chicago: University of Chicago Press.

Notes

1 One of the solutions to this problem was promised by other new compensatory technologies such as the electric dishwasher (Spigel 1992: 92). There was also the need to negotiate the potential threat to family unity that 'togetherness' could produce. One (commercially unsuccessful) response to the potential conflict that might arise from family viewing was Duoscope that incorporated two receivers, enabling the family to be together but indulge individual preferences (Spigel 1992: 71).

2 It is also worth noting that the link between TV and privatization presumes that TV watching is not a social activity beyond the family. However, when TVs are relatively scarce, TV watching can be anything but privatized as Spigel (1992: 127) notes. Jancovich et al. (2003) make similar points about TV in the UK in the 1950s while Miller (1992) offers more recent examples of collective viewing in Trinidad. Furthermore, claims about privatization also neglect how TV is also consumed in public spaces (see McCarthy 2001).

3 Given that Spigel's aim is to read TV's relationship to the domestic *historically*, it is important to note that this is not the end of the story. Her work demonstrates how the relationship between TV and the domestic is reworked and reimagined in different historical periods (see Spigel 2001a, 2001b and 2005).

4 There is a large body of scholarship on women and soap opera that highlights the relationship between 'the housewife', soaps and domestic life (for an overview of these debates, see Brunsdon 2000). Studies of later daytime American soaps have also sought to demonstrate how the formal features of soaps anticipate distracted viewing (Modleski 1984) although research on TV audiences has questioned whether we can read off how audiences use soap operas from an analysis of their formal features (Seiter et al. 1989; Gray 1992). Nonetheless, studying soap operas can offer one route into understanding domestic cultures. Geraghty (1991) and Brunsdon (1981) offer useful starting points for thinking about these issues.

5 It has also been claimed that in prime-time dramas centred on the workplace, characters interact as if they were members of a family (see Silverstone 1994). Other genres have more recently received attention in attempts to explore the relationship between TV and the domestic. For example, Brunsdon (2004) and O'Sullivan (2005), focusing on the UK, discuss the antecedents of the contemporary lifestyle shows with a focus on domestic life discussed in the last chapter.

6 Leal's study situates her analysis in terms of struggles over taste by considering how the TV has 'no positive aesthetic value' in the upper-class households she studies (Leal 1995: 318). Questions about TV, technology and taste are raised by studies of the public display of satellite dishes in the UK (Moores 1996; Brunsdon 1997).

7 Indeed, in the UK, attempts to change the timing of major national TV news programmes result in national debate.

8 An interesting example is offered by Diane Zimmerman Umble's (1992: 183) study of an Amish community in the USA. She argues that this group refused to have telephones in domestic spaces in order to maintain a sense of their own community and 'articulate distinct social boundaries' between themselves and the outside world.

7 | DISLOCATING PUBLIC AND PRIVATE

Introduction

The distinction between public and private has been central to the modern imagination and continues to structure many institutions, discourses and practices. However, the vigorous defence of the difference between public and private also demonstrates an anxiety that the boundaries between them may be far from fixed. Throughout this book I have problematized the idea that public and private spheres have clearly defined boundaries. Furthermore, I have demonstrated how the meanings of domestic cultures have not only been shaped by public industries, institutions, policies and representations but that domestic cultures have also been frequently outward-looking and have been used as the basis for interventions in public life. Just as domestic spaces are not *only* private, Anna McCarthy (2001: 121) argues that:

> public spaces are not purely and self-evidently public; they are, like every other cultural space, characterized by particular configurations of public and private. Indeed what makes the public/private division such a major category of social power is the fact that it is dynamic and flexible, varying from place to place.

The idea that home life is different to public life is still produced through a wide range of discourses and continues to inform everyday practices. Although some commentators have claimed that the significance of locality and a rooted sense of place is being eroded as we live in increasingly globalized societies characterized by mobility rather than stasis, empirical evidence suggests that not only is this experience of being mobile subjects more available to some more than others, but it also neglects the continuing importance of place for many people (for an overview see, for example, Morley 2000 and Tomlinson 1999). At the same time, and as I go on to discuss in more detail in the following section, domesticity itself may have become more mobile – for example, as new technologies enable people to take home with them wherever they go – and this may have produced a process in which elements of domesticity have become 'dislocated' (Morley 2003).

The idea of the dislocation – or, as Maria Fannin (2003) puts it, the 'displacing' – of domesticity also suggests that aspects of public life are becoming domesticated. If critics such as Silverstone (2006) have suggested that the processes by which technologies are domesticated within the home inevitably results in them being rendered safe and politically conservative, other critics such as Sharon Zukin have argued that the domestication of public space is also an inherently conservative process. For Zukin (1995: iv), 'domestication by cappuccino' refers to the privatization of public space in processes of urban gentrification. While she is clearly using the term domestication to refer to a process in which she believes that public spaces are sanitized and rendered safe and homogeneous, her use of domestication conflates two very different meanings of privatization – becoming more like the private sphere *and* coming under private ownership. Therefore, Zukin's reading of the domestication of public spaces as a negative process and a political problem depends on a conflation of two different meanings of the concept of private. This becomes clearer if we think about how privately owned quasi-public spaces such as shops and leisure complexes are not necessarily domesticated (although they may be). Likewise, while the homeless may domesticate pockets of the city by appropriating public spaces as quasi-domestic living spaces (see below), this does not mean that these spaces become privatized in the process.

My point here is that while the private sphere and domestic culture have frequently been seen as the same thing, private does not necessarily mean domestic. Mimi Sheller and John Urry (2003) make this clear when they highlight the wide range of ways in which the opposition between public and private has been invoked and mobilized. Therefore, while the private has certainly been identified with the domestic, it has also been identified with a range of other meanings such as 'the private sector' and 'private space'. For critics on the left, privatization is often seen as inherently negative because it is associated with processes through which aspects of economic, political, social and cultural life become increasingly shaped by privately owned economic interests (large corporations, and so on) rather than the State. However, it is misleading to simply conflate this conception of the private with an alternative meaning of the private as domestic. Indeed, Sheller and Urry (2003: 108) make the useful suggestion that we need to stop being constrained by the binary opposition between public and private. Instead, they argue that we should pay attention to the way in which ideas of public and private can no longer be identified with particular spaces but are increasingly mobile, considering processes in which there is a 'de-territorialization of publics and privates' that produce 'new hybrids of private-in-public and public-in-private' (see also Sheller 2004). I draw on these ideas in this chapter to explore moments and spaces in which the distinction between public and private – and domestic and non-domestic – have become increasingly blurred and produce new modes of cultural experience.

In the next section, I examine some of the ways in which the domestic has become mobile and de-territorialized so that values that have frequently been associated with domestic culture are used in spaces that are usually seen as non-domestic. The subsequent section discusses relationships between public and private in terms of the relationship between home and work. I explore how boundaries between home and work are frequently blurred, resulting in both the domestication of the workplace and the home becoming more like the workplace. In the final section I challenge the assumption that the idea of home is losing its significance in an increasingly complex, mobile and globalized world, and identify some of the ways in which people are reinvesting in – and transforming the meaning of – domesticity. Throughout the chapter I examine ways in which the boundaries between domestic and non-domestic spaces are drawn and redrawn, policed and negotiated, resisted and reinstated. In the process I demonstrate how distinctions between domestic and non-domestic – and private and public – can never be simply assumed but are continually in process.

Dislocating domesticity

Many critics who are interested in how elements of domestic culture have become mobile have focused on the role of media technologies in these processes of dislocation. While the last chapter explored how media technologies undergo processes of domestication, Morley (2003: 450) has also identified counter-processes in which there has been a 'de-domestication of media'. This suggests that we need to think about how the meanings of both media technologies and media consumption change as forms or practices that have been associated with domestic life become mobile. However, these processes of dislocation and displacing do not just apply to the media and the section goes on to explores how a range of forms, practices and values that have been associated with domestic culture have been mobilized within non-domestic spaces.

It would be easy to think that when domestic media move into the public sphere then they take with them 'domestic' meanings. However, these processes are far from straightforward. Anna McCarthy's research into the use of TV in 'nondomestic space' in the USA from the post-war period onwards demonstrates the sheer 'variability' in the way that TV is used (McCarthy 2001: 3, 10). For example, in places associated with 'trauma', TV can offer people 'the calming focus of the hearth' but, in other sites, there are strenuous attempts to divest TV of its domestic associations – in doctor's waiting rooms, the TV is sometimes surrounded by leaflets and used as an informational source on health (McCarthy 2001: 137, 201). However, the TV (as material culture) in public space may also be domesticated by people who want to take 'ownership' of their workspace. For example, they may be surrounded by an entourage of other significant objects, producing a 'decorative statement [that] is at once a form of public address . . . and simultaneously, a form of intensely personal meaning production' (McCarthy 2001: 126). By domesticating the workplace, we might make a public statement about our identity or use objects as a personal reminder of non-work values and relationships. For example, the display of a child's drawing in a workplace might achieve either of these aims. These processes of domestication through which 'individuals tactically fashion a sense of public and private within their workspaces' are, of course, not limited to TV (McCarthy 2001: 132). Research demonstrates how some people also create an entourage of personal objects and images around – and within – their computer workstations in order 'to humanize and domesticate the workplace' (Lupton and Noble 2002: 18; see also McCarthy 2004).

Some new technologies such as Walkmans and iPods have been seen to offer different kinds of opportunity to be 'private in public'. Michael Bull (2000: 24, 33) argues that the Walkman offers its users an opportunity to take 'home' with them wherever they go. Many of the terms that people in his study associated with their personal stereos are ones commonly associated with domestic cultures – for example, intimacy, security and individuality (Bull 2000: 24, 33). Likewise, iPods are also understood as a 'sanctuary' (Bull 2005: 354). It is not only the technologies themselves but the sounds people select to play on them that enable users to make home mobile. 'The use of music that has personal associations or connotations heightens these feelings' helping people to carry with them 'a "memory bank" of "significant narratives"' (Bull 2000: 24, 37). These technologies not only enable people to withdraw into private worlds but also to code the public in terms of the personal and domestic (see also du Gay et al. 1997).

Like Walkmans – although in different ways – mobile telephones offer their users the opportunity to be 'private in public', operating as a device to block out or recode the surrounding world although, at the same time, 'users can publicize their private information' (Humphreys 2005: 828). While both TVs and computers have been seen as technologies that offer the potential to persuade children to stay at home by making it a more inviting place, mobile telephones are often bought for children to enable them to maintain a connection with home. Therefore, although mobile telephones could be seen as a technology that privileges the experience of mobility over the importance of locality, this does not necessarily correspond with the ways in which they are used. Studies suggest that a primary use of mobile telephones is to maintain and enhance connections to friends and family, activities that also enable women's domestic roles as 'kin-keepers' to be maintained when they are not at home (Wei and Lo 2000; Katz and Aakhus 2002). Indeed, as John Tomlinson, argues, mobile telephones could be thought of as 'technologies of the hearth: as imperfect instruments by which people try – in conditions of mundane deterritorialization – to maintain something of the security of cultural location' (2001: [13]).

Cars enable people to be 'private in public' in different ways, operating as 'mobile "domestic" environments, bubbles of privacy moving through public spaces' (Sheller 2004: 44). Indeed, Sheller and Urry (2003) claim, cars also show the limitations of thinking in terms of public or private as they hybridize spaces and spheres. While 'private zones of domesticity [are] reproduced on the road through social relations' (Sheller and Urry 2003: 115) – for example, installing child-seats to protect and care for children – contemporary top-end cars can also operate as 'mobile leisure spaces, business places and communication devices' (Sheller 2004: 44). Yet these new in-car technologies are not straightforwardly geared to either domestic or non-domestic activities – the same mobile telephone can be used to negotiate business deals and plan a children's party. Indeed, cars, as Raymond Williams (1983) recognized, challenge any straightforward understanding of public and private because they enable us to operate in a domestic, privatized space while being mobile within the public sphere (see also Urry 2006).

However, thinking about how aspects of domestic cultures are mobilized in public space can also take other directions. In Chapter 2, I identified how distinctions between public and private were a modern invention. While the public monuments of modernism were frequently predicated on a rejection of domestic and 'homely' architecture – and while modernist architects frequently sought to rid domestic architecture of its 'homely' qualities – there is a longer pattern of exchange between the aesthetics of domestic and public spaces. Rybczynski (1987) highlights how a domestic aesthetic was used to make new technological developments like the train appear less alien and more safe in the Victorian period. For example, 'train compartments were designed to look like small parlours; wealthy businessmen had their own railway carriages, whose interiors were furnished like plush smoking rooms with panelled walls, easy chairs, and tasselled drapery' (Rybczynski 1987: 174).

A more recent example of the way elements of the domestic are mobilized in non-domestic space can be seen in contemporary café culture. Chains such as Starbucks create a homely ambience using stripped wood floors and 'comfy' brown leather sofas. These features not only attempt to associate a global chain with the more personalized forms of hospitality associated with domestic culture but they also signify that Starbucks' cafés are a safe space, distinguishing them from earlier American coffee houses that were often represented as 'marginal' and disreputable (see Lyons 2005). However, Starbucks aims to go beyond merely domesticating public space, claiming that it wants to create a form of hybrid space: 'Design at Starbucks is about creating a third place. Third place is where life happens, a place between home and work, a place people can go to feel at ease, relax, visit with others or enjoy some private time'.[1] Ray Oldenburg (2001), who is frequently credited with coining the term 'third place', is critical of Starbucks' appropriation of the concept. He points to a long tradition of 'third places' in American cultural life, located in spaces such as the neighbourhood bar or diner, that have been threatened by the increasing privatization of American culture (privatization he associates with both suburban domesticity and corporate cultures). Although the concept of the third place clearly invoke olders notions of 'community', in both Oldenburg's work and Starbucks' PR statements, these spaces offer the promise that we can hybridize elements of the domestic and the public while compensating for the seeming inadequacies of both.

Given associations between hospitality and home, it is perhaps not surprising that some parts of the catering and hotel industry have attempted to incorporate aspects of domestic culture in order to suggest a personalized service. Indeed, Roy Wood suggests that, during the twentieth century, hotels have become increasingly modelled on the home and offer private facilities such as in-room TVs and en-suite bathrooms (see Warde and Martens 2000: 132). The rise of the apartment-hotel could be seen to take this process further. However, this is not straightforward as it involves an attempt to fuse elements of cultures that have been constructed as antithetical. As Alan Warde (1997: 113) explains, the opposition between private and public spheres – and between care and convenience – generates a series of further oppositions

> Personalized service against commodified produce; lavishing care against saving time; expressive against instrumental work; particularistic attention against mass provision; and so forth. In each case, the first element of the antithesis conjures up familiar and homely love, the second the cold and impersonal world of capitalist rationalization.

It is for this reason that there are frequently attempts to add value to commercially produced foods by associating them with domestic culture: pubs advertise 'home-cooked' food and supermarkets offer 'homestyle' ranges of ready-meals (Warde 1997, 1999; Ashley et al. 2004). However, at the same time, we do not expect homestyle to mean that food is sometimes burned, or served with a family argument. Indeed, restaurant chains such as McDonalds have built their empires on offering an identical service wherever and whenever people visit and the rise of ready-meals has been associated with the publicization of private life.

Other parts of the hospitality industry seek to offer the experience of a 'home away from home'. For example, the rise of 'boutique hotels' that seek to distinguish themselves from the corporate anonymity of large hotel chains is partly attributed to the perception that they offer a more personal, homely and unique experience. Indeed, they can be seen to be *more* homely than people's actual homes by offering a 'nostalgic' experience of domestic life (McIntosh and Siggs 2005: 77–8). In a similar manner to Starbucks, these hotels are not 'real homes' but they accentuate aspects of domestic cultures in order to compensate for the feeling that people's 'real homes' fail to live up to the 'ideal home'. Commenting on the rise of the 'boutique-hotel look' as an aesthetic for domestic interiors, designer Page Ikeda observes that when people are 'on vacation and staying in these spaces, they feel relaxed. They want that same element in their homes' (Muther 2006: [1]). Therefore, if some forms of commercial provision seek to sell 'bubbles of domesticity' within the public sphere, then this domesticated public can also be used as a model to improve the domesticated private when people try to reproduce the boutique hotel look in their own living spaces. Home interiors shows advise people on how to reproduce this look to produce a 'top-end spec' and some boutique hotels now literally act as boutiques by selling accessories and furnishings to take away. However, this can mask the extent to which the daily services of a paid maid are required in order to achieve 'the look' (Muther 2006: [2]).

Ideas about a 'home away from home' also inform some of the public institutions that have taken over responsibility for managing aspects of life that occupy a position in limbo between public and domestic. For example, because old age and the process of dying may be at odds with contemporary images of the 'ideal home', these life stages are now frequently relocated to institutional public settings that represent themselves as 'a home from home' but where elements of domesticity frequently mask a rule-bound public institution (Hockey 1999b). More complex forms of hybridization of public and domestic can be found in the rise of ' "homelike" birthing rooms' in some hospitals in North America. Fannin (2003) analyses how these hospitals offer the opportunity to experience birth as if it were in a domestic setting but within a medicalized space. 'Hospital rooms have been transformed into "homelike" spaces, with hardwood floors, brightly coloured bedspreads, rocking chairs, and carefully designed cabinetry that hides medical equipment' and women are encouraged to bring in objects and sounds from home to further domesticate the room (Fannin 2003: 513). She identifies how this trend is a response to the rise of the 'home birth movement' among middle-class women that pressed for a more 'humane' experience of childbirth, and also an attempt by some hospitals to win over middle-class consumers by attempting to tie in women, who they see as gatekeepers over family health decisions, as loyal customers by offering them a pleasant experience of childbirth. In the process, the 'homelike' space seeks to articulate the technical/medical with the domestic, aiming to produce a hybrid and 'a "deinstitutionalized" space still firmly situated within an institution' and attempting 'to spatially mediate conflicts over the very meaning of reproduction through mobilization of signs of the domestic' (Fannin 2003: 518, 520). As Fannin identifies, these hybridized home-hospital spaces offer a choice for those who can afford it. This masks the extent to which home birth is not a lifestyle choice for women who lack the financial resources to pay hospital bills.

However, other forms of 'private in public' are less voluntary and highlight the limits placed on hybridizing public and private. Because 'homelessness brings the private into the streets' (Rosler cited in Morley 2000: 28), it represents a threat to spatial boundaries, resulting in numerous attempts to erase the presence of the homeless in order to 'purify' public space (Cloke et al. 2003: [6]).[2] The practices of the homeless can work to create 'domestic' spaces within and across the city – for example, 'shop doorways become sleeping places, public lavatories become bathrooms'(Cloke et al. 2003: [10]) – but these forms of 'domestic life' come with no rights to privacy from a 'public gaze' (Smith 1993: 105). Nonetheless, representations of homelessness can often work to reaffirm idealized notions of domestic life in which the home is equated with 'safety and security' and the streets with 'fear and danger' (Wardhaugh 1999: 96). Such images also represent the homeless as 'victims' because they are 'out of place' (see Hebdige 1993).

Unsurprisingly, some of the homeless people interviewed by Cloke et al. (2003) observe that institutional spaces such as hostels cannot be used or experienced as a home. However, for some homeless people, hostels may offer the opportunity to experience more of the values associated with domestic cultures than 'real' homes. As one homeless woman interviewed by Julia Wardhaugh (1999: 99) commented, 'I've got more privacy here than I got at bloody home. I know once my bedroom door here is closed no-one is going to come in, and if they do they're going to knock . . . I don't consider myself homeless'.

As I suggested in Chapter 1, cultural theorists have often celebrated the romantic and adventurous figure of the (masculine) traveller who rejects the conservatism and stasis associated with home and femininity (Wolff 1993). Yet not only is mobility less enjoyable 'when there is no home to which to return', the figure of the homeless woman is less easily accommodated within these images. Indeed, one of the key figures of feminine homelessness remains the 'bag lady' who 'carries everywhere with her a collection of objects that come to signify for her a "mobile home"' (Wardhaugh 1999: 94, 104). In this way, the figure of the homeless woman who is outside 'social and spatial boundaries of home, family and domesticity threatens to undermine the construction of the home as a source of identity and as a foundation of social order' (Wardhaugh 1999: 106). Therefore, while attributes associated with femininity and domesticity are being mobilized within the public – not least to make the public a friendlier place for women to consume – homeless women (along with the homeless more generally) mark one of the limits of this process of domestication.

Home as work, work as home

Throughout this book I have examined how the idea of public and private spheres that are spatially and temporally distinct has been crucial to modernity: public and private – and work and home – have not only been associated with different qualities but have also been defined through their difference to each other. Although these boundaries between public and private have always been blurred in practice, in everyday life a lot of work still goes into maintaining these distinctions (Nippert-Eng 1995). However, it has been argued that these boundaries are undergoing a series of wider social and cultural reconfigurations. First, some critics have argued that there has been an increasing domestication of the workplace and a corresponding 'workification' of domestic cultures (Hochschild 2000). Second, other research indicates how an increasing amount of economic activity is moving out of 'public' workspaces and into the home as the number of homeworkers rises, a shift that has been partly enabled by developments in information and communication technologies that enable workers to be connected to the workplace from their homes. Finally, as there is now an expectation that both men and women should engage in paid work in the public sphere, there has been insufficient attention to the implications that this has for domestic life. Who does the caring work associated with domestic life when all adults are increasingly expected to engage in paid work (McDowell et al. 2005)? In this section, I explore how all these processes have implications for thinking about contemporary domestic cultures. In particular, not only do I focus on the increasing permeability between the *spaces* of paid work and home but also on the increasing permeability between the *temporal* experiences of paid work and home.

The organization of social life into separate spheres rested on the idea that distinct boundaries between home and work are desirable in order to promote and protect the home as a 'haven' from the outside world. As I have also made clear, this depended on the classification of domestic labour within the home as 'not work' and the association of home with leisure, suggesting that feminine domestic labour wasn't 'real work' and masking the extent to which home could only be experienced as a site of leisure for the 'breadwinner'. However, although this opposition between home and work has been reproduced through (sometimes contradictory) discourses and structures, Christena Nippert-Eng (1995: 28) suggests that reproducing these distinctions in everyday life requires a considerable amount of labour:

> 'Home' and 'work' are conceptual categories, differently imposed by mentally and physically drawing boundaries around activities, self, things and people . . . The boundaries we draw reflect and reinforce our perceptions of what does and does not belong together (and under what circumstances), and what is the relationship between all of them.

Nippert-Eng argues that people differ in the extent to which they integrate or segregate home and work spaces – and experiences. For example, some people use (or may be required to use) clothes to maintain a distinction between their 'work self' and their 'home self' while others rarely get changed to mark this distinction. Some people maintain separate work and home diaries and calendars while others integrate the two. Some people may seek to domesticate the workplace by always using breaks as personal time or by bringing in food that is prepared at home or having family photographs on their desk. At the same time, they may risk being labelled 'unprofessional' if they bring too much of home into work. While some people may refuse to bring work home or answer work telephone calls at home, others may be more open (or have little choice but to) integrate home and work. Nippert-Eng's work demonstrates how the relationship between home and work isn't fixed but requires complex ongoing negotiations in everyday life (and as I write this at home the washing machine is beeping insistently to tell me that I need to turn it off and put the washing on the line).

For people who do paid work from home – either some or all the time – these boundaries can be difficult to maintain. Far from becoming simply privatized, the modern home can also become public-ized and increasingly hybrid when it becomes the site of paid labour, domestic life and leisure. This represents a different articulation of production and consumption to that associated with pre-industrial modes of production. Rather than being a mode of domestic production, contemporary home-work – even for the self-employed – is frequently governed by the temporal regimes of a post-Fordist capitalist economy. Although doing home-work isn't necessarily new – for example, forms of piece-work such as sewing and stuffing envelopes have long been done by women from home – the extent of home-work is new. While industrialization brought about new ways of conceptualizing time associated with the increasing dominance of clock-time and consequent new forms of time-discipline, this rested on a spatial segregation between work and home as different kinds of 'time zones' associated 'working time' and 'free time'. However, the disembedding mechanisms that Giddens associates with late modernity mean that 'activities become independent of the locations associated with them and are no longer defined by the location for which the activity is performed' (Kaufman-Scarborough 2006: 64). When work comes home 'workplace defined rhythms become part of daily life' (Kaufman-Scarborough 2006: 66). Furthermore, some critics suggest that work is now both spatially and temporally 'overflowing' from fixed locations as work not only intensifies but also undergoes a process of 'extensification' as it becomes redistributed 'across different spaces/scales and times' (Jarvis and Pratt 2006).

Studies of home-work suggest that people negotiate these forms of intrusion into domestic time and space through a range of ways of constructing and reworking spatial and temporal boundaries. For example, one of the homeworkers studied by Moores (1996: 49) created a distance between home and work by unplugging the telephone at night and weekends 'to defend her domestic privacy' while another wanted to be permanently available to people outside the home. Spaces within the home may be coded as 'work spaces' distinct from home spaces, although lack of room in many homes may make these spatial divides much more symbolic than physical. Indeed, similar activities can be coded as work or non-work depending on where and how they are performed. For example, in Katie Ward's (2006) research, one interviewee signalled her leisure use of the computer by moving away from her workspace and going downstairs where she drank coffee while surfing the Internet. Just as morning routines help to mark the transition between segregated home and work spaces, 'time discipline . . . through symbolic acts and artefacts' is often seen as key in managing transitions within the home. Yet homeworkers often find that the end of the working day – or working week – is more difficult to routinize (Tietze and Musson 2002: 324). However, while some people attempt to segregate spatial and temporal dimensions of work and home within their domestic space, other people have little choice – or may actively prefer – to merge work and home, constantly shifting between, and combining, paid work, domestic work and leisure, and research suggests that women tended to integrate activities rather more than men resulting in the experience of 'juggling and struggling' (Tietze and Musson 2002: 326; Kaufman-Scarborough 2006). While homeworking offers people the opportunity to 'save time' by working more intensively or multi-tasking – and offers opportunities to negotiate new relationships between home and work – these forms of integration can also make 'it harder to commit in a meaningful way to either arena' (Tietze and Musson 2002: 330).

In her analysis of how 'homes of the future' are imagined in discourses surrounding the networked 'smart house', Spigel examines how new ways of being 'public in private' have been envisaged. As the corporate symbols of the public sphere lose their symbolic power in the wake of 9/11, she argues, the smart house offers to become central to a networked universe, 'a place where home, community, marketplace, leisure and labour mutate into a commodified sphere of communication' (Spigel 2005: 412). She also suggests that the public-ization of domestic life in the smart house means that 'the normative rhythms of domestic time, vacation time, commute time and labour time are being altered' (Spigel 2005: 414). The smart house doesn't use labour-saving devices to offer time free from labour but offers more opportunities for multi-tasking, especially for women. These luxurious homes offer opportunities to be forever busy and forever engaged in some form of labour. Indeed, Spigel argues, while the affluent leisure class of the early twentieth century demonstrated their superiority through their ability to distance themselves from labour and engage in 'conspicuous consumption', these affluent smart-house dwellers of the early twenty-first century demonstrate their distinction through 'conspicuous production'. As 'work and home become co-extensive', occupants are 'meant to be working all the time' because 'being idle is now suspect' (Spigel 2005: 415).

If Spigel is more concerned with how domestic culture is envisioned in cutting-edge images of future living currently only available to particular sections of the wealthy, the idea that work and home have merged to create constantly busy subjects who make 'productive' use of their time appears to have a wider purchase. In the process, Arlie Russell Hochschild (2000) suggests, home is no longer experienced as a 'haven' from work and a site of leisure because the temporal demands of the industrial workplace have become part of contemporary domestic experience. Hochschild's research, first published in 1989, is based on interviews with management and employees at a large American company that prided itself on family-friendly policies designed to help their staff to achieve a 'work–life balance'. While there was considerable resistance to these policies among some managers, there was also resistance among employees: many employees found the experience of domestic life more problematic than work and they frequently opted to use work as a 'retreat' from home.

Indeed, Hochschild argues, the values associated within home and work appeared to be reversed. Work appeared to offer a sense of 'community' that the home environment seemed to lack. A sense of belonging to a workplace 'family' was engineered by the company but the experience of family was far more difficult to achieve at home. The company had installed numerous strategies to make its employees feel valued and rewarded them for good work while at home people felt undervalued and unrewarded: 'a tired parent flees a world of unresolved quarrels and unwashed laundry for the reliable orderliness, harmony and managed cheer of work' (Hochschild 2000: 44). Although fear of redundancies always threatens the security of work, with rising divorce rates, work still often appeared to offer more security than home. This would suggest a process in which the public was being domesticated and the domestic public-ized. This even took place at an aesthetic level. Executives who travel for work, she argues, were able to experience the hotel as a 'haven' from home because it gave them 'time free from personal responsibility'. Hotel chains reproduced the same familiar and homely environment wherever executives travelled and Hochschild (2000: 61) observes that some of their 'real' homes came to resemble these hotel rooms as people attempted to recreate the same sense of sanctuary.

Although the idea of work as haven from home appeared to be experienced across class lines within the company Hochschild studies, it clearly isn't applicable to all workplaces (see Brannen 2005 for an example). However, Hochschild's ideas about how domestic life has become less appealing because of the industrialization of domestic time have had a wider purchase. While the post-Fordist workplace demands self-motivated workers who are responsible for managing their own time, she argues, the temporal experience of home has become increasingly similar to the regimes associated with the Taylorized workplace (see Chapter 2). Just as industrial workers experienced their time on the job as fragmented, regimented and out of their control, the temporal experience of domestic life has become 'hurried and rationalized'(Hochschild 2000: 214). Home no longer represented a place where temporal rhythms are opposed to the market but was characterized by multi-tasking, juggling schedules, and managing appointments as aspects of domestic life needed to be 'outsourced' to commercial providers such as childminders and party planners, as people try to 'save' time in order to create 'leisure time' and 'quality time'.

Hochschild documents how the workers she studies find it increasingly difficult to schedule time for the 'quality' experience of family life. As I explained in Chapter 4, the experience of family life does not just happen but often requires complex co-ordination and scheduling that enables the family to come together around a dinner table or in front of a TV programme. Competing and intensifying demands on time – and the increasing mobility of household members – makes this task of co-ordinating domestic life an increasingly difficult one, and many people experience the sense that time is being 'squeezed' (Southerton 2003; see also Southerton et al. 2001). Research demonstrates that this is particularly the case for women who are often left to take responsibility for performing – and, in particular, managing – this 'second shift' when they come home from their 'first shift' at their place of paid work. As Hochschild et al. (2003: 8) argue, women feel 'more responsible for home and children' and have absorbed 'the "speed-up" in work and family life', maintaining a 'leisure gap' between men and women. While women who can afford to do so will often seek to 'outsource' childcare to others (and frequently have little choice but to do so), this in turn frequently involves employing working-class women – frequently from ethnic minorities – who are forced to combine first and second shifts for low levels of pay in undervalued jobs.

Hochschild (2000) suggests that the sheer intensity of the second shift creates the need to schedule a 'third shift' that people identified with 'quality' family time. However, the need to schedule an appropriate amount of family time is antithetical to traditional ideas of family time that see it as something to be 'given freely' (especially by women) and an index of a 'good' family life (Brannen 2005: 117). 'Failure' to live up to these ideals creates further pressures on domestic life (again experienced more acutely by women whose family is seen to symbolize their abilities as a mother). The pressure to 'save time' also produces an increasing anxiety about 'wasting time' (Southerton 2003: 12), echoing Spigel's (2005) ideas about 'conspicuous production'. Complaints about having 'not enough time' are also sometimes translated into the desire for a different experience of time. While one employee in Hochschild's study claimed that she 'didn't want to move to the country', she wished that she 'could bring some of that ease of country living home, where relationships come first' (2000: 52). I return to this pursuit of alternative temporal experiences in the next section.

For Hochschild et al. (2003: 213), the increasing pressures on home, and the consequential harried and fragmented experience of domestic life, produces a tension 'between the importance of a family's *need* for care and the *devaluation* of the work it takes to give that care, a devaluation of the work a home-maker once did' (and this is exacerbated by the increasing association between domestic work and unskilled paid domestic labour). Linda McDowell (2004: 146) identifies how this tension is also a result of **neo-liberal** government policies that reject state welfare provision and value 'free-market principles, . . . economic rationalism, competition, entrepreneurialism, individualism and independence'. Not only are these values antithetical to the ones traditionally associated with domestic cultures, but neo-liberalism also assumes that all members of society should be able to engage in paid work in the marketplace. This represents a shift in social policy from one modelled on an image of family units comprised of a male breadwinner and a female home-maker supported by state welfare provision to one in which paid work becomes the responsibility of all adults (McDowell et al. 2005: 220). While neo-liberal policies also emphasize 'family values' and 'the moral duty to be a good parent', they pay little attention to 'those resources that are outside the market – goods, services and labour exchanged voluntarily or for love, in the household and in the locality' (McDowell 2004: 146, 154).

Therefore, although these policies appear to promote equal opportunities for women in the workforce, they both devalue the contribution made by unpaid domestic labour to social life and devalue 'intangible' feminized practices such as caring. Furthermore, while emphasizing the responsibility of adults to be self-reliant by engaging in paid labour, these policies fail to acknowledge the extent to which many adults – and especially women – also have significant care responsibilities for children and fail to provide adequate support for easily available, accessible and affordable childcare provision. The extent to which there is a need to care for the elderly is also often overlooked. As Jenny Hockey (1999b: 108) observes in her work on the elderly, idealized images of familial domestic life tend to exclude 'aspects of family life such as disease and disability'. These policies also underestimate the extent to which women – who are also positioned as mothers as well as workers – feel a moral obligation to invest in practices of caring associated with mothering (McDowell et al. 2005).

Many workplaces now offer flexible working patterns to parents so that they can try to achieve 'work–life balance'. However, the implementation of these policies frequently relies on the discretion of managers. Furthermore, employees who opt to take advantage of flexible working risk being seen as lacking 'commitment' to their jobs and employers (Hochschild 2000; Perrons et al. 2005). The relatively low take-up of these policies is also explained by the extent to which caring work is afforded little social and cultural value because it is so closely associated with femininity and/or low-grade occupations performed by working-class, ethnic and migrant labour. An understanding of the crucial role that domestic life – and the roles and responsibilities associated with feminine domestic labour – plays in contemporary culture is essential if the idea of 'work–life balance' is to be realistic: 'an ethic of care needs to be part of policy' (McDowell et al. 2005: 232).

The concept of 'work–life balance' in its broadest sense suggests a balance between working life and other aspects of life. However, in most policies – and in the work of feminist critics such as Hochschild – it frequently comes to mean 'work – family' balance. In Chapter 1, I highlighted how domestic culture is frequently equated with familial culture, working to 'other' those who live outside of parent–child nuclear family units. Yet the language of 'work–life balance' is thoroughly familial. Hochschild's work continually slips between the terms 'home', 'family' and 'life' as if they were the same thing. This means that when Hochschild highlights the erosion of domestic culture through the penetration of values associated with the public sphere into home life, the domestic culture she suggests is worth preserving is a familial culture. While questions about how care can and should be valued and organized should be central to social policy, there is perhaps scope for a more expansive notion of care than one that simply reduces it to caring for children. If domestic life becomes synonymous with family life, this inevitably means that those who do not live in 'normal' families have no 'right to life'.

In this section, I have also highlighted processes through which domestic cultures become public-ized as domestic life becomes governed by the temporal rhythms formerly associated with the public sphere. If homes are increasingly frenzied places where people juggle different tasks at the same time, then many of the values that have been constructed as central to domestic culture are also seen to be under threat: home becomes increasingly indistinguishable from work. The lack of leisure and relaxation in the contemporary home could be seen to be an intensification of the experience of home as a site of labour for women rather than a wholesale change in domestic experience, although the demands of combining paid work and domestic work seems to suggest something more complex is going on. However, while the trends I have discussed in this section might suggest that domestic cultures are losing their significance, there are also other signs that suggest a reinvestment in domestic culture as a means of combating the problems associated with contemporary life. It is to these trends that I now turn.

Time for domesticity

Despite these pressures on domestic life – or maybe because of them – recent years have seen an expanding media interest in the domestic (see Chapter 5). The proliferation of formats and channels devoted to domestic life has also been accompanied by a fascination with 'domestic goddesses' such as Nigella Lawson and Martha Stewart and an increased participation in 'traditional' domestic activities such as knitting, cooking and crafts. While it would be easy to read these media representations as part of an intensification of processes in which domestic life is commodified, it is also possible to suggest that this fascination represents an attempt to make sense of the nature and significance of contemporary domestic culture. In this section, I want to explore some of the ways in which recent invitations to take time for domesticity can be seen as a response to the problems of domestic life identified in the last section. If some of the interviewees in Hochschild's study show a desire to run away from home as a way of coping with the pressures of modern domestic life, then I want to explore some counter-examples that represent a reinvestment in both traditional and new forms of domesticity as a way of combating the temporal pressures experienced by many people in contemporary domestic life.

The revival of interest in traditional domestic arts and crafts has been described as 'perversely time-consuming' (Campbell 2001: 4). However, but this seeming perversity can be seen as an attempt to carve out a different form of temporal experience within the contemporary home that enables domestic work and domestic leisure to be integrated rather than fragmented. As I have explored in more detail in earlier work (Hollows 2003b), Nigella Lawson's collection of baking recipes, *How to be a Domestic Goddess*, both identifies and attempts to combat the experience of time scarcity through indulging in the time-consuming – and largely 'non-essential' – activity of baking. Lawson (2000: vii) suggests that modern cookery has produced a

> mood . . . of skin-of-the-teeth efficiency, all briskness and little pleasure. Sometimes that's the best we can manage, but at other times we don't want to feel like a post-modern, post-feminist, overstretched woman but, rather, a domestic goddess trailing nutmeggy fumes of baking pie in our languorous wake.

If many modern femininities involve combining paid work and domestic labour, Lawson invokes a way of taking time out and winning space by spending an excessive amount of time on an activity like baking bread or making home-made bagels. Indulging in these activities can be seen as an attempt to produce 'temporal autonomy' by creating 'temporal niches', an attempt to control time 'in the face of uncontrollable and unpredictable durations and tempos' (Fine 1996: 55).

Lawson takes care to point out that she is not suggesting that women retreat into the home and become full-time home-makers. Nor is she suggesting that women take on responsibility for 'the second-shift'. Instead, she offers a way of using cooking and eating as a means of retreating from feminine responsibilities for time management and the experience of juggling domestic life by reclaiming domestic culture, 'enjoying life on purpose rather than by default' (Lawson 1999: 135). Richard Dyer argues that popular entertainments respond to 'particular inadequacies in society' by offering the experience of what alternative 'utopias' would *feel* like (Dyer 1985: 227). Nigella uses cooking as a means of imagining what 'temporal abundance' might feel like in response to contemporary problems of a 'time squeeze'. She offers the feeling of 'energy' that might be experienced when work and play are integrated that responds to feelings of exhaustion. She also shows how baking can conjure up feelings of 'intensity', 'the affectivity of living in response to the "dreariness" and "instrumentality" of the daily round' (Dyer 1985: 228). While these temporary solutions are undoubtedly more open to the middle classes who can create opportunities to experience alternative modes of domestic life by buying in the labour of working-class women to perform the less pleasurable aspects of domesticity, they nonetheless offer a means of imagining the value of domestic culture outside of the constraints of 'the time bind'.[3]

There has also been a resurgence of interest in traditional domestic crafts. Wendy Parkins identifies how the current vogue for knitting, like Nigella's baking, can also be understood as 'a reaction against the speed and dislocation of global postmodernity, part of an attempt to live differently at a different temporality, and to find meaning and identity in the practices of everyday life' (Parkins 2004a: 426). Like baking, the practice of knitting can be understood as a means of creating a 'temporal niche' for a 'slower, mindful use' of domestic time to those imposed by the intensification and extensifica-tion of working time (Parkins 2004a: 436). Parkins argues that 'knitting, with its connotations of pre-industrial domesticity, may seem to reinforce women's locatedness in the private sphere of the home but the resignification of knitting as leisure, as a way of creating space and time for the self, may provide an effective means of being in, but not of, the domestic' (Parkins, 2004a: 433). However, knitting is also portable, enabling it to be used to produce a temporal experience that has traditionally been associated with the domestic in public space (and, in the process, also making the domestic visible in public). While Parkins notes how the resignification of knitting as a 'hip' activity to be 'performed publicly' has been aided by its celebrity advocates (Parkins, 2004a: 430), knitting 'activists' have taken this further, thrusting knitting into public space. For example, one knitting group performs 'knit-ins' on a London underground line (Higgins 2005) while 'stitch 'n bitch' groups meet in pubs and clubs. This forms part of a wider network of 'craftivists' who consciously mobilize the homely values of knitting as a critique of consumer culture and as a form of eco-activism (Farry 2006). At the time of writing, knitters globally were being invited to contribute towards a giant pink blanket to cover a World War II tank in Copenhagen as a protest against military involvement in Iraq.[4]

These representations of cooking and knitting can be seen as an attempt to revalue domestic cultures and use what might be seen as 'traditional' elements of domestic culture to win time and space. However, in other responses to the increasing workifica-tion of home, it appears that the temporal pressures of contemporary domestic life can only be escaped by seeking a 'home from home'. While I have already discussed how one of the women in Hochschild's study yearned for an alternative sense of time that she associated with country living, another female employee struggling with the 'time bind' at home attempted to escape the demands of the clock by retreating to a weekend vacation home in the country for quality 'family time' (Hochschild 2000: 81). In Eric Hirsch's study of the domestic consumption of ICTs, he recounts the domestic life of the Simons who resist the idea of a separation between public and private spheres, seeing their home as a public space where they use technologies in order to be access-ible 24/7. However, from time to time, the Simons retreated to a second home in geographically remote Cornwall to create a space for a 'private' family life free from the intrusions of ICTs (the remoteness accentuated by their ability to go out on their boat while they were there) (Hirsch 1992: 214). In both these examples, the primary home has become too public, too busy and too demanding so that in order to experi-ence the values traditionally associated with domestic cultures, the residents need to establish a 'home from home', somewhere that represents a haven from their primary residence. For these people, 'quality' domestic time is only achieved through movement between different homes with different functions.

Some of the literature on second-home ownership backs up these ideas. Williams and McIntyre (2000: 397) argue that if primary homes are increasingly experienced as 'a terminus' and become 'thinned of meaning – reduced as it were to a staging area for daily life', then 'an alternative thicker, mythic second-home may be cultivated to recre-ate a place of attachment, identity, continuity, tradition and refuge, otherwise under-mined by modern lifestyles'. In many cases, the different meanings of primary and second homes is also a product of where they are located. Primary homes located in urban areas appear to be integrated with work while the more traditional and myth-ologized meanings of domestic culture associated with second homes are accentuated through their alternative locations. The second home in a holiday resort may accentu-ate the meaning of home as a space of family togetherness through leisure and relax-ation. The rural second home 'represents an escape *from* modernity and *towards* a sense of place, rootedness, identity and authenticity' (Williams and Kaltenborn 1999: 227). In this way, more traditional forms of domestic culture are produced in the country second home through association with the mythical qualities of the 'rural idyll'. This is not to argue that the countryside *is* pre-modern but to suggest that the appeal of the rural is often that it is *imagined* as a space that is rooted in tradition, offering a respite from the problems of modernity (see Bell 2006). Therefore, while I suggested earlier in this book that celebrations of mobility are frequently based on a rejection of home, the forms of mobility associated with moving between homes repre-sents 'an escape for home, not just from home' (Crouch cited in Williams and Kalten-born 1999: 227).

Second-home ownership is still confined to the relatively privileged minority: there are approximately 250 000 second homes in the UK, with more having been bought overseas. Davina Chaplin's (1999) study of British people with second homes in France demonstrates how people used the second home as a way to achieve a work–life balance by attempting to 'escape' the stresses of modern life. Owners claimed that their French holiday homes gave them an opportunity to escape the time bind by offering them a different temporal experience, free from fragmentation and the need to schedule and multi-task. In the process, they gained a sense of control over their time and an opportunity to experience 'family life'. Although these rural second homes offered an escape from modern experiences of work, owners used their leisure time to engage in what they saw to be 'meaningful' labour such as renovating and maintaining their homes and engaging in slow cooking. In this way, owners adopted a 'back to basics' approach and sought a 'pre-industrial' experience of domestic time in which production and reproduction are integrated and there is no dividing line between work and leisure (Chaplin 1999: 50; Williams and Kaltenborn 1999: 222). However, while the spread of second-home ownership is linked to an increased mobility which enables people to be both 'at home' and 'away', a mobility that is a product of modernity, it rests on the fantasy that it is possible to travel to rural areas within, or across, nations that remain magically outside of modernity (see Bell and Hollows 2007).

These temporary retreats into a 'real' domestic culture through a change of pace and location are also informed by wider ideas of slow living 'as the key to an enriched life, a deeper subjectivity and is closely linked to notions of authenticity bound up with everyday practices of domesticity' (Parkins 2004b: 258). The pursuit of slow living can also be seen in contemporary trends for 'voluntary simplicity' and 'downshifting' in which people attempt to escape the time bind by opting for simpler and more sustainable lifestyles, cutting back on paid work or seeking more 'meaningful' forms of labour (see Hollows 2006b). Advice manuals on downshifting frequently challenge the way in which working within corporate culture has become privileged over everyday domestic life, advising people on how to both leave 'the rat race' and reject the demands of consumer culture, what Ghazi and Jones (2004: 44) in one advice manual call 'the "work-spend-consume" straightjacket'. While such moves are frequently dependent on significant financial reserves that have been built up through the very practices they seek to undermine, they also can be seen as part of a wider critique of modern life that also seeks to reclaim and reprioritize elements of domestic cultures. 'By purposely adopting slowness, subjects seek to generate alternative practices of work and leisure, family and sociality' (Parkins 2004c: 364).

However, the ability to reclaim temporal niches and experience the pleasures of having time for domestic life, depends on being relatively rich in other resources that can be mobilized to alleviate time poverty. As I have already suggested, temporal inequalities are closely related to forms of economic inequality. In this chapter, I have also highlighted how our experience of time is also gendered. Evidence suggests that women continue to have substantially less 'free time' than men. Furthermore, as an increasing number of women combine paid labour with unpaid domestic labour, they also find it increasingly difficult to control the tempo of domestic life. The search for an experience of a slower domestic time, which enables people to experience another side of domestic life, should be understood in this context.

Much work has concentrated on the 'time squeeze' experienced by the professional middle classes as working hours increase in length. However, these classes have more access to economic capital that enables them to purchase other people's time to carry out some of the labour of maintaining everyday domestic life or to afford a second home that enables them to experience the space and time for domestic life. While the status accorded to 'conspicuous production' might signal the blurring of work and home among the affluent, and while the domestic time of the middle classes may be becoming increasingly Taylorized, this does not mean that the affluent are at the sharp end of temporal inequalities. This is because their levels of capital still afford them a degree of choice over how to spend their time and pace their life: they are able to choose between fast mobile living and slow localized living. The status given to 'conspicuous production' and a perpetual state of 'busyness' associated with living at speed generates its own forms of distinction while 'the unemployed, children, the elderly and women at home . . . are outside "fast time" for much of the time and hence maybe overlooked by the fast' (Parkins 2004c: 366; see also Massey 1994). The ability to choose slowness often depends on some degree of distance from necessity; spending time investing in domestic life is a luxury beyond many people's reach.

Conclusions

Throughout this book, I have emphasized that there is nothing new about the blurring of boundaries between public and private. In this chapter I have identified how a series of economic, social and cultural conditions have produced particular pressures that have both created new ways in which public and private have been de-territorialized and produced particular responses to the problem of managing relationships to both public and private in contemporary culture. However, the de-territorialization of aspects of both public and private life does not mean that it is redundant to talk about domestic cultures. As we have seen in this chapter, one response to the interpenetration of public and private has been to re-emphasize the importance of values that have a long-standing association with the domestic. While these values have frequently been identified as conservative, in this book I have hoped to demonstrate that there is nothing intrinsically culturally or politically conservative about domestic culture. While the Right have frequently represented domestic culture as a familial culture that plays a vital role in reproducing 'traditional' moral values, there is no inherent connection between domestic culture and these values – this is just one way in which the meaning of home has been imagined. Furthermore, as McDowell's (2004) work makes clear, the recognition that the caring work associated with domestic cultures has a value provides a crucial challenge to neo-liberal economic policies.

In this chapter I have drawn together debates about very different aspects of social and cultural life to think about how the idea of home, and the values associated with domesticity, continue to have a strong purchase in contemporary culture. The key issue is not to dismiss the significance of home as a sign of 'false consciousness' but to attend to the different ways in which we can imagine and practise domestic life. There is nothing inherently conservative or radical about domestic culture. Instead, it is necessary to think about the range of ways in which domestic cultures are represented, mobilized and lived. It is also necessary to think about who has access to the ability to invest in domestic life. As Young (1997: 161) argues, this 'calls for conceptualizing the positive values of home and criticizing a global society that is unable or unwilling to extend those values to everyone'.

Further reading

Fannin, M. (2003) Domesticating Birth in the Hospital: 'Family-centred' Birth and the Emergence of 'Homelike' Birthing Rooms, *Antipode*, 35(3): 513–35.

Hochschild, A. Russell (2000) *The Time Bind: When Work Becomes Home and Home Becomes Work*. New York: Owl Books.

Morley, D. (2003) What's Home Got to do With it? Contradictory Dynamics in the Domestication of Technology and the Dislocation of Domesticity, *European Journal of Cultural Studies*, 6(4): 435–58.

Parkins, W. (2004) Celebrity Knitting and the Temporality of Postmodernity, *Fashion Theory*, 8(4): 425–42.

Sheller, M. and Urry, J. (2003) Mobile Transformations of 'Public' and 'Private' Life, *Theory Culture and Society*, 20(3): 107–25.

Notes

1 Taken from an advertisement for a post as a Design Manager at Starbucks; http://www.jobster.com/outreach/jobs/jobDetails.html;jsessionid=3EA4E329A2CC3310618D1867E8DAEB3A?opportunity=5914416 (accessed 18 July 2006).

2 For some discussions of attempts to erase the homeless from urban spaces see, for example, Davis 1990; Hebdige 1993; Smith 1993; and Zukin 1995.

3 David Goldstein (2005) discusses Martha Stewart in relation to temporality, albeit from a different angle. Charlotte Brunsdon (2006) not only offers a useful comparison of Martha and Nigella but also discusses their relationship to leisure and labour. In her work on the representation of domesticity in chick-lit, Caroline J. Smith (2005: 675) not only distinguishes between the images of a seemingly perfect home offered by Martha and the 'lived messiness' represented by Nigella, but also explores how chick-lit novelists enable their heroines to negotiate a domestic culture in which they can 'attain the sentiments associated with domesticity' outside of 'traditional' family structures. Ann Mason and Marian Meyers (2001) have studied why Martha's version of domesticity appeals to her fans.

4 For some information on UK activist knitters, see www.castoff.info and www.knitchicks.co.uk. Stitch 'n bitch groups have their roots in third-wave feminism and were often influenced by Debbie Stoller's book *Stitch 'n Bitch: The Knitter's Handbook* (see Gillis 2005). Knitting is only one part of a wider resurgence of interest in crafts more generally and the interest in craft is frequently linked to a critique of consumerism and greener ways of living.

GLOSSARY

Abolition: a result of the passing of the Thirteenth Amendment to the Constitution of the United States that abolished slavery within the USA and deemed that one human being could not own another as property.

Affluent workers: a term adopted by some commentators in the post-war UK to describe an expanding group of skilled manual workers whose wages were comparable to white-collar workers. It was often assumed that this group were becoming more like the middle class in terms of their politics and values (see **embourgeoisement**) but a series of sociological studies also disputed this assumption.

Capitalist industrialization: while industrialization can take many forms, it is often closely associated with the emergence of capitalism, an economic system in which labour is organized as a commodity that can be bought and sold.

Communitarian: although communitarianism has many forms, this usage refers to a nineteenth-century American movement that advocated social reform through the construction of model housing developments located within 'natural' environments.

Diasporic: refers to social groups that have been geographically dispersed. The most commonly used example is of the Jewish people who became dispersed after their expulsion from their homeland.

Disembedding: used by Anthony Giddens to make sense of some of the effects of modernity. Disembedding happens because social relationships are no longer shaped by local contexts but instead become stretched across time and space. As a result, people have to increasingly place their trust in abstract systems.

Domestic feminism: is associated with nineteenth-century feminists who believed that women's caring role within the home – and their moral superiority to men – enabled them to make a valuable contribution to public affairs, particularly in matters relating to the home and morality.

Embourgeoisement: refers to the idea that middle-class ideas are becoming more widespread and was used in the UK in the 1950s and 1960s to explain a process through which the working class were allegedly adopting elements of middle-class culture, including middle-class voting patterns.

Ethnography: refers to a research method used across a range of social sciences that seeks to discover the meanings that people use to construct and make sense of their social and cultural worlds.

False consciousness: is often associated with the concept of ideology and seeks to explain why specific social groups accept their exploitation. However, many have criticized this concept on the grounds that it amounts to little more than the claim that people's perception of the world – or their place within it – is somehow 'false'.

First-wave feminism: is associated with a range of feminist activity in the nineteenth and early twentieth centuries. While many feminists of the period were involved in the political struggles to win suffrage for women, the feminist ideas produced in this period were diverse and there was no single feminist perspective on gender inequality.

Fordist: while Henry Ford is often credited with the introduction of the factory assembly-line (see also **Taylorism** and **rationalization**), this term is often used to refer to a system that emerged after the Great Depression of the 1930s that aimed to make capitalism into a more stable system and combined mass production with the conditions for mass consumption. Expert knowledge was used to regulate social, economic and cultural life.

Frankfurt School: a group of neo-Marxist scholars, many of whom relocated from Germany to the USA following the rise of Nazism. Associated scholars include Theodor Adorno, Max Horkheimer and Herbert Marcuse.

Gated Communities: apartment and housing complexes with secured entry systems that limit access to non-residents. In the USA in particular, the expansion of gated communities has resulted in large-scale housing developments with their own privatized facilities within heavily secured boundaries.

Heteronormativity: the idea of normative heterosexuality in which heterosexual familial arrangements are prescribed as the *only* acceptable way to live. This is reinforced through a range of social, cultural, legal and economic institutions and ideologies.

Levittowns: the construction company Levitt and Sons were responsible for producing a series of mass-produced and planned suburban developments in the post-war USA that came to be known as Levittowns. These suburbs frequently came to symbolize all that was supposedly wrong with suburbia.

Liberal feminism: a key strand of second-wave feminism. Liberal feminists argued that men and women needed to be given equal rights if gender equality was to be achieved and frequently used the legislative process in an attempt to bring about change.

Mass culture: although used more widely, this concept frequently involves a negative judgement. While mass culture has a longer history, it was used from the 1930s to the 1950s to refer to a situation in which the production and consumption of cultural forms had become economic and industrial activities that were governed by commercial interests. Mass culture was seen as a threat to both aesthetic standards and political life.

Mass man: with industrialization and urbanization, it has been argued, people live in increasingly large groups in which they come to identify with the figure of an anonymous and homogeneous mass man.

Mobile privatization: a term used by Raymond Williams to refer to the seemingly contradictory possibilities of modern life that were enabled by new technologies. For example, while TV consumption in the post-war period was centred on the family and in the home (hence privatized), TV also enabled new forms of mobility as people made imaginative journeys elsewhere. Similarly, the car enabled people to travel while remaining in their own private space.

Modernist: used to describe the movements across the arts associated with modernism, and frequently associated with avant-garde techniques that attempted to challenge people's understanding of the world. However, modernist architecture is often seen as an attempt to apply the ideas of reason and rationality to the design of buildings in order to make them more functional and efficient and, as a result, to reorder everyday life.

Moral economy: a term used by Roger Silverstone to describe the value systems that are created and mobilized within households. He uses the concept to make sense of the ways in which households take objects from the formal economy and use them within domestic space to construct and express the particular values of a household.

Narrowcasting: associated with the increasing proliferation of TV and radio channels that are seen to fragment the mass audience that has usually been associated with *broad*casting.

Nuclear family: a term coined in the post-war period to characterize living arrangements based on a married heterosexual couple and, usually two or three, dependent children. The nuclear family is distinguished from the extended family in which numerous generations live together, a living arrangement that is often seen to characterize traditional societies.

Ontological security: a concept used by Anthony Giddens to refer to a state in which people feel that there is a sense of routine order and continuity and so enables them to feel a sense of security and predictability in their daily existence.

Parlour: usually the front downstairs room in a house whose principle function is display. Despite being associated with the nineteenth-century middle classes in the UK, the parlour would continue to shape the ways in which many of the working class used domestic space in the twentieth century.

Post-Fordist: a type of production and a type of society that demonstrates a development from, or beyond, Fordism. If Fordism was closely associated with mass production and consumption then post-Fordism is associated with a shift towards increased flexibility. This is seen in a tendency towards small-batch production geared towards niche markets.

Public service broadcasting: based on the philosophy that broadcast media such as radio and TV should not just entertain but have a duty to educate and inform the public and so enable them to act as a 'responsible' citizens.

Public sphere: the bourgeois middle classes are often claimed to have divided their social world into the public and private spheres. If the private is often associated with the personal and domestic, the public sphere was seen as its opposite, the realm of work, politics and social gatherings.

Qualitative research: often distinguished from quantitative research that analyses data mathematically. Qualitative research seeks to understand the meanings behind human action through the analysis of qualitatively rich sources such as in-depth interviews.

Rationalization: fundamental to industrialization, this process involved the application of reason (rationality) to the organization of social activities. Rationalization took particular processes – such as the production of a specific object – and broke them down into a series of discrete tasks. It is therefore strongly associated with the ideas of the factory assembly-line but many critics have suggested that other aspects of social and cultural life have also become increasingly subject to rationalization.

Re-embedding mechanisms: a concept used by Anthony Giddens to explain how societies attempt to come to terms with some of the unsettling effects of disembedding. Re-embedding mechanisms attempt to 'pin down' abstract systems and make them appear to be more personal. For example, the human voice at the other end of a telephone answering system for a global corporation may generate a personal touch that helps us to place our trust in abstract systems.

Second-wave feminism: associated with the Women's Movements of the late 1960s and the 1970s. While second-wave feminism is associated with political activism that sought to call attention to the cause of gender inequalities, this was never a monolithic movement and there were a range of different feminist theories to explain how these inequalities were created and reproduced.

Section 28: a controversial amendment to the Local Government Act passed by the Conservative Government in 1988, Section 28, prohibited local authorities in the UK from 'promoting' homosexuality. This legislation has since been repealed.

Sexual division of labour (the): presumes that social roles are differentiated along the lines of sex and/or gender. For example, certain roles, responsibilities and tasks are seen as men's work and others are seen as women's work.

Social realism: although used more widely across a range of the arts, social realist cinema in the UK is associated with the British 'new wave' of the late 1950s and early 1960s. Influenced by the French *nouvelle vague* and documentary film-making practices, a number of film-makers claimed that their films exhibited a new 'realism' because they attempted to represent gritty subject matter, working-class characters and industrial, urban locales that had frequently been marginalized within cinema.

Taylorism: named after Frederick Taylor, this refers to the application of principles of scientific management in order to rationalize the production process and increase productivity.

Thatcherism: used to describe both a period of British history and a set of political ideologies associated with the Conservative Prime Minister from 1979 to 1990, Margaret Thatcher.

Urbanization: refers to the process by which an increasing number of people move to live in towns and suburbs alongside a corresponding decrease in the proportion of people living in rural locations.

BIBLIOGRAPHY

Abrams, M. and Rose, R. (1960) *Must Labour Lose?* Harmondsworth: Penguin.

Adorno, T. and Horkheimer, M. (1979) *Dialectic of Enlightenment*. London: Verso.

Ahmed, S. (1999) Home and Away: Narratives of Migration and Estrangement, *International Journal of Cultural Studies*, 2(3): 329–47.

Aksoy, A. and Robins, K. (2002) Banal Transnationalism: The Difference Television Makes. Transnational Communities Programme Working Paper Series; www.transcomm.ox.ac.uk/working%20papers/WPTC–02–08%20Robins.pdf (accessed 7 July 2007).

Anders, G. (1957) The Phantom World of TV, in D. Rosenberg and D. Manning White (eds) *Mass Culture: The Popular Arts in America*. New York: Free Press: 258–67.

Anderson, B. (1991) *Imagined Communities: Reflections on the Origin and Spread of Nationalism*. London: Verso.

Anon ([1922] 1986) 'The Reason for Good Housekeeping', in B. Braithwaite, N. Walsh and G. Davies (eds) *From Ragtime to Wartime: The Best of Good Housekeeping, 1922–1939*. London: Random House: 11.

Appadurai, A. (1986) Introduction: Commodities and the Politics of Value, in A. Appadurai (ed.) *The Social Life of Things*. Cambridge: Cambridge University Press: 3–63.

Ashley, B., Hollows, J., Jones, S. and Taylor, B. (2004) *Food and Cultural Studies*. London: Routledge.

Attfield, J. (1995) Inside Pram Town: A Case Study of Harlow House Interiors, 1951–61, in J. Attfield and P. Kirkham (eds) *A View From the Interior: Women and Design*. London: Women's Press: 215–38.

Attfield, J. (2000) *Wild Things: The Material Culture of Everyday Life*. Oxford: Berg.

Attwood, F. (2005) Inside Out: Men on the Home Front, *Journal of Consumer Culture*, 5(1): 87–107.

Baca Zinn, M. (1989) Common Grounds and Crossroads: Race, Ethnicity and Class in Women's Lives, *Signs*, 14(4): 856–74.

Bakardjieva, M. (2006) Domestication Running Wild: From the Moral Economy of the Household to the Mores of a Culture, in T. Berker, M. Hartmann, Y. Punie and K.

Ward (eds) *Domestication of Media and Technology*. Maidenhead: Open University Press: 62–79.

Barrett, M. and McIntosh, M. (1982) *The Anti-social Family*. London: Verso.

Baxter, J. (2000) The Joys and Justice of Housework, *Sociology*, 34(4): 609–31.

Beetham, M. (1998) The Reinvention of the English Domestic Woman: Class and 'Race' in the 1890s Woman's Magazine, *Women's Studies International Forum*, 21(3): 223–33.

Belk, R. (1995) *Collecting in a Consumer Society*. London: Routledge.

Bell, D. (2006) Variations on the Rural Idyll, in P.J. Cloke, T. Marsden and P. Mooney (eds) *Handbook of Rural Studies*. London: Sage: 149–60.

Bell, D. and Hollows, J. (2005) Making Sense of Ordinary Lifestyles, in D. Bell and J. Hollows (eds) *Ordinary Lifestyles: Popular Media, Consumption and Taste*. Maidenhead: Open University Press: 1–18.

Bell, D. and Hollows, J. (2007) Mobile Homes?, *Space and Culture*, 10(1): 22–39.

Bell, D. and Valentine, G. (1997) *Consuming Geographies: We are Where we Eat*. London: Routledge.

Benjamin, W. (1992) *Illuminations*. London: Fontana.

Bennett, T. (2002) 'Home' and Everyday Life, in T. Bennett and D. Watson (eds) *Understanding Everyday Life*. Oxford: Blackwell: 1–50.

Bentley, A. (1998) *Eating For Victory: Food, Rationing and the Politics of Domesticity*. Urbana: University of Illinois Press.

Bentley, A. (1999) Bread, Meat and Rice: Exploring Cultural Elements of Food Riots, Proceedings of the Conference Cultural and Historical Aspects of Food: Yesterday, Today, Tomorrow, Oregon State University, April 9–11.

Berger, B. (1960) *Working-class Suburb: A Study of Autoworkers in Suburbia*. Berkeley: University of California Press.

Berker, T., Hartmann, M., Punie, Y., and Ward, K. (2006) Introduction, in T. Berker, M. Hartmann, Y. Punie and K. Ward (eds) *Domestication of Media and Technology*. Maidenhead: Open University Press: 1–17.

Berman, M. (1983) *All That is Solid Melts into Air: The Experience of Modernity*. London: Verso.

Bhabha, H. (1997) Postscript: Bombs Away in Front-line Suburbia, in R. Silverstone (ed.) *Visions of Suburbia*. London: Routledge: 298–303.

Bianchi, S.M., Milkie, M.A., Sayer, L.C. and Robinson, J.P. (2000) Is Anyone Doing the House-work? Trends in the Gender Division of Household Labour, *Social Forces*, 79(1): 191–228.

Binkley, S. (2004) Everybody's Life is Like a Spiral: Narrating Post-Fordism in the Lifestyle Movement of the 1970s, *Cultural Studies-Critical Methodologies*, 4(1): 71–96.

Birdwell-Pheasant, D. and Lawrence-Zúñiga, D. (1999) Introduction: Homes and Families in Europe, in D. Birdwell-Pheasant and D. Lawrence-Zúñiga (eds) *House Life: Space Place and Family in Europe*. Oxford: Berg: 1–37.

Blumin, S.M. (1989) *The Emergence of the Middle Class: Social Experience in the American City, 1760–1900*. Cambridge: Cambridge University Press.

Blunt, A. and Dowling, R. (2006) *Home*. London: Routledge.

Bonner, F. (2003) *Ordinary Television: Analyzing Popular TV*. London: Sage.

Boorstin, D. (1962) *The Image: Or What Happened to the American Dream*. Harmondsworth: Penguin.

Bourdieu, P. (1984) *Distinction: A Social Critique of the Judgement of Taste*. London: Routledge.

Bourke, J. (1994) Housewifery in Working-class England, 1860–1914, *Past and Present*, 143(1): 167–97.

Bovill, M. and Livingstone, S. (2001) Bedroom Culture and the Privatization of Media Use. LSE Research Online; http://eprints.lse.ac.uk/archive/00000672 (accessed 5 August 2006).

Bowlby, R. (1992) *Still Crazy After All These Years: Women, Writing and Psychoanalysis*. London: Routledge.

Boys, J. (1995) From Alcatraz to the OK Corral: Images of Class and Gender in Housing Design, in J. Attfield and P. Kirkham (eds) *A View from the Interior: Women and Design*, updated edition. London: Women's Press: 39–54.

Braithwaite, B. and Walsh, N. (eds) (1990) *Food Glorious Food: Eating and Drinking with Good Housekeeping, 1922–42*. London: Random House.

Brannen, J. (2005) Time and the Negotiation of Work–Family Boundaries: Autonomy or Illusion?, *Time and Society*, 14(1): 113–31.

Brooke, S. (2001) Gender and Working-class Identity in Britain During the 1950s, *Journal of Social History*, 35: 774–95.

Brunsdon, C. (1978) 'It is Well Known that by Nature Women are Inclined to be Rather Personal', in Women Studies Group (eds) *Women Take Issue*. Centre for Contemporary Studies, Hutchinson: 18–34.

Brunsdon, C. (1981) *Crossroads*: Notes on a Soap Opera, *Screen*, 22(4): 32–7.

Brunsdon, C. (1997) *Screen Tastes: Soap Opera to Satellite Dishes*. London: Routledge.

Brunsdon, C. (2000) *The Feminist, the Housewife and the Soap Opera*. Oxford: Clarendon.

Brunsdon, C. (2001) Once More on the Insignificant, in C. Brunsdon, C. Johnson, R. Moseley and H. Wheatley, Factual Entertainment in British Television: The Midlands TV Research Group's '8–9 Project', *European Journal of Cultural Studies*, 4(1): 53–62.

Brunsdon, C. (2004) Taste and Time on Television, *Screen*, 45(2): 115–29.

Brunsdon, C. (2006) The Feminist in the Kitchen: Martha, Martha and Nigella, in J. Hollows and R. Moseley (eds) *Feminism in Popular Culture*. Oxford: Berg: 41–56.

Brunsdon, C. and Morley, D. (1978) *Everyday Television: 'Nationwide'*. London: BFI.

Buchli, V., Clarke, A. and Upton, D. (2004) Editorial, *Home Cultures*, 1(1): 1–4.

Buckingham, D. (2000) *After the Death of Childhood: Growing Up in the Age of Electronic Media*. Cambridge: Polity.

Bugge, A. Bahr (2003) *Cooking as Identity Work*. Oslo: SIFO.

Bugge, A. Bahr and Almås, R. (2006) Domestic Dinner: Representations and Practices of a Proper Meal Among Young Suburban Mothers, *Journal of Consumer Culture*, 6(2): 203–28.

Bull, M. (2000) *Sounding Out the City: Personal Stereos and the Management of Everyday Life*. Oxford: Berg.

Bull, M. (2004) Automobility and the Power of Sound, *Theory, Culture and Society*, 21(4/5): 243–59.

Bull, M. (2005) No Dead Air! The iPod and the Culture of Mobile Listening, *Leisure Studies*, 24(4): 343–55.

Burgoyne, J. and Clarke, D. (1983) You are What you Eat: Food and Family Reconstitution, in A. Murcott (ed.) *The Sociology of Food and Eating*. Aldershot: Gower.

Búriková, Z. (2006) The Embarrassment of Co-Presence: Au Pairs and Their Rooms, *Home Cultures*, 3(2): 99–122.

Cameron, D. (2007) Time to Make Marriage a Priority, *Daily Mail*, 11 July; http://www.conservatives.com/tile.do?def=news.show.article.page&obj_id=137541 (accessed 14 July 2007).

Campbell, D. (2001) Housewives' Choice?, *Trouble and Strife*, 42: 2–12.

Carey, J. (1992) *The Intellectuals and the Masses: Pride and Prejudice Among the Literary Intelligentsia. 1880–1939*. London: Faber.

Casey, E. and Martens, L. (2007) Introduction, in E. Casey and L. Martens (eds) *Gender and Consumption: Domestic Cultures and the Commercialization of Everyday Life*. Aldershot: Ashgate: 1–11.

Chambers, D. (2000) Representations of Familialism in the British Popular Media, *European Journal of Cultural Studies*, 3(2): 195–214.

Chaney, D. (1983) The Department Store as Cultural Form, *Theory Culture and Society*, 1(3): 22–31.

Chaplin, D. (1999) Consuming Work/Productive Leisure: The Consumption Patterns of Second Home Environments, *Leisure Studies*, 18(1): 41–55.

Chapman, T. (1999) Spoiled Home Identities: The Experience of Burglary, in T. Chapman and J. Hockey (eds) *Ideal Homes: Social Change and Domestic Life*. London: Routledge: 133–46.

Chapman, T. (2004) *Gender and Domestic Life: Changing Practices in Families and Households*. Basingstoke: Palgrave.

Chapman, T. and Hockey, J. (1999a) The Ideal Home as it is Imagined and as it is Lived, in T. Chapman and J. Hockey (eds) *Ideal Homes? Social Change and Domestic Life*. London: Routledge: 1–13.

Chapman, T. and Hockey, J. (1999b) *Ideal Homes? Social Change and Domestic Life*. London: Routledge.

Charles, N. (1995) Food and Family Ideology, in S. Jackson and S. Moores (eds) *The Politics of Domestic Consumption: Critical Readings*. Hemel Hempstead: Harvester Wheatsheaf: 100–15.

Charles, N. and Kerr, M. (1988) *Women, Food and Families: Power, Status, Love, Anger*. Manchester: Manchester University Press.

Cieraad, I. (1999) (ed.) *At Home: An Anthropology of Domestic Space*. Syracuse: Syracuse University Press.

Clarke, A. (1997) Tupperware: Suburbia, Sociality and Mass Consumption, in R. Silverstone (ed.) *Visions of Suburbia*. London: Routledge: 132–60.

Clarke, A. (1998) Window Shopping at Home: Classifieds, Catalogues and New Consumer Skills, in D. Miller (ed.) *Material Cultures: Why Some Things Matter*. London: UCL Press: 73–99.

Clarke, A. (1999) *Tupperware: The Promise of Plastic in 1950s America*. Washington: Smithsonian Institution Press.

Clarke, A. (2001) The Aesthetics of Social Aspiration, in D. Miller (ed.) *Home Possessions: Material Culture Behind Closed Doors*. Oxford: Berg: 23–46.

Cloke, P., Johnsen, S. and May, J. (2003) Journeys and Pauses: Tactical and Performative Spaces in the Homeless City, Homeless Places Project; http://www.geog.qmul.ac.uk/homeless/homelessplaces/users.html (accessed 15 August 2006).

Cohen, L. (1980) Embellishing a Life of Labour: An Interpretation of the Material Culture of American Working-class Homes, 1885–1915, *Journal of American Culture*, 3(4): 752–5.

Cohen, L. (2003) *A Consumer's Republic: The Politics of Mass Consumption in Postwar America*. New York: Vintage.

Cott, N. (1977) *The Bonds of Womanhood: 'Woman's Sphere' in New England, 1780–1835*. New Haven: Yale University Press.

Couldry, N. (2005) The Extended Audience: Scanning the Horizon, in M. Gillespie (ed.) *Media Audiences*. Maidenhead: Open University Press: 183–222.

Cowan, R. Schwartz (1983) *More Work for Mother: The Ironies of Household Technology from the Open Hearth to the Microwave*. New York: Basic.

Coward, R. (1980) 'This Novel Changes Lives': Are Women's Novels Feminist Novels?, *Feminist Review*, 5: 53–64.

Cox, R. (2006) *The Servant Problem: Domestic Employment in a Global Economy*. London: I.B. Tauris.

Cross, G. (1997) The Suburban Weekend: Perspectives on a Vanishing Twentieth Century Dream, in R. Silverstone (ed.) *Visions of Suburbia*. London: Routledge: 109–31.

Csikszentmihalyi, M and Rochberg-Halton, E. (1981) *The Meaning of Things: Domestic Symbols and the Self*. Cambridge: Cambridge University Press.

Daniels, S. and Rycroft, S. (1993) Mapping the Modern City: Alan Sillitoe's Nottingham Novels, *Transactions of the Institute of British Geographers*, 18: 460–80.

Davidoff, L. (2003) Gender and the Great Divide: Public and Private in British Gender History, *Journal of Women's History*, 15(1): 11–27.

Davidoff, L. and Hall, C. (2002) *Family Fortunes: Men and Women of the English Middle Class, 1780–1850*, 2nd edn. London: Routledge.

Davis, B. (2000) *Home Fires Burning: Food, Politics and Everyday Life in World War I Berlin*. Chapel Hill: University of North Carolina Press.

Davis, M. (1990) *City of Quartz: Excavating the Future in Los Angeles*. London: Verso.

Delphy, C. (1984) *Close to Home: A Materialist Analysis of Women's Oppression*. London: Hutchinson.

De Solier, I. (2005) TV Dinners: Culinary Television, Education and Distinction, *Continuum*, 19(4): 465–81.

DeVault, M. (1991) *Feeding the Family: The Social Organization of Caring as Gendered Work*. Chicago: University of Chicago Press.

Dhoest, A. (2007) Identifying With the Nation: Viewer Memories of Flemish TV Fiction, *European Journal of Cultural Studies*, 10(1): 55–73.

DiMaggio, P. (1982) Cultural Entrepreneurship in Nineteenth-century Boston, *Media, Culture and Society*, 4(1): 33–50.

Dobash, R. and Dobash, R. (1980) *Violence Against Wives*. New York: Free Press.

Dobash, R. and Dobash, R. (1992) *Women, Violence and Social Change*. London: Routledge.

Donzelot, J. (1979) *The Policing of Families: Welfare Versus the State*. London: Hutchinson.

Douglas, M. (1991) The Idea of Home: A Kind of Space, *Social Research*, 58(1): 288–307.

Du Gay, P., Hall, S., Janes, L., Mackay, H. and Negus, K. (1997) *Doing Cultural Studies: The Story of the Sony Walkman*. London: Sage.

Duncan, S., Edwards, R., Reynolds, T. and Alldred, P. (2003) Motherhood, Paid Work and Partnering: Values and Theories, *Work, Employment and Society*, 17(2): 309–30.

Dupuis, A. and Thorns, D.C. (1998) Home Ownership and the Search for Ontological Security, *Sociological Review*, 46(1): 24–47.

Dyer, R. (1985) Entertainment and Utopia, in B. Nichols (ed.) *Movies and Methods: Volume II.* Berkeley: University of California Press: 200–32.

Dyhouse, C. (1986) Mothers and Daughters in the Middle Class Home, c. 1870–1914, in J. Lewis (ed.) *Labour and Love: Women's Experience of Home and Family Life, 1850–1940.* Oxford: Blackwell: 27–48.

Dyhouse, C. (1989) *Feminism and the Family in England, 1880–1939.* Oxford: Blackwell.

Echols, A. (1989) The Taming of the Id: Feminist Sexual Politics, 1968–83, in C. Vance (ed.) *Pleasure and Danger.* London: Pandora: 50–72.

Ehrenreich, B. (1983) *The Hearts of Men: American Dreams and the Flight from Commitment.* London: Pluto.

Ehrenreich, B. and Hochschild, A. Russell (2003) (eds) *Global Women: Nannies, Maids, and Sex Workers in the New Economy.* New York: Metropolitan Books.

Fannin, M. (2003) Domesticating Birth in the Hospital: 'Family-centred' Birth and the Emergence of 'Homelike' Birthing Rooms, *Antipode*, 35(3): 513–35.

Farry, E. (2006) ¡Viva Las Craftivistas!, *The Guardian*, 29 May; http://arts.guardian.co.uk/features/story/0,,1785059,00.html (accessed 7 July 2006).

Featherstone, M. (1991) *Consumer Culture and Postmodernism.* London: Sage.

Felski, R. (2000) *Doing Time: Feminist Theory and Postmodern Culture.* New York: New York University Press.

Fine, G.A. (1996) *Kitchens: The Culture of Restaurant Work.* Berkeley: University of California Press.

Firestone, S. (1979) *The Dialectic of Sex: The Case for Feminist Revolution.* London: Women's Press.

Flynn, B. (2003) Geography of the Digital Hearth, *Information, Communication and Society*, 6(4): 551–76.

Fog Olwig, K. (1999) Travelling Makes a Home: Mobility and Identity Among West Indians, in T. Chapman and J. Hockey (eds) *Ideal Homes: Social Change and Domestic Life.* London: Routledge: 73–83.

Fortier, A-M. (2001) 'Coming Home': Queer Migrations and Multiple Evocations of Home, *European Journal of Cultural Studies*, 4(4): 405–24.

Forty, A. (1986) *Objects of Desire: Design and Society, 1750–1980.* London: Thames and Hudson.

Freeman, J. (2004) *The Making of the Modern Kitchen: A Cultural History.* Oxford: Berg.

Friedan, B. (1963) *The Feminine Mystique.* New York: Dell.

Furlong, R. (1995) There's No Place Like Home, in M. Lister (ed.) *The Photographic Image in Digital Culture.* London: Routledge: 170–87.

Gans, H.J. (1967) *The Levittowners: How People Live and Politic in Suburbia.* New York: Pantheon.

Garvey, P. (2001) Organized Disorder: Moving Furniture in Norwegian Homes, in D. Miller (ed.) *Home Possessions: Material Culture Behind Closed Doors.* Oxford: Berg: 47–68.

Gauntlett, D. and Hill, A. (1999) *TV Living: Television, Culture and Everyday Life.* London: Routledge.

Geraghty, C. (1991) *Women and Soap Opera: Studying Prime-time Soap Operas.* Cambridge: Polity.

Ghazi, P. and Jones, J. (2004) *Downshifting: The Bestselling Guide to Happier, Simpler Living.* London: Hodder and Stoughton.

Giard, L. (1998) Doing Cooking, in M. de Certeau, L. Giard and P. Mayol, *The Practice of Everyday Life, Volume 2: Living and Cooking*. Minneapolis: University of Minnesota Press: 149–247.

Giddens, A. (1990) *The Consequences of Modernity*. Cambridge: Polity.

Giddens, A. (1991) *Modernity and Self-identity: Self and Society in the Late Modern Age*. Cambridge: Polity.

Gilbert, D. and Preston, R. (2003) Stop Being So English: Suburbia and National Identity, in D. Gilbert, D. Matless and B. Short (eds) *Geographies of British Modernity: Space and Society in the Twentieth Century*. Oxford: Blackwell: 187–203.

Giles, J. (1995) *Women, Identity and Private Life, 1900–1950*. Basingstoke: Macmillan.

Giles, J. (2004) *The Parlour and the Suburb: Domestic Identities, Class, Femininity and Modernity*. Oxford: Berg.

Gillespie, M. (1989) Technology and Tradition: Audio-visual Culture Among South Asian Families in West London, *Cultural Studies*, 3(2): 226–39.

Gilligan, C. (1982) *In a Different Voice*. Cambridge: Harvard University Press.

Gillis, S. (2005) Which Domestic Goddess are you? (Post)feminism and the Fetishization of the Domestic, paper presented at the Society for Cinema and Media Studies Conference, University of London, March–April.

Glucksmann, M. (1990) *Women Assemble: Women Workers and the New Industries in the Interwar Years*. London: Routledge.

Goldsack, L. (1999) Haven in a Heartless World? Women and Domestic Violence, in T. Chapman and J. Hockey (eds) *Ideal Homes? Social Change and Domestic Life*. London: Routledge: 121–32.

Goldstein, D. (2005) Recipes for Living: Martha Stewart and the New American Subject, in D. Bell and J. Hollows (eds) *Ordinary Lifestyles: Popular Media, Consumption and Taste*. Milton Keynes: Open University Press: 47–62.

Gordon, S. (2004) 'Boundless Possibilities': Home Sewing and the Meanings of Women's Domestic Work in the United States, 1890–1930, *Journal of Women's History*, 16(2): 68–91.

Gordon, J. and McArthur, J. (1985) American Women and Domestic Consumption, 1800–1920: Four Interpretative Themes, *Journal of American Culture*, 8(3): 35–46.

Gorman-Murray, A. (2006a) Queering Home or Domesticating Deviance? Interrogating Gay Domesticity Through Lifestyle Television, *International Journal of Cultural Studies*, 9(2): 227–47.

Gorman-Murray, A. (2006b) Gay and Lesbian Couples at Home: Identity Work in Domestic Space, *Home Cultures*, 3(2): 145–68.

Gorman-Murray, A. (2006c) Homeboys: Uses of Home by Gay Australian Men', *Social and Cultural Geography*, 7(1): 53–69.

Gray, A. (1992) *Video Playtime: The Gendering of a Leisure Technology*. London: Routledge.

Gray, A. (2003) *Research Practice for Cultural Studies*. London: Sage.

Gregson, N. and Lowe, M. (1994) *Servicing the Middle Class: Class, Gender and Waged Domestic Labour in Contemporary Britain*. London: Routledge.

Gullestad, M. (1995) Home Decoration as Popular Culture: Constructing Homes, Genders and Classes in Norway, in S. Jackson and S. Moores (eds) *The Politics of Domestic Consumption: Critical Readings*. Hemel Hempstead: Harvester Wheatsheaf: 321–35.

Gunn, S. (2005) Translating Bourdieu: Cultural Capital and the English Middle Class in Historical Perspective, *British Journal of Sociology*, 56(1): 49–64.

Gurney, C.M. (1999) Lowering the Drawbridge: A Case Study of Analogy and Metaphor in the Social Construction of Home-ownership, *Urban Studies*, 36(10): 1705–22.

Haddon, L. (1992) Explaining ICT Consumption: The Case of the Home Computer, in R. Silverstone and E. Hirsch (eds) *Consuming Technologies: Media and Information in Domestic Spaces*. London: Routledge: 82–96.

Haddon, L. (2006) Empirical Studies Using the Domestication Framework, in T. Berker, M. Hartmann, Y. Punie, and K. Ward (eds) *Domestication of Media and Technology*. Maidenhead: Open University Press: 103–22.

Hall, P. (1996) *Cities of Tomorrow: An Intellectual History of Urban Planning and Design in the Twentieth Century*, updated edition. Oxford: Blackwell.

Hall, S. (1983) The Great Moving Right Show, in S. Hall and M. Jacques (eds) *The Politics of Thatcherism*. London: Lawrence and Wishart: 19–39.

Hand, M. and Shove, E. (2004) Orchestrating Concepts: Kitchen Dynamics and Regime Change in *Good Housekeeping* and *Ideal Home*, 1922–2002, *Home Cultures*, 1(3): 1–22.

Hareven, T.K. (2002) The Home and Family in Historical Perspective, in T. Bennett and D. Watson (eds) *Understanding Everyday Life*. Oxford: Blackwell: 34–9.

Harley, S. (1990) The Good of the Family and Race: Gender, Work and Domestic Roles in the Black Community, 1880–1930, *Signs*, 15(2): 336–49.

Hartley, J. (1997) The Sexualization of Suburbia: The Diffusion of Knowledge in the Postmodern Public Sphere, in R. Silverstone (ed.) *Visions of Suburbia*. London: Routledge: 180–216.

Hayden, D. (1982) *The Grand Domestic Revolution: A History of Feminist Designs for American Homes, Neighbourhoods and Cities*. Cambridge, MA: The MIT Press.

Hayden, D. (2004) *Building Suburbia: Green Fields and Urban Growth, 1820–2000*. New York: Vintage.

Hebdige, D. (1979) *Subculture: The Meaning of Style*. London: Methuen.

Hebdige, D. (1988) *Hiding in the Light: On Images and Things*. London: Routledge.

Hebdige, D. (1989) After the Masses, in S. Hall and M. Jacques (eds) *New Times: The Changing Face of Politics in the 1990s*. London: Lawrence & Wishart: 76–93.

Hebdige, D. (1993) Redeeming Witness: In the Tracks of the Homeless Vehicle Project, *Cultural Studies*, 7(2), 173–223.

Hecht, A. (2001) Home Sweet Home: Tangible Memories of an Uprooted Childhood, in D. Miller (ed.) *Home Possessions: Material Culture Behind Closed Doors*. Oxford: Berg: 123–45.

Hepworth, M. (1999) Privacy, Security and Respectability: The Ideal Victorian Home, in T. Chapman and J. Hockey (eds) *Ideal Homes? Social Change and Domestic Life*. London: Routledge: 17–29.

Hewitt, N. (2002) Taking the True Woman Hostage, *Journal of Women's History*, 14(1): 156–62.

Higgins, C. (2005) Political Protest Turns to the Radical Art of Knitting, *The Guardian*, 31 January; http://arts.guardian.co.uk/news/story/0,,1402062,00.html (accessed 7 July 2006).

Highmore, B. (2002) *Everyday Life and Cultural Theory: An Introduction*. London: Routledge.

Highmore, B. (2004) Homework: Routine, Social Aesthetics, and the Ambiguity of Everyday Life, *Cultural Studies*, 18(2–3): 306–27.

Hill, J. (1986) *Sex, Class and Realism: British Cinema, 1956–63*. London: BFI.

Hirsch, E. (1992) The Long Term and the Short Term of Domestic Consumption: An Ethnographic Case Study, in R. Silverstone and E. Hirsch (eds) *Consuming Technologies: Media and Information in Domestic Spaces*. London: Routledge: 208–26.

Hobson, D. (1980) Housewives and the Mass Media, in S. Hall, D. Hobson, A. Lowe and P. Willis (eds) *Culture, Media, Language: Working Papers in Cultural Studies, 1972–79*. London: Hutchinson: 105–14.

Hochschild, A. Russell (2000) *The Time Bind: When Work Becomes Home and Home Becomes Work*. New York: Owl Books.

Hochschild, A. Russell with A. Machone (2003) *The Second Shift*. London: Penguin.

Hockey, J. (1999a) Houses of Doom, in T. Chapman and J. Hockey (eds) *Ideal Homes: Social Change and Domestic Life*. London: Routledge: 147–60.

Hockey, J. (1999b) The Ideal of Home: Domesticating the Institutional Space of Old Age and Death, in T. Chapman and J. Hockey (eds) *Ideal Homes: Social Change and Domestic Life*. London: Routledge: 108–18.

Hoggart, R. (1958) *The Uses of Literacy: Aspects of Working Class Life with Special Reference to Publications and Entertainments*. Harmondsworth: Penguin.

Holliday, R. (2005) Home Truths?, in D. Bell and J. Hollows (eds) *Ordinary Lifestyles: Popular Media, Consumption and Taste*. Maidenhead: Open University Press: 65–81.

Hollis, P. (1979) *Women in Public: The Women's Movement 1850–1900*. London: Allen and Unwin.

Hollows, J. (2000) *Feminism, Femininity and Popular Culture*. Manchester: Manchester University Press.

Hollows, J. (2002) The Bachelor Dinner: Masculinity, Class and Cooking in *Playboy*, 1953–61, *Continuum*, 16(2): 143–55.

Hollows, J. (2003a) Oliver's Twist: Leisure, Labour and Domestic Masculinity, in *The Naked Chef, International Journal of Cultural Studies*, 6(2): 229–48.

Hollows, J. (2003b) Feeling Like a Domestic Goddess: Postfeminism and Cooking, *European Journal of Cultural Studies*, 6(2): 179–202.

Hollows, J. (2006a) Science and Spells: Cooking, Lifestyle and Domestic Femininities in British *Good Housekeeping* in the Inter-war Period, in D. Bell and J. Hollows (eds) *Historicizing Lifestyle*. Aldershot: Ashgate: 21–40.

Hollows, J. (2006b) Can I Go Home Yet? Feminism, Post-feminism and Domesticity, in J. Hollows and R. Moseley (eds) *Feminism in Popular Culture*. Oxford: Berg: 97–118.

Hollows, J. (2007) The Feminist and the Cook: Julia Child, Betty Friedan and Domestic Femininity, in E. Casey and L. Martens (eds) *Gender and Consumption: Domestic Cultures and the Commercialization of Everyday Life*. Aldershot: Ashgate: 33–48.

hooks, bell (1991) *Yearning: Race, Gender and Cultural Politics*. Boston: Turnaround.

Horsfield, M. (1997) *Biting the Dust: The Joys of Housework*. London: 4th Estate.

Horton, J.O. (1986) Freedom's Yoke: Gender Conventions Among Antebellum Free Blacks, *Feminist Studies*, 12(1): 51–76.

Humble, N. (2001) *The Feminine Middlebrow Novel, 1920s to mid-1950s: Class, Domesticity and Bohemianism*. Oxford: Oxford University Press.

Humble, N. (2005) *Culinary Pleasures: Cookbooks and the Transformation of British Food*. London: Faber.

Humpherys, L. (2005) Cellphones in Public: Social Interactions in a Wireless Era, *New Media and Society*, 7(6): 810–33.

Hunt, P. (1995) Gender and the Construction of Home Life, in S. Jackson and S. Moores (eds) *The Politics of Domestic Consumption: Critical Readings*. Hemel Hempstead: Harvester Wheatsheaf: 301–13.

Jack, F. ([1922] 1990) 'A Seasonable Lunch', in B. Braithwaite and N. Walsh (eds) *Food Glorious Food: Eating and Drinking with Good Housekeeping, 1922–42*. London: Random House: 10–11.

Jack, F. ([1924] 1990) Cookery as a Career for Women, in B. Braithwaite and N. Walsh (eds) *Food Glorious Food: Eating and Drinking with Good Housekeeping, 1922–42*. London: Random House: 38–9.

Jackson, K.T. (1985) *Crabgrass Frontier: The Suburbanization of the United States*. New York: Oxford University Press.

Jackson, P. (1993) Towards a Cultural Politics of Consumption, in J. Bird, B. Curtis, T. Putnam, G. Robertson and L. Tickner (eds) *Mapping the Futures: Local Cultures, Global Change*. London: Routledge: 207–28.

Jackson, S. and Moores, S. (1995) Introduction, in S. Jackson and S. Moores (eds) *The Politics of Domestic Consumption*. Hemel Hempstead: Harvester Wheatsheaf: 1–21.

Jancovich, M. and Faire, L. with Stubbings, S. (2003) *The Place of the Audience: Cultural Geographies of Film Consumption*. London: BFI.

Jarvis, H. and Pratt, A.C. (2006) Bringing it All Back Home: The Extensification and 'Overflowing' of Work: The Case of San Francisco's New Media Households, *Geoforum*, 37(3): 331–9.

Jenkins, H. (2001) Participatory Vs. Broadcast Media, *re:constructions: reflections on humanity and media after tragedy*; http://web.mit.edu/cms/reconstructions/interpretations/particip. html (accessed 5 May 2006).

Johnson, L. and Lloyd, J. (2004) *Sentenced to Everyday Life: Feminism and the Housewife*. Oxford: Berg.

Johnson, R. (1986) The Story so Far: and Further Transformations?, in D. Punter (ed.) *Introduction to Contemporary Cultural Studies*. Harlow: Longman: 277–313.

Johnston, L. and Valentine, G. (1995) Wherever I Lay My Girlfriend, That's my Home: The Performance and Surveillance of Lesbian Identities in Domestic Environments, in D. Bell and G. Valentine (eds) *Mapping Desire: Geographies of Sexualities*. London: Routledge: 99–113.

Katz, J.E. and Aakhus, M.A. (2002) (eds) *Perpetual Contact: Mobile Communication, Private Talk, Public Performance*. Cambridge: Cambridge University Press.

Kaufman-Scarborough, C. (2006) Time Use and the Impact of Technology: Examining Workspaces in the Home, *Time and Society*, 15(1): 57–80.

Kemmer, D. (1999) Food Preparation and the Division of Labour Among Newly-married and Cohabiting Couples, *British Food Journal*, 101(80): 570–9.

Kenyon, L. (1999) A Home From Home: Students' Transitional Experience of Home, in T. Chapman and J. Hockey (eds) *Ideal Homes? Social Change and Domestic Life*. London: Routledge: 84–95.

Kerber, L. (1988) Separate Spheres, Female Worlds, Woman's Place: The Rhetoric of Women's History, *Journal of American History*, 75(1): 9–39.

Kiros, T. (2004) *Falling Cloudberries: A World of Family Recipes: Book 2*. London: Murdoch Books.

Klinger, B. (2006) *Beyond the Multiplex: Cinema, New Technologies and the Home*. Berkeley: University of California Press.

Knight, P.G. (1997) Naming the Problem: Feminism and the Figuration of Conspiracy, *Cultural Studies*, 11(1): 40–63.

Kopytoff, I. (1986) The Cultural Biography of Things: Commoditization as Process, in A. Appadurai (ed.) *The Social Life of Things: Commodities in Cultural Perspective*. Cambridge: Cambridge University Press: 64–94.

Laermans, R. (1993) Learning to Consume: Early Department Stores and the Shaping of Modern Consumer Culture (1860–1914), *Theory Culture and Society*, 10(4): 79–102.

Laing, S. (1986) *Representations of Working-class Life: 1957–1964*. Basingstoke: Macmillan.

Lally, E. (2002) *At Home with Computers*. Oxford: Berg.

Langhamer (2000) *Women's Leisure in England, 1920–60*. Manchester: Manchester University Press.

Lawson, N. (1999) *How to Eat: The Pleasures and Principles of Good Food*. London: Chatto & Windus.

Lawson, N. (2000) *How to be a Domestic Goddess: Baking and the Art of Comfort Cooking*. London: Chatto & Windus.

Leadbetter, C. (1989) Power to the Person, in S. Hall and S. Jacques (eds) *New Times: The Changing Face of Politics in the 1990s*. London: Lawrence and Wishart: 37–49.

Leal, O. Fachel (1995) Popular Taste and Erudite Repertoire, in S. Jackson and S. Moores (eds) *The Politics of Domestic Consumption*. Hemel Hempstead: Harvester Wheatsheaf: 314–20.

Leavitt, S.A. (2002) *From Catherine Beecher to Martha Stewart: A Cultural History of Domestic Advice*. Chapel Hill: University of North Carolina Press.

Lee, M. (1993) *Consumer Culture Reborn: The Cultural Politics of Consumption*. London: Routledge.

Lehtonen, T.-K. (2003) The Domestication of New Technologies as a Set of Trials, *Journal of Consumer Culture*, 3(3): 363–85.

Lemor, A.M. Rosso (2006) Making a 'Home': The Domestication of Information and Communication Technologies in Single Parents' Households, in T. Berker, M. Hartmann, Y. Punie and K. Ward (eds) *Domestication of Media and Technology*. Maidenhead: Open University Press: 165–84.

Light, A. (1991) *Forever England: Femininity, Literature and Conservatism Between the Wars*. London: Routledge.

Livingstone (1992) The Meaning of Domestic Technologies: A Personal Construct Analysis of Familial Relations, in R. Silverstone and E. Hirsch (eds) *Consuming Technologies: Media and Information in Domestic Spaces*. London: Routledge: 113–30.

Livingstone, S. (2005) In Defence of Privacy: Mediating the Public/Private Boundary at Home, London: LSE Research Online; http://eprints.lse.ac.uk/archive/00000505 (accessed 4 August 2006).

Lovell, T. (1990) Landscapes and Stories in 1960s British Realism, *Screen*, 31(4): 357–76.

Low, S. (2003) *Behind the Gates: Life, Security and the Pursuit of Happiness in Fortress America*. New York: Routledge.

Lupton, D. (1996) *Food, The Body and the Self*. London: Sage.

Lupton, D. and Noble, G. (2002) Mine/Not Mine: Appropriating Personal Computers in the Academic Workplace, *Journal of Sociology*, 38(1): 5–23.

Lury, C. (1996) *Consumer Culture*. Cambridge: Polity.

Lyons, J. (2005) 'Think Seattle, Act Globally': Speciality Coffee, Commodity Biographies and the Promotion of Place, *Cultural Studies*, 19(1): 14–34.

McCarthy, A. (2001) *Ambient Television: Visual Culture and Public Space*. Durham: Duke University Press.

McCarthy, A. (2004) Geekospheres: Visual Culture and Material Culture at Work, *Journal of Visual Culture*, 3(2): 213–21.

McClintock, A. (1995) *Imperial Leather: Race, Gender and Sexuality in the Colonial Contest*. London: Routledge.

Macdonald, D. (1963) *Against the American Grain*. London: Victor Gollancz.

McDowell, L. (2004) Work, Workfare, Work/Life Balance and an Ethic of Care, *Progress in Human Geography*, 28(2): 145–63.

McDowell, L., Ray, K., Perrons, D., Fagan, C. and Ward, K. (2005) Women's Paid Work and Moral Economies of Care, *Social and Cultural Geography*, 6(2): 219–35.

McElvoy (forthcoming) Property TV: The (Re)Making of Home on National Screens, *European Journal of Cultural Studies*.

McFeeley, M. Drake (2001) *Can She Bake a Cherry Pie? American Women and the Kitchen in the Twentieth Century*. Amherst: University of Massachusetts Press.

McIntosh, A.J and Siggs, A. (2005) An Exploration of the Experiential Nature of Boutique Accommodation, *Journal of Travel Research*, 44(1): 74–81.

McKibbin, R. (1999) Mondeo Man in the Driving Seat, *London Review of Books*, 21(19): 30.

McRobbie, A. (1981) Settling Accounts with Subcultures: A Feminist Critique, in T. Bennett, G. Martin, C. Mercer and J. Woollacott (eds) *Culture, Ideology and Social Process: A Reader*. London: Batsford: 111–23.

McRobbie, A. (2004) Post-feminism and Popular Culture, *Feminist Media Studies*, 4(3): 255–64.

McRobbie, A. and Garber, J. (1978) 'Girls and Subcultures', in S. Hall and T. Jefferson (eds) *Resistance Through Rituals: Youth Subcultures in Post-war Britain*. London: Hutchinson: 209–22.

Madigan, R. and Munro, M. (1999) 'The More we are Together': Domestic Space, Gender and Privacy, in T. Chapman and J. Hockey (eds) *Ideal Homes? Social Change and Domestic Life*. London: Routledge: 61–72.

Malos, E. (1980) (ed.) *The Politics of Housework*. London: Allison and Busby.

Marcoux, J-S. (2001) The Refurbishment of Memory, in D. Miller (ed.) *Home Possessions: Material Culture Behind Closed Doors*. Oxford: Berg: 69–86.

Marston, S. (2000) The Social Construction of Scale, *Progress in Human Geography*, 24(2): 219–42.

Martens, L. and Casey, E. (2007) Afterword: Gender, Consumer Culture and Promises of Betterment in Late Modernity, in E. Casey and L. Martens (eds) *Gender and Consumption: Domestic Cultures and the Commercialization of Everyday Life*. Aldershot: Ashgate: 219–42.

Martens, L. and Scott, S. (2005) 'The Unbearable Lightness of Cleaning': Representations of Domestic Practices and Products in *Good Housekeeping* Magazine (UK): 1951–2001, *Consumption, Markets and Culture*, 8(3): 371–409.

Martens, L., Southerton, D. and Scott, S. (2004) Bringing Children (and Parents) into the Sociology of Consumption: Towards a Theoretical and Empirical Agenda, *Journal of Consumer Culture*, 4(2): 155–82.

Mason, A. and Meyers, M. (2001) Living with Martha Stewart: Chosen Domesticity in the Experience of Fans, *Journal of Communication*, December: 801–23.

Massey, D. (1993) Power-geometry and a Progressive Sense of Place, in J. Bird, B. Curtis, T. Putnam, G. Robertson and L. Tickner (eds) *Mapping the Futures: Local Cultures, Global Change*. London: Routledge: 59–69.

Massey, D. (1994) *Space, Place and Gender*. Cambridge: Polity.

Matless, D. (1998) *Landscape and Englishness*. London: Reaktion.

Matrix (1984) *Making Space: Women and the Man-made Environment*. London: Pluto.

Matthews, G. (1987) *'Just a Housewife': the Rise and Fall of Domesticity in America*. New York: Oxford University Press.

Medhurst, A. (1997) Negotiating the Gnome Zone: Versions of Suburbia in British Popular Culture, in R. Silverstone (ed.) *Visions of Suburbia*. London: Routledge: 240–68.

Metcalfe, A. (2006a) 'It Was the Right Time to Do it': Moving House, the Life-course and *Kairos, Mobilities*, 1(2): 243–60.

Metcalfe, A. (2006b) Moving House, Haunted Homes: On Past Times, Previous Occupants and Current Lives, unpublished paper.

Meyerowitz, J. (1994) Beyond *The Feminine Mystique*: A Reassessment of Postwar Mass Culture, 1946–58, in J. Meyerowitz (ed.) *Not June Cleaver: Women and Gender in Postwar America, 1946–60*. Philadelphia: Temple University Press: 229–62.

Meyrowitz, J. (1985) *No Sense of Place: The Impact of Electronic Media on Social Behaviour*. New York: Oxford University Press.

Mies, M. and Shiva, V. (1993) *Ecofeminism*. Halifax, Nova Scotia: Fernwood.

Miller, D. (1988) Appropriating the State on the Council Estate, *Man*, 23(2): 353–72.

Miller, D. (1992) The Young and the Restless in Trinidad: A Case of the Local and the Global in Mass Consumption, in R. Silverstone and E. Hirsch (eds) *Consuming Technologies: Media and Information in Domestic Spaces*. London: Routledge: 163–82.

Miller, D. (1994) *Material Culture and Mass Consumption, 2nd edn*. Oxford: Blackwell.

Miller, D. (1995) (ed.) *Acknowledging Consumption: A Review of New Studies*. London: Routledge.

Miller, D. (1998) *A Theory of Shopping*. Cambridge: Polity.

Miller, D. (2001a) Behind Closed Doors, in D. Miller (ed.) *Home Possessions: Material Culture Behind Closed Doors*. Oxford: Berg: 1–19.

Miller, D. (2001b) Possessions, in D. Miller (ed.) *Home Possessions: Material Culture Behind Closed Doors*. Oxford: Berg: 107–21.

Miller, D. (2001c) (ed.) *Home Possessions: Material Culture Behind Closed Doors*. Oxford: Berg.

Mills, C. Wright (1956) *The Power Elite*. New York: Oxford University Press.

Mitchell, J. (1999) The British Main Meal in the 1990s: Has it Changed its Identity?, *British Food Journal*, 101(11): 871–3.

Modleski, T. (1984) *Loving With a Vengeance: Mass-produced Fantasies for Women*. London: Routledge.

Moisio, R., Arnold, E.J. and Price, L.L. (2004) Between Mothers and Markets: Constructing Family Identity Through Homemade Food, *Journal of Consumer Culture*, 4(3): 361–84.

Moores, S. (1993) *Interpreting Audiences: The Ethnography of Media Consumption*. London: Sage.

Moores, S. (1996) *Satellite Television and Everyday Life: Articulating Technology*. Luton: John Libbey.

Moores, S. (2000) *Media and Everyday Life in Modern Society*. Edinburgh: Edinburgh University Press.

Moores, S. (2005) *Media/Theory: Thinking About Media and Communications*. London: Routledge.

Moores, S. (2006) Media Uses and Everyday Environmental Experiences: A Positive Critique of Phenomenological Geography, paper presented at the MeCCSA Annual Conference, January, Leeds Metropolitan University.

Moores, S. and Qureshi, K. (2000) Identity, Tradition and Translation, in S. Moores (ed.) *Media and Everyday Life in Modern Society*. Edinburgh: Edinburgh University Press: 117–34.

Moran, J. (2004) Housing, Memory and Everyday Life in Contemporary Britain, *Cultural Studies*, 18(4): 607–27.

Moran, J. (2005a) The Strange Birth of Middle England, *Political Quarterly*, 76(2): 232–40.

Moran, J. (2005b) *Reading the Everyday*. London: Routledge.

Morgan, D. (1999) Risk and Family Practices: Accounting for Change and Fluidity in Family Life, in E. Silva and C. Smart (eds) *The New Family*? London: Sage: 13–30.

Morley, D. (1986) *Family Television: Cultural Power and Domestic Leisure*. London: Comedia.

Morley, D. (1991) Where the Global Meets the Local: Notes from the Sitting Room, *Screen*, 32(1): 1–15.

Morley, D. (1992) *Television, Audiences and Cultural Studies*. London: Routledge.

Morley, D. (2000) *Home Territories: Media, Mobility and Identity*. London: Routledge.

Morley, D. (2001) Belongings: Space, Place and Identity in a Mediated World, *European Journal of Cultural Studies*, 4(4): 425–8.

Morley, D. (2003) What's Home Got to do With it? Contradictory Dynamics in the Domestication of Technology and the Dislocation of Domesticity, *European Journal of Cultural Studies*, 6(4): 435–58.

Morley, D. with Silverstone, R. (1992) Domestic Communication: Technologies and Meanings, in D. Morley *Television, Audiences and Cultural Studies*. London: Routledge: 201–12.

Mort, F. (1988) Boy's Own? Masculinity, Style and Popular Culture, in R. Chapman and J. Rutherford (eds) *Male Order: Unwrapping Masculinity*. London: Lawrence and Wishart: 193–219.

Mort, F. (1989) The Politics of Consumption, in S. Hall and S. Jacques (eds) *New Times: The Changing Face of Politics in the 1990s*. London: Lawrence and Wishart: 160–72.

Moseley, R. (2000) Makeover Takeover on British Television, *Screen*, 41(3): 299–314.

Moseley, R. (2001) Real Lads Do Cook But Some Things are Still Hard to Talk About: The Gendering of 8–9, in C. Brunsdon, C. Johnson, R. Moseley and H. Wheatley, Factual Entertainment in British Television: The Midlands TV Research Group's '8–9 Project', *European Journal of Cultural Studies*, 4(1): 32–40.

Moyal, A. (1995) The Gendered Use of the Phone: An Australian Case Study, in S. Jackson and S. Moores (eds) *The Politics of Domestic Consumption*. Hemel Hempstead: Harvester Wheatsheaf: 258–73.

Moynihan, D. P. (1986) *Family and Nation*. New York: Harcourt Brace Jovanovich.

Murcott, A. (1983) Cooking and the Cooked: A Note on the Domestic Preparation of Meals, in A. Murcott (ed.) *The Sociology of Food and Eating*. Aldershot: Gower: 178–93.

Murcott, A. (1995) 'It's a Pleasure to Cook for Him': Food, Mealtimes and Gender in some South Wales Households, in S. Jackson and S. Moores (eds) *The Politics of Domestic Consumption: Critical Readings*. Hemel Hempstead: Harvester Wheatsheaf: 89–99.

Murdoch, G., Hartmann, P. and Gray, P. (1992) Contextualizing Home Computing: Resources and Practices, in R. Silverstone and E. Hirsch (eds) *Consuming Technologies: Media and Information in Domestic Spaces*. London: Routledge: 146–60.

Muther, C. (2006) Home Sweet Home: Guests are Emulating the Boutique Hotel Look in Their Own Homes, *Boston Globe*, 23 February.

Myerson, J. (2005) *Home: The Story of Everyone Who Ever Lived in Our House*. London: Harper Perennial.

Nava, M. (1997) Modernity's Disavowal: Women, the City and the Department Store, in P. Falk and C. Campbell (eds) *The Shopping Experience*. London: Sage: 56–91.

Nippert-Eng, C.E. (1995) *Home and Work: Negotiating Boundaries Through Everyday Life*. Chicago: University of Chicago Press.

Nixon, S. and Du Gay, P. (2002) Who Needs Cultural Intermediaries?, *Cultural Studies*, 16(4): 495–500.

Nordenmark, M. and Nyman, C. (2003) Fair or Unfair? Perceived Fairness of Household Division of Labour and Gender Equality Among Women and Men, *European Journal of Women's Studies*, 10(2): 181–209.

Oakley, A. (1974) *The Sociology of Housework*. London: Martin Robertson.

Oakley, A. (1976) *Housewife*. Harmondsworth: Penguin.

Oates, C.J. and McDonald, S. (2006) Recycling and the Domestic Division of Labour: Is Green Pink or Blue?, *Sociology*, 40(3): 417–33.

Oerton, S. (1997) 'Queer Housewives'? Some Problems in Theorizing the Division of Domestic Labour in Lesbian and Gay Households, *Women's Studies International Forum*, 20(3): 421–30.

Oldenburg, R. (2001) (ed.) *Celebrating the Third Place: Inspiring Stories about the 'Great Good Places' at the Heart of our Communities*. New York: Marlow and Company.

Oliver, J. (2000) *The Return of the Naked Chef*. London: Michael Joseph.

Oliver, P., Davis, I. and Bentley, I. (1981) *Dunroamin: The Suburban Semi and its Enemies*. London: Pimlico.

Orwell, G. (1983) *The Penguin Complete Novels of George Orwell*. Harmondsworth: Penguin.

O'Sullivan, T. (1991) Television Memories and Cultures of Viewing, 1950–65, in J. Corner (ed.) *Popular Television in Britain*. London: BFI: 159–81.

O'Sullivan, T. (2005) From Television Lifestyle to Lifestyle Television, in D. Bell and J. Hollows (eds) *Ordinary Lifestyles: Popular Media, Consumption and Taste*. Maidenhead: Open University Press: 21–34.

Packard, V. (1957) *The Hidden Persuaders*. Harmondsworth: Penguin.

Packard, V. (1961) *The Status Seekers*. Harmondsworth: Penguin.

Parkins, W. (2004a) Celebrity Knitting and the Temporality of Postmodernity, *Fashion Theory*, 8(4): 425–42.

Parkins, W. (2004b) At Home in Tuscany: Slow Living and the Cosmopolitan Subject, *Home Cultures*, 1(2): 257–74.

Parkins, W. (2004c) Out of Time: Fast Subjects and Slow Living, *Time and Society*, 13(2/3): 363–82.

Partington, A. (1993) Popular Fashion and Working-class Affluence, in J. Ash and E. Wilson (eds) *Chic Thrills: A Fashion Reader*. Berkeley and Los Angeles: University of California Press: 145–61.

Partington, A. (1995) The Designer Housewife in the 1950s, in J. Attfield and P. Kirkham (eds) *A View From the Interior: Women and Design*. London: Women's Press: 206–14.

Pells, R. (1989) *The Liberal Mind in a Conservative Age: American Intellectuals in the 1940s and 1950s, Second edition*. Middletown: Wesleyan University Press.

Perrons, D., Fagan, C., McDowell, L., Ray, K. and Ward, K. (2005) Work, Life and Time in the New Economy: An Introduction, *Time and Society*, 14(1): 51–64.

Petridou, E. (2001) The Taste of Home, in D. Miller (ed.) *Home Possessions: Material Culture Behind Closed Doors*. Oxford: Berg: 87–104.

Pink, S. (2004) *Home Truths: Gender, Domestic Objects and Everyday Life*. Oxford: Berg.

Polenberg, R. (1986) *One Nation Divisible: Class, Race, and Ethnicity in the United States Since 1938*. Harmondsworth: Penguin.

Poster, M. (1988) *Jean Baudrillard: Selected Writings*. Stanford: Stanford University Press.

Probyn, E. (1993) Choosing Choice: Winking Images of Sexuality in Popular Culture, in S. Fisher and K. Davis (eds) *Negotiating at the Margins: Gendered Discourses of Resistance*. New Brunswick, NJ: Rutgers University Press: 278–94.

Purbrick, L. (2007) *The Wedding Present: Domestic Life Beyond Consumption*. Aldershot: Ashgate.

Rakow, L. (1992) *Gender on the Line: Women, the Telephone and Community Life*. Urbana: University of Illinois Press.

Rappaport, E. (2000) *Shopping for Pleasure: Women in the Making of London's West End, 1860–1914*. Princeton: Princeton University Press.

Ravetz, A. with Turkington, R. (1995) *The Place of Home: English Domestic Environments, 1914–2000*. London: E. and F.N. Spon.

Reay, D. (2004) Gendering Bourdieu's Concepts of Capitals, *Sociological Review*, 52(52): 57–74.

Reiger, K. (1985) *The Disenchantment of the Home: Modernizing the Australian Family 1880–1940*. Melbourne: Oxford University Press.

Reimer, S. and Leslie, D. (2004) Identity, Consumption and the Home, *Home Cultures*: 1(2): 187–208.

Riesman, D. (1961) *The Lonely Crowd: A Study of the Changing American Character*. New Haven: Yale University Press.

Riley, D. (1983) *War in the Nursery: Theories of the Child and the Mother*. London: Virago.

Ronald, R. (2004) Home Ownership, Ideology and Diversity: Re-evaluating Concepts of Housing Ideology in the Case of Japan, *Housing Theory and Society*, 21(2): 49–64.

Roos, G., Prättälä, R. and Koski, K. (2001) Men, Masculinity and Food: Interviews with Finnish Carpenters and Engineers, *Appetite*, 37(1): 47–56.

Rose, G. (2003) Family Photographs and Domestic Spacings: A Case Study, *Transactions of the Institute of British Geographers*, 28: 5–18.

Rowbotham, S. (1996) Introduction: Mapping the Women's Movement, in M. Threkfall (ed.) *Mapping the Women's Movement: Feminist Politics and Socialist Transformation in the North*. London: Verso: 1–15.

Ryan, M. (1981) *The Cradle of the Middle Class: The Family in Oneida County, New York, 1790–1865*. Cambridge: Cambridge University Press.

Rybczynski, W. (1987) *Home: A Short History of an Idea*. Harmondsworth: Penguin.

Saunders, P. (1990) *A Nation of Home Owners*. London: Unwin Hyman.

Savage, M., Barlow, J., Dickens, P. and Fielding, T. (1992) *Property, Bureaucracy and Culture: Middle-class Formation in Contemporary Britain*. London: Routledge.

Savage, M., Bagnall, G. and Longhurst, B. (2001) Ordinary, Ambivalent and Defensive: Class Identities in the Northwest of England, *Sociology*, 35(4): 875–92.

Scannell, P. (1996) *Radio, Television and Modern Life: A Phenomenological Approach*. Oxford: Blackwell.

Scannell, P. (2000) For-Anyone-as-Someone Structures, *Media, Culture and Society*, 22(1): 5–24.

Segal, L. (1983) The Heat in the Kitchen, in S. Hall and M. Jacques (eds) *The Politics of Thatcherism*. London: Lawrence and Wishart: 207–15.

Segal, L. (1987) *Is the Future Female? Troubled Thoughts on Contemporary Feminism*. London: Virago.

Segal, L. (1988) Look Back in Anger: Men in the 1950s, in R. Chapman and J. Rutherford (eds) *Male Order: Unwrapping Masculinity*. London: Lawrence and Wishart: 68–96.

Seiter, E. (1999) *Television, New Media and Audiences*. Oxford: Clarendon.

Seiter, E., Borchers, H., Kreutzner, G. and Warth, E. (1989) 'Don't Treat Us Like We're So Stupid and Naïve': Towards an Ethnography of Soap Opera Viewers, in E. Seiter, H. Borchers, G. Kreutzner and E. Warth (eds) *Remote Control: Television, Audiences and Cultural Power*. London: Routledge: 223–47.

Sheller, M. (2004) Mobile Publics: Beyond the Network Perspective, *Environment and Planning D: Society and Space*, 22: 39–52.

Sheller, M. and Urry, J. (2003) Mobile Transformations of 'Public' and 'Private' Life, *Theory Culture and Society*, 20(3): 107–25.

Short, F. (2006) *Kitchen Secrets: The Meaning of Cooking in Everyday Life*. Oxford: Berg.

Shove, E. and Southertone, D. (2000) Defrosting the Freezer: From Novelty to Tradition, *Journal of Material Culture*, 5(3): 301–19.

Silva, E. (1999) Transforming Housewifery: Dispositions, Practices and Technologies, in E. Silva and C. Smart (eds) *The New Family?* London: Sage: 46–65.

Silva, E. (2000a) The Cook, the Cooker and the Gendering of the Kitchen, *Sociological Review*, 48(4): 612–28.

Silva, E. (2000b) The Politics of Consumption @ Home: Practices and Dispositions in the Uses of Technologies, Pavis Papers in Social and Cultural Research, No. 1; http://www.open.ac.uk/socialsciences/pavis/papers.php (accessed 4 April 2006).

Silva, E. (2007) Gender, Class, Emotional Capital and Consumption in Everyday Life, in E. Casey and L. Martens (eds) *Gender and Domestic Consumption: Domestic Consumption and the Commercialization of Everyday Life*. Ashgate: Aldershot: 141–59.

Silva, E. and Smart, C. (1999) The 'New' Family Practices and Politics of Family Life, in E. Silva and C. Smart (eds) *The New Family?* London: Sage: 1–12.

Silverstone, R. (1994) *Television and Everyday Life*. London: Routledge.

Silverstone, R. (1997) Introduction, in R. Silverstone (ed.) *Visions of Suburbia*. London: Routledge: 1–25.

Silverstone, R. (2006) Domesticating Domestication: Reflections on the Life of a Concept, in T. Berker, M. Hartmann, Y. Punie and K. Ward (eds) *Domestication of Media and Technology*. Maidenhead: Open University Press: 229–48.

Silverstone, R., Hirsch, E. and Morley, D. (1992) Information and Communication Technologies and the Moral Economy of the Household, in R. Silverstone and R. Hirsch (eds) Consuming Technologies: *Media and Information in Domestic Spaces*. London: Routledge: 15–31.

Skeggs, B. (1997) *Formations of Class and Gender: Becoming Respectable*. London: Sage.

Skeggs, B. (2004) *Class, Self, Culture*. London: Routledge.

Slater, D. (1997) *Consumer Culture and Modernity*. Cambridge: Polity.

Smith, C.J. (2005) Living the Life of a Domestic Goddess: Chick Lit's Response to Domestic Advice Manuals, *Women's Studies*, 34(8): 671–99.

Smith, N. (1993) Homeless/Global: Scaling Places, in J. Bird, B. Curtis, T. Putnam, G. Robertson and L. Tickner (eds) *Mapping the Futures: Local Cultures, Global Change*. London: Routledge, 87–119.

Southerton, D. (2001) Consuming Kitchens: Taste, Context and Identity Formation, *Journal of Consumer Culture*, 1(2): 179–203.

Southerton, D. (2003) Squeezing Time: Allocating Practices, Coordinating Networks and Scheduling Society, *Time and Society*, 12(1): 5–25.

Southerton, D., Shove, E. and Warde, A. (2001) 'Harried and Hurried': Time Shortage and the Co-ordination of Everyday Life, CRICC Discussion Paper 47, Manchester: Centre for Research on Innovation and Competition; http://www.cric.ac.uk/cric/Abstracts/dp47.htm (accessed 27 June 2006).

Sparke, P. (1995) *As Long as it's Pink: The Sexual Politics of Taste*. London: Pandora.

Spigel, L. (1992) *Make Room for TV: Television and the Family Ideal in Postwar America*. Chicago: University of Chicago Press.

Spigel, L. (2001a) Media Homes: Then and Now, *International Journal of Cultural Studies*, 4(4): 385–411.

Spigel, L. (2001b) *Welcome to the Dreamhouse: Popular Media and Postwar Suburbs*. Durham: Duke University Press.

Spigel, L. (2005) Designing the Smart House: Posthuman Domesticity and Conspicuous Production, *European Journal of Cultural Studies*, 8(4): 403–26.

Stacey, J. (1986) Are Feminists Afraid to Leave Home? The Challenge of Conservative Pro-family Feminism, in A. Oakley and J. Mitchell (eds) *What is Feminism*? Oxford: Blackwell: 219–48.

Stacey, J. (1991) Promoting Normality: Section 28 and the Regulation of Sexuality, in S. Franklin, C. Lury and J. Stacey (eds) *Off-centre: Feminism and Cultural Studies*. London: Harper Collins Academic: 284–304.

Stanko, E. (1985) *Intimate Intrusions: Women's Experiences of Male Violence*. London: Routledge and Kegan Paul.

Stokes, J. (1999) *On Screen Rivals*. London: Macmillan.

Sullivan, O. (2000) The Division of Domestic Labour: Twenty Years of Change? *Sociology*, 34(3): 437–56.

Tagg, J. (1981) Power and Photography – A Means of Surveillance: The Photograph as Evidence in Law, in T. Bennett, G. Martin, C. Mercer and J. Woollacott (eds) *Culture, Ideology and Social Process: A Reader*. London: Batsford: 285–308.

Taylor, L. (2005) It was Beautiful Before You Changed it All: Class, Taste and the Transformative Aesthetics of the Garden Lifestyle Media, in D. Bell and J. Hollows (eds) *Ordinary Lifestyles: Popular Media, Consumption and Taste*. Maidenhead: Open University Press: 113–27.

Taylor, P. (1979) Daughters and Mothers – Maids and Mistresses: Domestic Service Between the Wars, in J. Clarke, C. Critcher and R. Johnson (eds) *Working Class Culture: Studies in History and Theory*. London: Hutchinson: 121–39.

Thornton, S. (1995) *Club Cultures: Music, Media and Subcultural Capital*. Cambridge: Polity.

Tietze, S. and Musson, G. (2002) When 'Work' Meets 'Home': Temporal Flexibility as Lived Experience, *Time and Society*, 11(2/3): 315–34.

Tincknell, E. (2005) *Mediating the Family: Gender, Culture and Representation*. London: Arnold.

Tolson, A. (1990) Social Suveillance and Subjectification: The Emergence of Subculture in the Work of Henry Mayhew, *Cultural Studies*, 4(2): 113–27.

Tomlinson, A. (1990) Home Fixtures: Doing-it-yourself in a Privatized World, in A. Tomlinson (ed.) *Consumption, Identity and Style: Marketing, Meanings and the Packaging of Pleasure*. London: Routledge: 57–73.

Tomlinson, J. (1999) *Globalization and Culture*. Cambridge: Polity.

Tomlinson, J. (2001) Instant Access: Some Cultural Implications of 'Globalizing' Technologies, University of Copenhagen, Global Media Cultures, Working Papers 13.

Tosh, J. (1996) New Men? The Bourgeois Cult of Home, *History Today*, December: 9–15.

Tosh, J. (1999) *A Man's Place: Masculinity and the Middle-class Home in Victorian England*. London: Yale University Press.

Umble, D. Zimmerman (1992) The Amish and the Telephone: Resistance and Reconstruction, in R. Silverstone and E. Hirsch (eds) *Consuming Technologies: Media and Information in Domestic Spaces*. London: Routledge: 183–94.

Urry, J. (2006) Inhabiting the Car, *Sociological Review*, 54 (s1): 17–31.

Usherwood, B. (1997) Transnational Publishing: The Case of *Elle Decoration*, in M. Nava, A. Blake, I. MacRury and B. Richards (eds) *Buy This Book: Studies in Advertising and Consumption*. London: Routledge: 178–90.

VanEvery, J. (1997) Understanding Gendered Inequality: Reconceptualizing Housework, *Women's Studies International Forum*, 20(3): 411–20.

Vickery, A. (1993) From Golden Age to Separate Spheres? A Review of the Categories and Chronology of English Women's History, *The Historical Journal*, 36(2): 383–414.

Walker, D. (1999) The Right to Buy, *The Guardian*, January 5: 15.

Walker, L. (2002) Home Making: An Architectural Perspective, *Signs*, 27(3): 823–35.

Walkerdine, V. and Lucey, L. (1989) *Democracy in the Kitchen: Regulating Mothers and Socializing Daughters*. London: Virago.

Walkowitz, J. (1992) *City of Dreadful Delights*. London: Virago.

Walks, R. A. (2005) City-Suburban Electoral Polarization in Great Britain, 1950–2001, *Transactions of the Institute of British Geographers*, 30: 500–517.

Walsh, K. (2006) British Expatriate Belongings: Mobile Homes and Transnational Homing, *Home Cultures*, 3(2): 123–44.

Ward, K. (2006) The Bald Guy Just Ate an Orange: Domestication, Work and Home, in T. Berker, M. Hartmann, Y. Punie and K. Ward (eds) *Domestication of Media and Technology*. Maidenhead: Open University Press: 145–64.

Warde, A. (1997) *Consumption Food and Taste: Culinary Antinomies and Commodity Culture*. London: Sage.

Warde, A. (1999) Convenience Food: Space and Timing, *British Food Journal*, 101(7): 518–27.

Warde, A. (2002) Setting the Scene: Changing Conceptions of Consumption, in S. Miles, A. Anderson and K. Meethan (eds) *The Changing Consumer: Markets and Meanings*. London: Routledge: 10–24.

Warde, A. and Hetherington, K. (1993) A Changing Domestic Division of Labour: Issues of Measurement and Interpretation, *Work, Employment and Society*, 7(1): 23–45.

Warde, A. and Martens, L. (1998) A Sociological Approach to Food Choice: The Case of Eating Out, in A. Murcott (ed.) *The Nation's Diet: The Social Science of Food Choice*. Harlow: Longman: 129–44.

Warde, A. and Martens, L. (2000) *Eating Out: Social Differentiation, Consumption and Pleasure*. Cambridge: Cambridge University Press.

Wardhaugh, J. (1999) The Unaccommodated Woman: Home, Homelessness and Identity, *Sociological Review*, 47(1): 91–108.

Webster, W. (1998) *Imagining Home: Gender, 'Race' and National Identity, 1945–64*. London: UCL Press.

Wei, R. and Lo, V.-H. (2000) Staying Connected While On the Move: Cellphone Use and Social Connectedness, *New Media and Society*, 8(1): 53–72.

Welter, B. (1966) The Cult of True Womanhood: 1820–1860, *American Quarterly*, 18(2): 151–74.

Wheelock, J. (1992) Personal Computers, Gender and an Institutional Model of the Household, in R. Silverstone and E. Hirsch (eds) *Consuming Technologies: Media and Information in Domestic Spaces*. London: Routledge: 97–116.

Whelehan, I. (2005) *The Feminist Bestseller*. Basingstoke: Palgrave.

Wiese, A. (1999) The Other Suburbanites: African American Suburbanization in the North Before 1950, *Journal of American History*, 85(4): 1495–524.

Wieten, J. and Pantti, M. (2005) Obsessed with the Audience: Breakfast Television Revisited, *Media, Culture and Society*, 27(1): 2001–39.

Williams, D.R. and Kaltenborn, B.P. (1999) Leisure Places and Modernity: The Use and Meaning of Recreational Cottages in Norway and the USA, in D. Crouch (ed.) *Leisure Practices and Geographic Knowledge*. London: Routledge: 214–30.

Williams, D.R and McIntyre, N. (2000) Where Heart and Home Reside: Changing Constructions of Place and Identity, paper delivered at Trends 2000, the 5th Outdoor Recreation and Tourism Trends Symposium, September, Lansing, Michigan; www.prr.msu.edu/trends2000/pdf/williams.pdf (accessed 8 August 2006).

Williams, J. (1991) Domesticity as the Dangerous Supplement of Liberalism, *Journal of Women's History*, 2(3): 69–88.

Williams, J. (2000) *Unbending Gender: Why Family and Work Conflict and What to do about it*. New York: Oxford University Press.

Williams, R. (1974) *Television, Technology and Cultural Form*. London: Fontana.

Williams, R. (1983) *Towards 2000*. London: Chatto and Windus.

Williams, R. (1997) Culture is Ordinary, in A. Gray and J. McGuigan (eds) *Studying Culture: An Introductory Reader*. London: Arnold: 5–14.

Willis, P. (1977) *Learning to Labour: How Working Class Kids Get Working Class Jobs*. Farnborough: Saxon House.

Willmott, P. and Young, M. (1960) *Family and Class in a London Suburb*. London: Routledge and Kegan Paul.

Wilson, E. (1985) *Adorned in Dreams: Women and Modernity*. London: Virago.

Winship, J. (1987) *Inside Women's Magazines*. London: Pandora.

Winstanley, A., Thorns, D.C. and Perkins, H.C. (2002) Moving House, Creating Home: Exploring Residential Mobility, *Housing Studies*, 17(6): 813–32.

Wood, H., Skeggs, B. and Thumin, N. (forthcoming) 'Its Just Sad': Mediated Intimacy and the Emotional Labour of Reality Television, in S. Gillis and J. Hollows (eds) *Feminism, Domesticity and Popular Culture*. New York: Routledge.

Woodward, I. (2003) Divergent Narratives in the Imagining of the Home Amongst Middle-class Consumers: Aesthetics, Comfort and the Symbolic Boundaries of Self and Home, *Journal of Sociology*, 39(4): 391–412.

Wooler, M. and F. ([1922] 1990) 'The Business of Housekeeping: Making a Budget', in B. Braithwaite and N. Walsh (eds) *Food Glorious Food: Eating and Drinking with Good Housekeeping, 1922–42*. London: Random House: 9.

Wolff, J. (1993) On the Road Again: Metaphors of Travel in Cultural Criticism, *Cultural Studies*, 7(2): 224–39.

Wylie, P. (1942) *Generation of Vipers*. New York: Rinehart and Co.

Young, I.M. (1997) *Intersecting Voices: Dilemmas of Gender, Political Philosophy, and Policy*. New Jersey: Princetown University Press.

Young, M. and Willmott, P. (1962) *Family and Kinship in East London*. Harmondsworth: Penguin.

Zukin, S. (1995) *The Culture of Cities*. Cambridge, MA: Blackwell.

INDEX

Critical Readings
MORAL PANICS AND THE MEDIA

Chas Critcher (ed)

First developed by Stanley Cohen in 1972, 'moral panic' is a key term in media studies, used to refer to sudden eruptions of indignant concern about social issues. An occurrence of moral panic is characterized by stylized and stereotypical representation by the mass media and a tendency for those in power to claim the moral high ground and pronounce judgement. In this important book, Chas Critcher brings together essential readings on moral panics, which he locates in contemporary debates through an editor's introduction and concise section introductions.

The first section discusses moral panic models and includes contributions on the history and intellectual background of the concept. Differences in thinking between British and American moral panic scholarship are also examined. A second section features important case studies, including AIDS, Satanism, drugs, paedophilia and asylum seekers. This is followed by readings that look at themes such as the importance of language, rhetoric and discourse; the dynamics of media reporting and how it affects public opinion; and the idea of the 'risk society'. Finally, readings critique and debate the use and relevance of moral panic models.

Critical Readings: Moral Panics and the Media is a valuable resource for students and researchers in media studies, criminology and sociology.

Essays by: David L. Altheide, Nachman Ben-Yehuda, Joel Best, Theodore Chiricos, John Clarke, Stan Cohen, Chas Critcher, Mary deYoung, Julie Dickinson, Erich Goode, Johanna Habermeier, Stuart Hall, Sean P. Hier, Tony Jefferson, Philip Jenkins, Hans Mathias Kepplinger, Jennifer Kitzinger, Daniel Maier-Katkin, Angela McRobbie, Peter Meylakhs, Suzanne Ost, Bryan Roberts, Liza Schuster, Stephen Stockwell, Kenneth Thompson, Sarah L. Thornton, Sheldon Ungar, Simon Watney, Jeffrey Weeks, Michael Welch, Paul Williams.

352pp   0 335 21807 5 (EAN: 9 780335 218073) Paperback

          0 335 21808 3 (EAN: 9 780335 218080) Hardback

CULTURE ON DISPLAY
THE PRODUCTION OF CONTEMPORARY VISITABILITY

Bella Dicks

a welcome addition to a growing body of scholarly writing . . . a comprehensive critical survey of the literature on cultural heritage and tourism and associated issues in the fields of cultural and media studies over the previous decade. These concepts and issues are clearly presented and exemplified in the case studies of numerous sites of cultural display . . .

Southern Review

- Why is culture so widely on display?
- What are the major characteristics of contemporary cultural display?
- What is the relationship between cultural display and key features of contemporary society: the rise of consumerism; tourism; 'identity-speak'; globalization?
- What can cultural display tell us about current relations of self and other, here and there, now and then?

Culture on Display invites the reader to visit culture. Reflecting on the contemporary proliferation of sites displaying culture in visitable form, it offers fresh ways of thinking about tourism, leisure and heritage.

Bella Dicks locates diverse exhibitionary locations within wider social, economic and cultural transformations, including contemporary practices of tourism and travel, strategies of economic development, the staging of identities, globalization, interactivity and relations of consumerism. In particular, she critically examines how culture becomes transformed when it is put on display within these contexts. In each chapter, key theoretical issues of debate, such as authenticity, commodification and representation, are discussed in a lively and accessible manner.

This is an important book for undergraduate and postgraduate students of cultural policy, cultural and media studies and sociology, as well as academic researchers in this field. It will also be of considerable value to students of sociology of culture, cultural politics, arts administration and cultural management.

248pp   0 335 20657 3 (Paperback)   0 335 20658 1 (Hardback)